# CONSCRIPTION AND CONFLICT
# IN THE CONFEDERACY

SOUTHERN CLASSICS SERIES
JOHN G. SPROAT, *General Editor*

# CONSCRIPTION AND CONFLICT IN THE CONFEDERACY

ALBERT BURTON MOORE

*with a new introduction by*
WILLIAM GARRETT PISTON

UNIVERSITY OF SOUTH CAROLINA PRESS

Published in Cooperation with the Institute for Southern Studies and the
South Caroliniana Society of the University of South Carolina

Introduction copyright © 1996 University of South Carolina

First published 1924 by Macmillan Co.

Published in Columbia, South Carolina, by the
University of South Carolina Press
in cooperation with the Institute for Southern Studies and
the South Caroliniana Society of the University of South Carolina

Manufactured in the United States of America

00  99  98  97  96  5  4  3  2  1

Library of Congress Cataloging-in-Publication Data
Moore, Albert Burton, 1887–1967.
    Conscription and conflict in the Confederacy / Albert Burton
Moore, with a new introduction by William Garrett Piston.
        p.    cm. — (Southern classics series)
    Originally published: New York : Macmillan Co., 1924.
    Includes bibliographical references and index.
    ISBN 1–57003–152–5 (pbk.)
    1. Confederate States of America.    Army—Recruiting, enlistment,
etc.   2. Draft—Confederate States of America.    I. Title.
II. Series.
E545.M82   1996
973.7′42—dc20                                                    96-26451

TO MY FATHER AND MOTHER
JAMES DAVID AND FRANCES ESTES MOORE
WITH GRATITUDE

# CONTENTS

GENERAL EDITOR'S PREFACE . . . . . . ix

INTRODUCTION BY WILLIAM GARRETT PISTON    xi

I  THE MILITARY SYSTEM OF THE CONFEDERACY TO APRIL, 1862 . . . . . . . . . . . . . 1

II  THE FIRST CONSCRIPTION ACT AND ITS RECEPTION . . . . . . . . . . . . . 12

III  SUBSTITUTION . . . . . . . . . . . 27

IV  STATUTORY EXEMPTION (1862–1864) . . . . 52

V  STATUTORY-EXECUTIVE EXEMPTION . . . . 83

VI  THE FRUITS OF THE FIRST CONSCRIPTION ACT    114

VII  THE SECOND ACT AND THE PROBLEMS OF ENFORCEMENT . . . . . . . . . . . 140

VIII  THE COURTS AND CONSCRIPTION . . . . . 162

IX  THE DUAL SYSTEM . . . . . . . . . 191

X  THE DUAL SYSTEM (Continued) . . . . . 207

XI  CONFEDERATE VERSUS STATE AUTHORITY IN THE LOWER SOUTH . . . . . . . . . . . 228

XII  CONFEDERATE VERSUS STATE AUTHORITY IN GEORGIA AND NORTH CAROLINA . . . . . 255

XIII  CONFEDERATE VESUS STATE AUTHORITY IN THE UPPER SOUTH . . . . . . . . . . . 297

XIV  THE CONCLUDING YEAR . . . . . . . 305

XV  THE LAST DAYS . . . . . . . . . . 336

XVI  DID CONSCRIPTION FAIL? . . . . . . . 354

# GENERAL EDITOR'S PREFACE

Because national military conscription conflicted directly with the doctrine of states' rights, inevitably it created greater problems for the Confederacy than for the Union. Some seventy years after it was written, A. B. Moore's comprehensive study remains the standard work on the subject. Now, in a discerning introduction to this Southern Classics edition, William Garrett Piston puts Moore's work in a new and better perspective required by more recent scholarship on the Civil War.

*     *     *

Southern Classics returns to general circulation books of importance dealing with the history and culture of the American South. Under the sponsorship of the Institute for Southern Studies and the South Caroliniana Society of the University of South Carolina, the series is advised by a board of distinguished scholars whose members suggest titles and editors of individual volumes to the general editor and help to establish priorities in publication.

Chronological age alone does not determine a title's designation as a Southern Classic. The criteria include, as well, significance in contributing to a broad understanding of the region, timeliness in relation to events and moments of peculiar interest to the American South, usefulness in the classroom, and suitablity for inclusion in personal and institutional collections on the region.

JOHN G. SPROAT
General Editor, *Southern Classics*

# INTRODUCTION

First published in 1924 and reprinted in 1963, Albert Burton Moore's *Conscription and Conflict in the Confederacy* remains the only comprehensive study of conscription in the Confederacy and is indispensable for anyone who wishes to understand the background to the Confederacy's remarkable military achievements and the complex course of the would-be nation's internal politics. It has been a standard source for more than three generations of Civil War scholars. When Frank L. Owsley wrote his influential *State Rights in the Confederacy* (1925), he considered Moore's treatment of conscription so thorough that he did not go into great detail on the subject himself. Oswley agreed with Moore's argument that the problems caused by centralizing tendencies inherent in conscription demonstrated the fundamental weakness of attempting to establish on the basis of state rights doctrine a nation strong enough to wage a prolonged war. Although Moore credited the Confederacy's conscription with a high degree of success, his discussions of the friction between state governors and President Jefferson Davis, the wrangling between the state and national judicial systems, and the problems of establishing an effective bureaucracy to implement conscription have been cited by other scholars as evidence of the South's overall failure in the Civil War.

Born on a plantation in Belk, Alabama, in 1887, Moore attended Alabama Polytechnic Institute, which later became Auburn University. He received a B.S. in 1911 and an M.S. in 1912, then continued his education at the University of Chicago, earning an A.M. in 1915 and a Ph.D. in 1921. His teaching career, which spanned more than forty-five years, began while he was still in school. He served as an instructor in history while at Alabama Polytechnic, and from 1919 to 1923 he taught at the Iowa State College for Agricultural and Mechanical Arts—which later became Iowa State University—rising to the rank of associate professor. In 1923, at age thirty-six, he came to the University of Alabama to chair the history department, a position he held for the next twenty-eight years. He resigned as chair in 1951 and retired in 1958. He was also dean of the graduate school from 1925 to 1958. A long-time supporter of school athletics, he served two terms as president of the National Collegiate Athletic Association where he secured the adoption of a uniform code of ethics for athletic scholarships.

A descendant of Confederate veterans, Moore watched as the last soldiers who had participated in the Civil War passed to their reward. It is not surprising that much of his scholarship and community service was related to Southern history. *Conscription and Conflict in the Confederacy*, his first work, was followed by a monograph, *History of Alabama and Its People* (1927), and a textbook, *History of Alabama* (1935), which was used in the state's universities for thirty years. After his retirement from teaching, Moore was executive director of the Alabama Civil War Centennial Commission and served successively as vice-chair, chair, and director of the Confederate States Centennial Conference. He was on the national advisory committee of the Civil War Centennial Commission; vice-president and member of the executive committee of the Southern Heritage Foundation; a director of the Jefferson Davis Foundation; and a member of the board of advisory directors of

the Papers of Jefferson Davis. Prior to his death at Tusca-
loosa in 1967, he was honored with a joint resolution of
thanks for his service to the state by the Alabama legislature.

*Conscription and Conflict in the Confederacy* remains
Moore's most significant achievement. Although of obvious
importance, the topic is potentially a dry one. Fortunately
for Moore the cast of characters involved—the president,
members of congress, state governors, newspaper editors,
and, of course, the common soldiers—were frequently
acerbic and sometimes eloquent when expressing their
views on conscription. The author's judicious quotations
from their letters and speeches not only enliven the narrative, but they also convey a sense of the turmoil and passion
surrounding the debate. For instance, even the harshest
modern critic of Jefferson Davis will feel some sympathy
for the Confederate president when reading about the actions of governors Joseph E. Brown of Georgia and Zebulon
B. Vance of North Carolina.

Moore's approach is straightforward. He begins with a
chapter on the Confederate military up to April 1862, then
studies the First and Second Conscription Acts and the
troublesome systems of substitutions and exemptions. The
middle third of the book examines the Confederate national
and state courts in relation to conscription and the difficulties created when the Confederate armies, the state militia,
and the Conscription Bureau competed for recruits. The
last third of the book explores the conflict between state
and central authority and details the ultimate collapse of
conscription in the wake of Confederate military failure.

Moore's concluding chapter, "Did Conscription Fail?,"
provides a final analysis and summary of his themes. Moore
begins with the assumption that the South seceded in order

to preserve state rights and never escaped the paradox of having to submit to centralization in order to protect those rights. The state rights doctrine severely inhibited or compromised the ability of the Confederacy to assemble armies and wage war. The initial forces were raised by the states, with colonels appointed by the governors and lower-ranking officers elected by the enlisted men. This process made leadership a matter of popularity rather than talent, reducing the efficiency of Confederate arms throughout the war. The state governors retained a proprietary interest in "their" troops even after they entered Confederate service, pestered the administration constantly, and generally added to Davis's problems. When conscription was adopted, conflict between the state and central government grew rapidly.

Because Confederate records are incomplete, Moore tends to avoid statistics. But he considers conscription a success in the sense that, despite the system's flaws, the South placed an extremely high percentage of its white male population of military age under arms. By requiring the twelve-month volunteers to remain in the army, the First Conscription Act saved the Confederacy from collapse during the desperate summer of 1862. Almost equally important, the new law spurred thousands of men to volunteer during 1862 in order to avoid the social stigma of being drafted. This produced a body of volunteers who formed the core of the Southern armies throughout 1863 and 1864. Strengthened by the Second Conscription Act, the system produced a substantial body of men to supplement the volunteers, allowing the South to wage heroic campaigns despite ever-worsening conditions and increasing odds. Moore notes that many historians believe that conscription drove away more men that it brought in, that the alienation caused by the imposition of centralized authority on a populace of rugged individualists was counterproductive, and that the animosity it engendered between the authorities in Richmond and the state governors fatally weakened the Confederacy. Moore agrees with much of this assessment, but argues that despite its faults no other system could have produced better results.

Together with Owsley's previously mentioned work, *Conscription and Conflict* was cited by historians in the 1920s and 1930s who argued that the South had "died of state rights." But the influence of Moore's work has not been limited to a particular school of thought or interpretation, for it is cited by almost every historian who touches upon conscription. Examples range from general histories of the war and the Confederacy, such as E. Merton Coulter, *The Confederate States of America, 1861–1865* (1950), Frank E. Vandiver, *Their Tattered Flags* (1970), Emory Thomas, *The Confederate Nation, 1861–1865* (1979), and James M. McPherson, *Battle Cry of Freedom: The Civil War Era* (1988), to specialized studies like Georgia Lee Tatum, *Disloyalty in the Confederacy* (1934), Mary Spencer Ringold, *The Role of State Legislatures in the Confederacy* (1966), Thomas A. Alexander and Richard E. Beringer, *The Anatomy of the Confederate Congress* (1972), Paul D. Escott, *After Secession: Jefferson Davis and the Failure of Confederate Nationalism* (1978), and Marshall L. De Rosa, *The Confederate Constitution of 1861* (1991).

Readers of *Conscript and Conflict* should bear in mind the time and circumstances of Moore's writing. Like many Southern authors of his generation, he can be accused of searching for an internal key to the Confederate defeat in order to avoid any suggestion that the North actually beat the South in a fair fight. When reading Moore's criticisms of the Confederate Conscription Bureau one should also remember that the author had witnessed the massive conscription programs of World War I, which efficiently placed tens of millions of European men into service. Even the United States's draft, which began late and lasted only nineteen months, procured over three million men in short order. Moore praises the United States selective service system because decisions concerning exemptions were made at the community level by a draft board composed of local citizens. By comparison, the Confederate system, by which decisions were made in Richmond and potential conscripts were exempted by classification, seemed peculiarly designed to alienate the maximum number of people.

The most remarkable feature of Moore's study, however, is his open and forthright admission that a large number of Southerners never supported the Confederacy, that a substantial number did so only reluctantly, and that many others, who served gallantly at first, failed to remain faithful to the end. His discussion of desertion and resistance to conscription shows a side of the war not seen in the generals' memoirs, regimental histories, and campaign studies with which the reading public of the 1920s was familiar. Although he praises the soldiers, there is nothing nostalgic in his study. It is modern and professional, free from "moonlight and magnolia."

Current scholarship suggests that some of Moore's assumptions should be modified. While Moore sees state rights as the central issue of the conflict, scholars writing since the 1950s emphasize the role of slavery. Closer to Moore's focus on conscription, however, is the question of whether the intense state identification of Confederate soldiers was as great a liability as he indicates. Compared to the selective service system that the United States used between 1917 and 1918, which mingled anonymous recruits from every geographic region to produce a truly national army, the Confederate system seems not only inefficient, but directly counterproductive to producing the sense of nationalism the Confederacy needed in order to survive. Not only were military units initially raised by the states, after conscription was instituted the draftees were assigned not to national units (the Confederate Regular Army), but to pre-existing units of their native states, thus maintaining state identification and retaining state loyalties. The practice of electing officers detracted from efficiency, while state governors proved meddlesome.

Recently, however, Civil War historians have argued that more was gained than lost by allowing Confederate military units to retain their state identity. Reid Mitchell, Gerald F. Linderman, and others have emphasized the positive role of community in raising troops and sustaining them, at least in the early part of the war. The basic unit was the company, raised in a specific village, town, or county, usually by a prominent local citizen whose initiative was rewarded by his election to captain. Prior to leaving for the front, the company almost always received a flag made by the local women. This was ordinarily presented during a public ceremony with highly religious overtones at which the men pledged to uphold the honor of the community. Local pride fused with state pride as companies were brought together to form regiments. When the First Conscription Act required these men to serve beyond their original twelve-month commitment, very few of them deserted, thanks to their community-based sense of honor. As Mitchell notes in *Civil War Soldiers* (1988), however, as the war dragged on even community was not enough to hold the Confederate units's sense of honor together.

In their work *Why the South Lost the Civil War* (1986),

Richard E. Beringer, Herman Hattaway, Archer Jones, and William N. Still, Jr., have re-examined the whole question of state rights and the Confederate war effort. They state that historians "have sometimes let the colorful characters involved in the controversy blind them to a clear understand of what those characters did when they were not arguing with other Confederates. Far from damaging Confederate staying power or subtracting from Confederate will, state rights put in action was very likely an important reason why power and will lasted as long as they did." State governors may have been jealous of central government prerogatives, but they did more to assist than to hinder. States not only raised the initial armies, but their continued support of state units freed the central government from many burdens early in the war. The state militia, sometimes portrayed as a refuge for draft dodgers and political cronies of the governor, provided valuable emergency service and freed the national armies from the defense of nonessential territory.

Moore concentrates on conscription in the Confederacy. He makes no comparisons to the Union's problem-plagued experiences, nor does he provide context by discussing fully the history of militia conscription by states and colonies prior to the Civil War. But his study remains a valuable contribution to the overall history of conscription in America. As memories of the draft in relation to World War II, Korea, and Vietnam gradually fade, the generation that has known only an all-volunteer United States Army would do well to remember the crucial period Moore examines, when Americans (in this case, Southerners), first struggled with one of the most important issues in democratic government: can the central government compel its citizens to kill?

WILLIAM GARRETT PISTON

# CONSCRIPTION AND CONFLICT
# IN THE CONFEDERACY

# CONSCRIPTION AND CONFLICT IN THE CONFEDERACY

## CHAPTER I

### THE MILITARY SYSTEM OF THE CONFEDERACY TO APRIL 6, 1862

IMMEDIATELY after the Confederate Government was organized the problem of defense was taken over by the General Government. Probably no government was ever confronted with a greater task. It had to raise an army in the face of the enemy and to establish the productive agencies necessary to equip it and place it in the field. Moreover, it was sure to be embarrassed by the principle of States' rights, and by the fact that volunteers, believing that the war would last only a few months, would not enlist for a long term.

On February 28th, the Provisional Congress passed an act empowering the President to "assume control of all military operations in every State." It also authorized him to receive from the several States all the arms and munitions in their possession, and to receive for a period of twelve months or more, and in such numbers as he deemed necessary, the State troops that might be tendered or that might volunteer by the consent of their States.[1] This act was very inadequate, but in view of

[1] These forces, unlimited by law as to numbers, were to be received in organized units. The President was given authority to appoint the general officers. O. R. ser. IV, vol. I, 114-117.

the high regard for State sovereignty and the belief that secession could be accomplished without the shedding of blood a stronger one could scarcely be expected.

When the danger of collision with the Federal Government became more apparent, more effective measures were taken to strengthen the Confederate arms. On March 6th, an act was passed which was clearly designed for the contingency of war. It authorized the President to "employ the militia, military, and naval forces of the Confederate States," and to call for and accept volunteers, not to exceed 100,000, either as cavalry, mounted riflemen, artillery, or infantry to serve for twelve months. They were to be employed to "repel invasion, maintain the rightful possession of the Confederate States,—and to secure the public tranquillity and independence against threatened assault." The term of the militia when called into service was extended to a period not exceeding six months; and the States were deprived of the power, recognized by the act of February 28th, to prevent volunteering. However, to compensate them for this loss of power they were given the right, in derogation of the sovereign powers of the Confederate Government, to appoint the officers of the volunteer troops. These troops, officered by their own choice, as in the militia, when mustered into the service were to be regarded in all respects as a part of the provisional army of the Confederate States.[2]

Soon after the engagement at Fort Sumter other measures were adopted. The President was authorized, May

[2] On this same date, March 6th, the regular army was created, but, except for the officers, it was never raised. It was merely an organization on paper.

6th, to receive into the service, "without the delay of a formal call upon the respective States,—such companies, battalions, or regiments—as may tender themselves," to serve for any length of time he might prescribe. He was empowered to use the whole land and naval forces in the prosecution of the war. Two days later he was authorized to accept, without regard to the place of enlistment, as many volunteers of all arms as he deemed necessary "for and during the existing war, unless sooner discharged." [3] These acts embodied two noteworthy features: first, the principle of short enlistments, which President Davis steadily opposed from the beginning,[4] was abandoned; and, second, the principle of election of officers which jeopardized efficient leadership was sanctioned by this, the first effort to raise a Confederate force independently of the States.[5] It was retained in one form or another throughout the war, and not only proved to be a drag at times upon efficient leadership but produced friction between the State authorities and the Government.

These acts were inspired by the fact of real war, and they represent the initial step in the parting of the ways, so far as State potency in the prosecution of the war was concerned. It is rather striking that before the war was a month old the Delegates to the Provisional Congress, fresh from a people who had just taken a desperate step upon the principle of the sovereign power of their States,

[3] O. R. ser. IV, vol. I, 302. See same source, page 281, for act of May 6th.

[4] Message to Congress, February 22, 1862. Richardson, *Messages and Papers of the Confederacy*, I, 190.

[5] The President was given power to appoint the field and staff officers and to commission the company officers elected by the enlisted men.

concluded that it would be the part of wisdom not to shy at any measure necessary to the success of secession, even though such measure should be incompatible with the political creed espoused. The people must, if necessary, submit to the paradoxical logic of establishing the principle of States' rights or decentralization by a process of centralization. It is true that these acts did not go a long way toward sacrificing States' rights for the success of the revolution, but they were freighted with significance for those who could see and read the signs of the times. The hazy convictions, soon to be clarified and deepened, which gave rise to these acts explain the tame submission of the masses of a proud, brave, and high-spirited people to many acts of the Confederate Government that were scarcely less than despotic.

The fall of Fort Sumter caused much excitement. It reinforced the confidence in Confederate arms and aroused a spirit of immoderate buoyancy. The patriotic response in the North to President Lincoln's call for 75,000 troops was paralleled in the South by the response to President Davis' call for volunteers. The call was met with such alacrity that President Davis found it necessary to reject many applications for service.

Enthusiasm ran high because of the general apprehension that the war would be terminated in a month or two by a grand march of the Confederate forces to Washington. The people were reminded by the press that nothing was more "probable than that President Davis will soon march an army through North Carolina and Virginia to Washington. Those of our volunteers who have decided to join the Southern Army as it shall press through our borders, had better organize at once for that purpose, and keep their arms, accoutrements, uniforms, ammunition and knapsacks in constant readiness." [6]

Then, too, the victory in the first battle of Manassas produced a wonderfully thrilling sensation throughout the Confederacy, so that the *esprit de corps* of the masses in the summer of 1861 has rarely, if ever, been excelled. President Lincoln's call for 75,000 troops, his projects for increasing the strength of the Federal army and navy, and his blockade policy, all of which seemed palpable infractions of the Constitution, mobilized many of the so-called "overt-actists" for the defense of the Southern cause. In their minds these acts justified the distrust of the Lincoln Government which had led to secession. To the masses, of whatever political faith and scruples about secession, it now seemed clear that President Lincoln was determined to make an "unholy crusade" against the South and Southern institutions by any means, fair or foul. This produced a determination in the bosoms of patriots never to yield. Everywhere men boasted that the people would suffer complete annihilation sooner than make terms with the "Abolition Power upon the basis of reconstruction." When it should become necessary every man of every age and condition in life intended to abandon his business, give up all purposes of private advantage, shoulder his gun, and give his whole time and energies to the defense of the Southern soil. Rather than let the enemy possess one city or village the last Southerner would pour out the current of life freely, "that he might not live to behold himself the serf of the Puritan or the father and companion of slaves." [7] Yes, every man would fight and "die in the

[6] Richmond *Enquirer,* April 13, 1861.
[7] Columbus *Sun,* July 18, 1863.

trenches" when necessary. This was the spirit when the war was new; but, as we shall see, many of these "do or die" patriots were to be found later in the ranks of the so-called "stay at home gentry."

While enthusiasm was running high the recruiting of the army caused the Confederate authorities no deep concern. The training and equipping of men, particularly the latter, constituted the really difficult military problem. Men volunteered readily and all requisitions on the States were promptly complied with,—the governors oftentimes having more men at their disposal than were requisitioned. The Richmond *Enquirer* of August 8, 1861, said that it had been ascertained from official data that there were not less than 210,000 men in the field.

The huge preparations of the Federal Government led the Confederate Congress to pass, August 8th, another act of recruitment. This act authorized and directed the President to "employ the militia, military and naval forces and to ask for and accept the services of any number of volunteers not exceeding 400,000 to serve for a period of not less than twelve months nor more than three years." These volunteers were to be organized under the act of March 6th. It will be noted that the principle of enlistments for the war was abandoned in favor of enlistments for one to three years.

Toward the end of the year Congress became gravely concerned about the twelve-months' men whose terms of enlistment were soon to expire. The backbone of the Confederate army was in danger of being broken just at the moment when the ever-expanding Federal forces were swinging into full operation. The Confederacy could not afford to lose the services of these seasoned and experienced troops; so Congress set about to induce them to reënlist. An act was passed December 11th offering them a bounty of $50 and a furlough of sixty days with transportation to and from their homes, if they would enlist for two or three years or for the war. By way of further inducement it also promised that all troops reënlisting should, when their original terms of enlistment expired, have the right to reorganize themselves into companies, battalions, and regiments and elect their officers. The latter feature has led Major-General Upton to characterize the act as "An Act to disorganize and dissolve the Provisional Army." [8] The bounty inducement was made to include all State troops that might enlist for more than two years in the Confederate service, and to all voluntary recruits for three years or the war. [9]

Having passed an act which it believed would hold those who were already in the army, Congress next turned its attention to recruiting the depleted ranks of the companies "in the service for the war." It passed an act December 19th authorizing the Secretary of War to detail company commissioned officers for the purpose of recruiting the war-time companies. With the bounty provision of the act of December 11th as a bait it was expected that they would secure the needed volunteers.

Several military acts were passed during January and February, nearly all of which touched upon the question of recruitment. [10] Bounties were offered to volunteers and they were granted the privilege of electing their officers and of serving with troops from their respective States. Field commanders were empowered to detail recruiting parties to secure volunteers for the depleted

[8] *Military Policy of the United States*, 460.
[9] The policy of receiving recruits for the duration of the war, which was discontinued in August, was revived by this act.
[10] Acts of January 22d, 23d, 27th, and 29th, and February 17th.

companies which were in the service for three years or for the war; [11] and the President was authorized to appoint and commission field officers or captains to raise regiments, squadrons, battalions, or companies.[12] The President was authorized, also, to receive volunteers singly as well as in organized units, and to call upon the States for troops not to exceed the number already authorized by law. Every conceivable means of securing men was adopted, save that of compulsion.

The Provisional Congress expired on February 18th, having spent its last hours deliberating upon the subject of bounties. In its final act, the day before, it prescribed that a bounty should be paid to each recruit or reënlisted volunteer, as soon as pronounced by a surgeon to be fit for military service.

Thus it is seen, the Provisional Congress, which convened in its fifth and final session, November 18, 1861, gave most of its attention to the subject of recruiting the army. Acts were passed in rapid succession for this purpose; and from the beginning of the session to the end, furloughs and bounties were almost incessantly juggled with as stimulants to reënlistment and volunteering.

The military system during the first year of the war was one of rapid adjustment by legislative enactment to contingencies as they arose; and this, of course, predicated much legislation and many irregularities. The frequent changes and amendments rendered the system so

[11] This quite wisely made field commanders judges as to whether recruiting parties could safely be detached from their commands or not. Since December 19th, the Secretary of War had had the power of making these details.

[12] This was a design, of course, to utilize the personal influence of men in their communities. The prospect of a command would appeal to their vanity and ambition, and through their personal appeal many men would be induced to volunteer.

complicated as often to make it difficult to determine with exactness the meaning of the law.[13]  It is clear, however, that the Government was feeling its way into a definite line of action, even if there was a conspicuous lack of continuity of development in regard to some essentials. The development, which was toward centralization, was occasionally interrupted by a conscious concession to the principle of State sovereignty.  Congress, as it marched onward under the pressure of circumstances into the exercise of the substance of military power, occasionally interrupted itself to do obeisance with a stroke of the pen to the darling principle of State sovereignty and autonomy.  It was just these little interruptions that tended to befog matters and to inject irregularities here and there.

Building from the ground with any material at all, and against many obstacles, the Provisional Congress threw together the framework of an army.  This mosaic organization, created by the joint action of the Confederate and State governments, gave a good account of itself at Bethel, Bull Run, Springfield, Lexington, Leesburg, Belmont, and elsewhere.  This was a matter of sincere gratulation to all interested in the Southern cause, and did much to maintain a healthy war spirit.

However, as the first year of the war drew to a close the condition of affairs was serious for the Confederates. The zeal with which men sprang to arms at the outbreak of hostilities had begun to wane.  Absence from home, the privations of camp life, and the arduous duties and dangers of the service were no longer dreams; they had become painful realities to many persons.  The war

---

[13] President's Message to Congress, March 28, 1862.  Richardson, *Messages and Papers of the Confederacy*, I, 205.

had not closed, nor had Washington been reached. Volunteers were coming in slowly, and many men were taking advantage of their short terms to retire from military service. Some of the twelve-months' men were at home on furlough while the enemy was pressing on into the valleys of the Cumberland and the Tennessee, and many others were preparing to go home after the expiration of their terms of enlistment not to return unless forced back.[14]  There was good reason for the action of these men. Contemplating a short war, they had rushed off madly to the battlefront without making provisions for the care of their families. They felt that they should at least have a month or two in which to go home and adjust matters there, and many of them felt that it was only just that they should retire and let those who had not yet served have their turn.

The Confederate Congress convened at Richmond February 18th and addressed itself to the tremendous task before it. A powerful army had to be built within the span of a few weeks out of the fragments left over from the encounters of the previous year. Two things were imperative: first, large numbers of recruits had to be added, and they must be secured from a people in

[14] The twelve-months' men were generally estimated at one-third of the entire force in the field. Hon. A. H. Kenan asserted, in an address before the Georgia legislature, September 7th, 1862, that 200,000 of the 300,000 men in the field were twelve-months' men (*Southern Confederacy,* November 15, 1862). Referring to this matter, Secretary of War Randolph said that by the middle of the preceding May the terms of enlistment of 148 regiments of the twelve-months' men would have expired. "There was good reason," he observed, "to believe that a large majority of the men had not reënlisted, and of those who had reënlisted a very large majority had entered corps which could never be assembled, or, if assembled, could not be prepared for the field in time to meet the invasion actually commenced." O. R. ser. IV, vol. II, 43. See same source, 280-81, for a corroboratory statement by the new Secretary of War, J. A. Seddon.

whose souls the belligerent fires had been made less rampant by the unexpected length and magnitude of the struggle; and, second, uniformity must be introduced into the military organizations by establishing a complete centralized control over them, but the State authorities would certainly challenge any scheme of centralization which would invest the Richmond Government with all military power and make of them mere lookers-on in the stirring scenes of the tragic drama. The task was truly Herculean. The degree of success with which it was done will appear in the succeeding chapters.

# CHAPTER II

WHEN the first Congress convened the proud and hopeful Confederacy, whose flag had floated vauntingly in sight of the Federal Capital, seemed to be tottering to its fall. Forts Henry and Donelson had fallen into Federal hands in February and all defenses upon the upper Mississippi had to be abandoned; Nashville and Memphis had become the unresisting prey of the invaders; and the army of defense was retreating to the confines of Mississippi and Alabama. As if to add a crowning stroke of adversity to the Confederate cause in the West, New Orleans, the commercial emporium of the South, and the forts that guarded the mouth of the Mississippi after a feeble resistance had passed into the possession of the foe. While on the retrograde movement the Army of the West fought the battle of Shiloh (April 6th) and then retreated to Corinth.

If things were going badly for the Confederate cause in the West, they were little more encouraging in the East. Roanoke Island, the key to the inland waters of North Carolina, had been captured and General Mc-Clellan was ready when the grip of winter was broken to move on Richmond with every assurance of success that numbers, discipline, organization, and equipment could afford.

Something quick and decisive had to be done. It was imperative that the dissolving Confederate forces should be solidified and enlarged, but, as was pointed out in the preceding chapter, this was no easy task under the conditions that obtained. It was asserted by Congressman David Clopton of Alabama that volunteers were not filling the ranks as rapidly as they were being depleted.[1]

At this juncture the Confederate Congress proved its mettle. In spite of the theory of the independence and sovereignty of the States—thus far had unforeseen exigencies driven it—it passed by a vote of more than two to one [2] an act (April 16th) declaring every able-bodied white man between the ages of 18 and 35 to be subject to the military service of the Confederate States. Thus it was left for the national legislature in a governmental system, the very woof and filling of whose texture was the principle of State sovereignty and independence, to exploit and explain the extent of the power of general governments to raise and support armies.

President Davis urged conscription upon Congress for several reasons.[3] First, he thought it was imperative as a means of retrieving the mistake of short term enlistments.[4] Second, it was necessary to have uniformity

[1] Columbus *Sun*, July 12, 1863. For corroboratory evidence see Secretary of War's report. O. R. ser. IV, vol. II, 42, 279.

[2] *Journal* of the Confederate Congress, II, 154; V, 228.

[3] Message to Congress, March 28, 1863, Richardson, *Messages and Papers*, I, 206. Vice-President Stephens claimed that President Davis brought great pressure to bear on Congress to pass the conscript act (Johnston and Browne, *Life of A. H. Stephens*, 409). See Col. A. Roman's *The Military Operations of General Beauregard*, II, 433, for a similar contention.

[4] He wrote to Governor Brown that "the passage of the law was not only necessary, but . . . absolutely indispensable; that numerous regiments of 12 months' men were on the eve of being disbanded, whose places would not be supplied by new levies in the face of superior numbers of the foe without entailing the most disastrous results; that the position of our armies was so critical as to fill the bosom of every patriot with the liveliest apprehension." *Appleton's Annual Cyclopædia*, 1862, 243-4.

and regularity in the military system; a well balanced and sympathetically coördinated military machine could not be created by the independent action of twelve governments. He had early become an exponent of a simple and uniform military system with a centralized control, and he urged it with fervor upon Congress from the beginning of 1862. Third, he thought the act was necessary to secure an equal distribution of the burdens of war. Without it the ardent and patriotic would pay more than their debt of military service.[5]

The conscription act was passed about one month before the expiration of the term of enlistment of 148 regiments of the twelve-months' men. All white men within the age limits at the time the President should call for them were declared to be in the military service of the Confederate States for three years, unless they were entitled to exemption. Likewise those persons of conscript age who were already in the army were to be continued in the service for three years from the date of their original enlistment, unless the war should sooner terminate.[6] The twelve-months' men, especially affected by this act, were given the privilege to reorganize themselves and elect their officers. The furlough and bounty act of the preceding December was retained for their benefit, and if they preferred not to use the furlough they might receive in lieu of it the commutation value in money of the transportation charge. Thirty days of grace were allowed in which companies, squadrons, and

[5] He was not willing that youths under 18 and men over 35 should be conscribed; they should be kept at home as a reserve for home defense, "ready to be called out in case of emergency, and to be kept in the field only while the emergency exists."

[6] Those in the service who were under or above the conscript age were required to remain in the service for a period of 90 days, unless their places could sooner be filled by other recruits within the conscript age.

battalions might be raised by the volunteer method, with the privilege of electing their officers. This gave those of conscript age an opportunity to avoid the odium of being forced into service. The privilege of volunteering into units already in the field was allowed, provided one volunteered before he was enrolled.

The President was given power, with the consent of the governors of the various States, to employ the State officers for the enrollment of conscripts, but in any State where the State officers were not available he was authorized to use Confederate officers. The actual procedure in enrollment was left to the discretion of the Secretary of War. When enrolled, conscripts were to be assigned by him to those companies already in the service from their respective States until each company was filled to the maximum number. In case any State did not have enough units in the field to absorb its conscripts the excess was to be held in reserve, and the depleted ranks of companies in the field from that State were to be replenished by lot at intervals of three months. The reserves were allowed to remain at home pending their call by the President. Thus the general plan was not to organize the recruits in force as separate bodies; but in the event of an emergency the President was given power to call out and organize the entire reserve, allowing each man the right to combine with others from his State, and each unit the privilege of electing its officers. It is significant that the States' rights feeling and the preferences of individuals were respected by the provision that conscripts would be incorporated into organizations from their respective States.

The act allowed conscripts to employ able-bodied men, not of conscript age, as substitutes. But the substitute device could not be trusted to conserve the talent and labor necessary to keep the civil service and the essential industries going. Consequently an exemption act was passed, five days after the enactment of the conscript law, which exempted most of the civil service retinue of the Confederate and State governments and a large number of professional and industrial classes.[7]

It will be observed that the conscription act made two radical changes in the method of raising armies in the Confederacy. First, it dispensed with the instrumentality of the States in the recruitment of the armies; that is, it substituted the direct call for the call through the States. Second, it made compulsory enlistment the cardinal principle of military service, although voluntary enlistments were still allowed under certain conditions.

Congress passed the act primarily to retain the twelve-months' men, notwithstanding the original conditions of their enlistment, and secondarily to force other able-bodied men into service. This was a severe test of the patriotism and devotion of the twelve-months' troops. After nearly a year's experience with the diseases, privations, and hardships of the soldiers' life they were fondly anticipating a return to their homes where they could, temporarily at least, enjoy their habitual comforts and pleasures. They had, too, for self-justification, the unanswerable plea that they had borne their part of the burdens and dangers and that it was time for those equally interested and capable, who had as yet remained at home, to take their turns at the front. How great the sacrifice involved in the renunciation of their hoped-for release and pleasures may be more easily felt than de-

[7] See page 53 below.

scribed. "Yet was there scarce a murmur of disappointment and disaffection, and not an instance, as far as known, of resistance or revolt." [8]

The passage of the first conscription act aroused universal attention and interest. Many wild rumors concerning its contents were soon extant, and the War Office and newspaper editors were deluged with questions. Some of the answers by newspapers, antedating as they did the publication of the regulations necessary to put the act into operation, were misleading and served to agitate anxious and uneasy minds. Some of the newspapers took advantage of popular anxiety and misapprehension to accelerate enlistment. Strained interpretations were made to convince the able-bodied young man that the best thing he could do would be to volunteer at once.

There was a variety of opinion concerning conscription. Fundamentally, however, it did not harmonize with the individualistic instincts of Southerners and with their conception of genuine manhood. In language which became familiar to our ears when we entered the World War, it was often pointed out that the flower and youth of the country should have been allowed to volunteer before the disgrace of a draft was fastened upon them. It is a safe assumption that conscription could not have been adopted by a popular referendum, although the Columbus *Sun* of April 22, 1862, asserted that the press and the people as a whole indorsed conscription.

[8] Secretary of War to the President, January 3, 1863, O. R. ser. IV, vol. II, 281. President Davis said in an address before the Mississippi legislature, December 26, 1862, that they were willing to serve on if all the delinquents were forced into the army. *Southern Confederacy*, January 16, 1863.

Generally speaking, where the law pressed most heavily opposition to it was strongest. Conscription was quite naturally received with favor by those who had already volunteered and by their families at home.[9] Every able-bodied man at home who was not courageous and patriotic enough to volunteer, they thought, ought to be forced into the army. As regards those not in the army, their attitude depended on circumstances. If they were exempted or could easily employ substitutes there was a tendency not to object seriously to conscription, for it was obvious that more men were needed at the front and any system of recruiting which took $A$ and left $B$ did not alarm the latter, unless he were a detached States' rights doctrinaire. Those who could stay out of the army under color of the law were likely to be advocates of a more numerous and powerful army, and were most eloquent expounders of the principle that the war must not cease until the "atrocious foe" had been driven from the sacred soil of the South and a grand and glorious independence had been established. Not so with many of those who were not favored with position and wealth. They grudgingly took up their arms and condemned the law which had snatched them from their homes, as dear as life itself to them, and forced them to incur the dangerous and onerous burdens of the soldier's life, while their neighbors whose lives and families were not dearer to them were left at home. The only difference was the circumstance of position and wealth,

[9] President Davis wrote Governor Vance, November 1, 1862, that the conscript act had not been popular anywhere outside of the army. "There . . . it served to check the discontent which resulted from retaining the twelve-months' men beyond their term of original engagement." But in the same letter he rejoices over the evidence of popular support of any measure necessary for victory. O. R. ser. IV, vol. II, 154.

and perhaps these were just the things that had caused heartburnings in the more peaceful times.[10]

The sentiment of thousands in the upland counties, who had little interest in the war and who were not accustomed to a rigid centralized control, was probably well expressed by the following quaint epistle addressed to President Davis by a conscript at Camp Chowan, North Carolina:

> "Headquarters 'Scalp-Hunters'
>                   Camp Chowan, N. C., January 11.
>
> Excellency Davis:
>
> It is with feelings of undeveloped pleasure that an affectionate conscript intrusts this sheet of confiscated paper to the tender mercies of a Confederate States mail-carrier, addressed as it shall be to yourself, O Jeff, Red Jacket of the Gulf and Chief of the Six Nations—more or less. He writes on the stump of a shivered monarch of the forest, with the pine trees wailing round him,' and 'Endymion's planet rising on the air.' To you, O Czar of all Chivalry and Khan of Cotton Tartery! he appeals for the privilege of seeking, on his own hook, a land less free—a home among the hyenas of the North. Will you not halt your 'brave columns' and stay your gorgeous career for a thin space? and while the admiring world takes a brief gaze at your glorious and God forsaken cause, pen for the happy conscript a furlough without end? Do so, and mail it, if you please to that

[10] The following little lampoon taken from the *Southern Literary Messenger*, May, 1862, is a mild representation of their attitude toward those who framed the conscript law:

"The Conscription Bill, Its Beauty"

"Let us hail in this crisis the prosperous Omen
That our Senate shows virtue higher than Roman;
It has spurned all titles of honor—for rather
Than claim that each member be called 'Conscript father'
All self-aggrandizement they lay on the shelves,
And declare all men 'Conscripts', excepting *themselves.*"

city the windy, wandering Wigfall didn't winter in, called for short Philadelphia.

The Etesian winds sweeping down the defiles of the Old Dominion and over the swamps of Suffolk come moaning through the pines of the Old State laden with music and sigh themselves away into sweet sounds of silence to the far-off South. Your happy conscript would go to the far-away North whence the wind comes and leave you to reap the whirlwind with no one but your father the devil to rake and bind after you. And he's going.

It is with intense and multifariously proud satisfaction that he gazes for the last time upon our holy flag— that symbol and sign of an adored trinity cotton, niggers, and chivalry. He still sees it in the little camp on the Chowan, tied to the peak of its palmetto pole, and floating out over our boundless confederacy, the revived relic of ages gone, banner of our King of few days and full of trouble. And that pole in its tapering uprightness typifying some of the grandest beauties of our national-ity; its peak pointing hopefully toward the tropical stars and its highest end—run into the ground. Relic and pole, good-bye. 'Tis best the conscript goes; his claim to chivalry has gone before him. Behind he leaves the legitimate chivalry of this unbounded nation centered in the illegitimate son of a Kentucky horse-thief.

But a few more words, illustrious President, and he is done done gone.

Elevated by their sufferings and suffrages to the high-est office in the gift of the great and exceeding free people, you have held your position without a change of base, or purpose of any sort, through weary months, of war and want, and woe; and though every conscript would unite with the thousands of loyal and true men in the South in a grand old grief at your downfall, so too will they sink under the calamity of an exquisite joy when you shall have reached that eminent meridian whence all progress is perpendicular.

And now, bastard President of a political abortion, farewell.

'Scalp-hunters,' relic, pole, and chivalrous Confederates in crime, good-bye.   Except it be in the army of the Union, you will not again see the conscript.

NORM. HARROLD,
of Ashe County, N. C." [11]

As a rule the leading newspapers supported the conscription act.[12]   There were some, like the *Southern Confederacy*, that favored the principle of conscription but opposed the exercise of the power of it by the Confederate Government.   They counseled acquiescence and obedience, however, for the sake of the Confederate cause but thought that the Administration and Congress should be held to a strict accountability for it.   Still others, notably the Augusta *Constitutionalist*, the North Carolina *Standard*, and the Montgomery *Mail* were uncompromising in their denunciation of Confederate conscription. They challenged both the constitutionality and necessity of it.

A few extracts will serve to illustrate the line of argument by the press in support of conscription.   The Columbus *Sun* observed: "Among the first to approve it, further reading and reflection has confirmed us in our conviction of its overwhelming necessity to meet the press-

[11] This letter was picked up by a member of the Mounted Rifles in a deserted Confederate camp on the Chowan River, about thirty miles from Winton.   It was headed: "Read it if you want to, you thieving scalp-hunter, and forward, post-paid, to the lord high chancellor of the devil's exchequer on earth, Jeff Davis, Richmond, Va." Moore, *Rebellion Record* (Rumors and Events), vol. VII, 87-88.

[12] The act was contrary to the States' rights tenets of the *Mercury* and *Examiner*, but they embraced it because it seemed to be the only practicable way by which the Confederacy could defend itself at that moment and ultimately take up the offensive which they had since the summer of 1861 urged upon the Administration.

ing exigencies of the country and to enable us to repel
the enemy now invading our soil. The South should form
itself into one great camp of instruction—every man
capable of bearing arms should be a pupil." [13] The
*Southern Confederacy* regretted to see some of its con-
temporaries opposing it "on the merits of the question.
It should have been adopted at the commencement of
the war. It is the only just, equitable, and practicable
method of raising and keeping up the army, and we hope
the people everywhere will approve it. It treats all
alike, and puts every man in the Confederate States upon
an equal footing. In volunteering, thousands of eager,
patriotic men get into service who are physically unfit
to perform military duty," while "there are others who
are physically able, but will never volunteer. . . . Conscription will reach them as it will all other classes." It
was of the opinion that "the State governments and not
the general government, should exercise it. The Confederate Government ought to control the army after it
is raised, and turned over to it by the States, but . . . the
States should proceed in their own way to furnish" their
quotas, "and in our judgment that way should be by conscription." [14] "As a means of equalizing the necessary
military duties of any people," observed the Clarke
County (Alabama) *Journal,* "conscription is the fairest
and best mode of raising men; volunteering the most
unequal and unjust, and levies by States the most uncertain and hazardous." It makes the "unpatriotic perform the same duty as the most devoted citizen, and
brings the rich to the same level with the poor. . . .
Levies of troops by States in the Revolutionary War were

[13] April 22, 1862.
[14] April 20, 1862.

almost an absolute failure." [15]    The *Examiner* thought the law a "stringent one, but it is based on a necessity, which could not be avoided, and none should be disposed to avoid the responsibilities which it imposes and which its necessity has long pointed out." [16]

Many men, among whom were some of the most eminent jurists and statesmen of the country, thought the act was unconstitutional and they challenged the necessity for passing it.    The opposition of such men as Vice-President Stephens, Toombs, Brown, Orr, Foote, Judge Pearson, and Oldham predicated a troubled future for conscription.    Stephens thought that the Confederate Government had legal authority only to make requisition upon the States when it needed more men than it could raise by voluntary enlistment, hence "the Conscription Act was a very bad policy."    He feared that it would result in conflict with the governors and check the ardor of the people.    "Conscripts," he predicted, "will go into battle as a horse goes from home; volunteers, as a horse goes towards home: you may drive the latter hard and it does not hurt him." [17]    Governor Brown engaged President Davis in a long and tedious correspondence in

[15] May 5, 1864.

[16] Quoted in the Clarke County *Journal*, June 26, 1862. The *Confederate Union*, which was one of the opposition papers, said, May 6th, that it was a well-known fact that there were not enough arms to arm all of the troops already in the field. "Thus men cannot be used and they will be taken at a time which will cause many thousand acres of land to lie idle." *Southern Confederacy*, May 9, 1862. The opposition papers based their arguments primarily upon the unconstitutionality of the act. The *Standard* had another reason; namely, "This is a war of people against arbitrary power—let it be fought by volunteers . . . standing armies, raised by the draft, are the adjuncts and supporters of despotism." January 22, 1862, quoted by Clarence C. Douglass in the Trinity College *Historical Papers*, Series 14, 9.

[17] Johnston and Browne, *Life of Alexander H. Stephens*, 409, 415; Phillips, *Toombs, Stephens, Cobb Correspondence*, 598.

which he protested against conscription with all the power of his pen. He regarded it as a "bold and dangerous usurpation by Congress of the reserved rights of the States." To his good friend, the Vice-President, he wrote that he was sure his position was that of the old States' rights leaders and he was willing to stand or fall upon their doctrines. "I entered into this revolution," he said, "to contribute my humble mite to sustain the rights of the States and prevent the consolidation of Government, and I am still a rebel till this object is accomplished, no matter who may be in power." [18] Linton Stephens, brother of the Vice-President, expressed the sentiments of leading oppositionists when he told the Georgia legislature that the essence of conscription was the "right to take away the fighting men of the States against the wills of both the citizens and the States"; that sovereign States could not be coerced in such manner, even though "all the judicial tribunals on earth" should affirm that they could.[19]

It was often charged by the enemies of conscription and of the Administration that if a necessity for conscription existed it was intentionally created. Had not General Toombs offered a bill in Congress in the fall of 1861 which provided for the replenishing of the armies by

[18] Phillips, *Toombs, Stephens, Cobb Correspondence,* 597. Brown's correspondence with the President is recorded in the Official Records, ser. IV, vols. I and II; *Confederate Records of the State of Georgia,* vol. III, 167-352; and Fielder's *Life and Times of Joseph E. Brown,* 355-397.

[19] *Southern Confederacy,* November 15, 1862. Someone who wrote frequently to the *Confederacy* under the pen name of "Silver Grey,"—a sort of political seer, apparently—was highly displeased with the conscription act. It was his opinion that it had "opened another Pandora's box," that it would chill the enthusiasm of patriots, deprive the harvests of harvesters, and the farms and homes of persons necessary to control the slaves. As to the legal character of the act he observed: "It is a measure more despotic and more flagrantly unconstitutional than was ever attempted by the Government with which we are at war."

the "old recognized constitutional mode of requisitions upon the States for troops," leaving to the States their constitutional right to  appoint and commission their officers? [20]   It was "deliberately and intentionally" rejected in order that the military power might be centralized.  "The appointment of officers was the milk in the cocoanut" which the Administration sought.[21]  The Athens *Banner* admitted the necessity for conscription but said that it resulted from "criminal dillydallying while the Philistines were coming upon us." [22]

Over against this strong opposition to the conscription act lay the endorsement of a large number of reputed States' rights men.  The support of such stalwarts as Rhett, Yancey, Wigfall, and Pollard went a long way toward making conscription acceptable to the people.[23] Senator Yancey's position probably astonished some of his colleagues and friends.  He had not a single doubt that the act was constitutional and said that he had not

[20] Col. A. Roman says that President Davis opposed bills in January, 1862, for authorizing another call upon the States for troops. *Op. cit.* vol. II, 432.

[21] Linton Stephens' speech before the Georgia legislature, quoted in the *Southern Confederacy*, November 15, 1862.  The Augusta *Constitutionalist* made a similar charge, October 30th.

[22] Quoted in *Southern Confederacy*, September 26, 1862.  Congressman A. H. Kenan of Georgia said that Congress had been dilatory in order "to hold the twelve-months' men who were now seasoned.  To have lost these would have meant defeat."—Address before Georgia legislature, Southern *Confederacy*, November 15, 1862.

[23] The Cabinet and most of the leaders of Congress endorsed it (O. R. ser. IV, vol. I, 1133).  Senator Wigfall endorsed conscription on the floor of the Senate in spite of the fact that he had formerly threatened in burning oratory to have King Cotton humble the North, and the world, if need be, in defense of States' rights.  He "could not admit that the Southern States were joined in a 'loose league'" (*Mercury*, April 2, 1862). The Columbus *Sun* (April 18, 1862) reported that the Virginia legislature had endorsed conscription and expressed a willingness to coöperate with the Confederate authorities in the passing of laws to give full effect to it.

heard or read an argument against it that was tenable.[24]

Some influential leaders who had predilections against Confederate conscription yielded to it as a necessity. For example, Honorable Hershel V. Johnson of Georgia said that with perils on every hand he could do nothing less than waive his objections to the conscription act and yield to it a "cheerful acquiescence." The only other alternative, he warned, was annulment, but "nullification is folly, and secession is disintegration." [25]

[24] *Journal of the Congress of the Confederate States,* II, 154; Richmond *Enquirer,* September 10, 1862.

[25] *Southern Confederacy,* October 7, 1862. Congressman Kenan appealed to the editors of the *Southern Federal Union* to desist from their opposition. "Let us not yet stand," he said, "separate as the waves but one as the ocean." The question of States' rights could be adjusted after independence had been won. Savannah *Republican,* May 15, 1862.

# CHAPTER III

## SUBSTITUTION

THE practice of substitution, previously allowed by the Confederate Government and by some of the States, was continued by the conscription act.[1]  It was provided that persons not liable for service might be received as substitutes for those who were, under regulations issued by the Secretary of War.  Apparently it was intended to mollify the harshness of the conscript law, but more particularly to reserve skill and talent for service in the essential industries.  It would give an advantage, of course, to the individual who had accumulated wealth, but likely he had succeeded through his enterprise and efficiency and was just the person whose services were needed at home.  The policy, however, was not generally understood and accepted.  It required a keener analysis of the collateral requisites of the war and more self-effacement than the public could make.  It was not popularized by the fact that many of those who had money sought substitutes whether their talents could be used to advantage behind the battle lines or not.

The process of substitution was fairly simple.[2]  The

[1] Substitution was allowed by the Confederate Government as early as October, 1861.  Men who had volunteered were allowed to employ substitutes at the rate of one-per-company-per month (O. R. ser. IV, vol. I, 694).  The practice was apparently abolished by order of the War Department, March 5th of the following year (*Ibid.*, 971).  Some of the States that had raised their quotas by draft also allowed substitution (*Ibid.*, 967, 975).

[2] O. R. ser. IV, vol. I, 1099.

person employing the substitute accompanied him to the camp of instruction where he was enrolled, if found to be lawfully exempt from military duty and pronounced by the surgeon to be in all respects fit for service. Then the former, the "principal" so-called, was given a certificate of discharge by the commandant of the camp.[3]

Noncommissioned officers and privates might with the permission of their captains procure substitutes, provided that no company should receive more than one substitute per month.[4]   The latter provision caused a good deal of discontent among those who volunteered after the passage of the conscription act and procured substitutes before enrollment began. After the publication of the one-substitute-per-company-per-month clause[5] the enrolling officers held them subject to service, notwithstanding they had substitutes in their places. Vice-President Stephens wrote a letter to the Secretary of War, July 17th, on behalf of this class of persons in Georgia. He suggested that instructions should be given to Major Dunwoody to exempt every person liable to conscription, "who honestly and bona fide [had] a substitute not liable to conscription in his place." He thought that when for want of proper information proper form had not been followed, but "the substance obtained, any evil ensuing ought to be corrected, for if these parties had waited a few weeks and reported themselves to Major Dunwoody with their substitutes, they could, I take it for granted, have been received without question."[6]

Although the chief purpose of substitution was to

---

[3] Conscripts were not allowed to employ a substitute after having been mustered into service. O. R. ser. IV, vol. I, 1099.

[4] O. R. ser. IV, vol. I, 1093.

[5] *Ibid.*, 1093.

[6] *Ibid.*, vol. II, 6.

utilize the potentialities of men along industrial lines, there was from the beginning, as might have been expected, a general propensity to regard it through purely private considerations. The average man of draft age thought of it as an opportunity to escape service; he thought of what it might mean to him in the way of comfort and security, and not of what his exemption might mean to the common weal. Hence, once he secured his freedom by it, he became a perfectly normal, private, being and turned himself to the exploitation of the business opportunities created by the war. Having absolved himself from the business of war, he was likely to turn to the business of profiteering, and of preaching the then beautiful gospel of the extermination of the "Yankees." [7]

Some of those who had wealth and could not secure immunity under the exemption act made a rush for substitutes, and in their anxiety to procure them they were not very scrupulous about complying with the law. The character of the substitutes mattered not at all to them. Any substitute that could keep a would-be "principal" out of the army was a good substitute. From the beginning the substitute market was buoyant, so great was the demand for substitutes. The market price of a soldier, it is said, soon mounted to from $1,500 to $3,000.[8] In July, 1863, Jones noticed advertisements in the newspapers offering $4,000 for substitutes, and one man in Hanover County, Virginia, offered a farm of 230 acres. By

[7] *Southern Confederacy,* October 3, 1862; *Examiner,* January 4 and 18, 1864; Savannah *Republican,* January 26, 1864; O. R. ser. IV, vol. II, 586.

[8] Columbus *Sun,* December 25, 1863; Moore, *Rebellion Record,* VIII (Rumors and Incidents), p. 46; Lossing, *The Civil War in America,* III, 96. It is said that the bounty for substitutes started at $150. *Appleton's Annual Cyclopædia,* 1862, 246. Expressed in terms of gold the price would be about a third less than indicated above. Schwab, *The Confederate States of America,* 167.

the latter part of the year the price had risen to $6,000.[9]
In the case of Curtis, Judge Pearson spoke of substitutes
receiving as much as $5,000 to $10,000.[10] The newspapers carried many advertisements for substitutes like
"want ads" in our present dailies, and sometimes a would-
be substitute advertised for employment, though this was
rare.[11] To employ a substitute or to accept services as
one was regarded by many, and almost universally so in
army circles,[12] as highly reprehensible; so the parties did
not usually disclose their names when advertising. Trans-
actions were usually made through newspapers, mercan-
tile firms, banks, and business offices. "The procuration

[9] *Diary*, vol. I, 387; II, 85. Reduced to a gold basis the $4,000 substi-
tute would be worth $425 to $450, and the $6,000 substitute at the latter
part of the year would probably be worth less than $400. Schwab, 166-
167. In all probability the prices mentioned in the advertisements were
higher than those usually paid for substitutes. The fact that they were
fancy prices would be a good reason for mentioning them.

[10] 60 N. C., 180.

[11] Apparently the few persons who advertised their services were those
who took advantage of the demand for substitutes to ask extortionate
prices. The following examples will illustrate the character of the advertisements. Others may be found in Wallace P. Reed's *History of
Atlanta;* and in many of the leading newspapers.

### "A Substitute Wanted!

"A substitute wanted for the war. Call at the store of Brown, Fleming & Co., Masonic Building, a few doors below the Trout House. Call
at once. A liberal sum will be paid. *Southern Confederacy,* May 3,
1862."

### "Wanted!

"Anyone wishing to act as a substitute for a man subject to the conscript act, will receive the following compensation: a likely negro boy
and five hundred dollars. Address B., Appeal Office. Vicksburg *Whig,*
August 6, 1862."

### "A Substitute!

"I will serve as a substitute in the Confederate service for two thousand five hundred dollars, or in the militia for one thousand five hundred
dollars. For further information apply to Thomas Allen, Depot Agent at
Duck Hill. Moore, *Rebellion Record,* VIII (Rumors and Incidents), 46."

[12] O. R. ser. IV, vol. II, 996.

of substitutes [became] a regular business;"[13] and like other kinds of business, it developed its brokers and its agents, some of whom became reputed for their disregard of law and of the canons of decent business.[14]

Many unnaturalized foreigners, boys of 18, diseased men, and old men unfit for service were employed as substitutes, and the practice did not cease when orders forbidding it were promulgated.[15] Moreover, men between the ages of 18 and 35, legally incompetent to serve as substitutes, were accepted as such, and principal's certificates were forged by able-bodied men who could not employ substitutes.[16] Many of the companies organized after the passage of the conscription act enrolled substitutes at will, and principals did not always, as required

---

[13] O. R. ser. IV, vol. II, 45; Reed, *History of Atlanta*, 122.

[14] The *Dispatch* (June 24, 1862) said there were "immense frauds and villainy being carried on" in Richmond "in buying and selling substitutes by men who make a regular business of the nefarious trade." The Adjutant General of Virginia attested to the same fact, and added that most of the substitutes were "vagabond foreigners and other persons of the same stamp who deserted as soon as they were mustered into service." Pamphlet, Boston Athenæum, cited in *Rhodes*, vol. V, 438.

The business became so vicious before the end of 1862 that an order was issued forbidding the employment of substitute agents. A violation of the order made the principal, substitute, and agent liable to service, and the money paid to the substitute and agent confiscable to the Government. The offender was also liable to any punishment that a court martial might impose. In June of 1863 the Superintendent of Conscription indorsed the project of employing expert detectives to apprehend substitute agents "in their habitual fraud." O. R. ser. IV, vol. II, 583, 611; *Appleton's Annual Cyclopædia*, 1862.

[15] Order after order was published to prevent these abuses but they persisted until substitution was abolished. O. R. ser. IV, vol. II, 45, 73, 78, 611, 670.

[16] O. R. ser. IV, vol. II, 670, 940, 946. Lossing, *The Civil War in America*, III, 96. Some persons who were exempted engaged themselves as substitutes. It was held, *in re Curtis*, that such action forfeited the right to exemption and hence the party involved became liable to service; and that such action was a perversion of the law and must be prevented *proprio vigore*. 60 N. C. 180.

by law, report to the camps of instruction with their substitutes.[17]

Substitutes gleaned by these illegal devices were for the most part a worthless lot.[18] They went into the army not to fight but to get the principal's bounty, and then to desert at the first opportunity. Some became professional substitutes; that is, they learned the art of bartering their bodies for a handsome sum and then deserting from the ranks to negotiate another lucrative trade.[19] It was said that some unnaturalized foreigners became very proficient in this sort of enterprise.[20]

Needless to say that substitution, if allowed to pursue these channels, would soon reduce greatly the strength of the army. The common soldier and the officers generally sustained an unmitigated contempt for both the principal and the substitute.[21] Both were to their minds contumacious cowards and moral weaklings;[22] and patriotic women hissed and groaned at the mention of their names. Generals did not care to have their armies cumbered with substitutes. I have been told by some of those who served in General Jackson's command that he

[17] O. R. ser. IV, vol. I, 1130; vol. II, 7.

[18] Ibid., 45, 996; The Examiner, quoted in the Clarke County Democrat, January 11, 1863.

[19] See O. R. ser. IV, vol. II, 996, for the statement of the Secretary of War to the President concerning this fact. The Adjutant General of Virginia reported (September 1, 1863) that many of the substitutes who deserted "played the same game over again as often as they had a chance to do so." Pamphlet, Boston Anthenæum (quoted in Rhodes, vol. V, 438).

[20] The Independent, August 29, 1863; O. R. ser. IV, vol. II, 45.

[21] "Generals don't care to have their commands encumbered with substitutes." Richmond Examiner, quoted in Clarke County Democrat, January 11, 1863. See also Columbus Weekly Sun, September 1, 1862.

[22] The Weekly Sun, November 11, 1863; Clarke County (Ala.) Journal, May 14, 1863.

had only a few substitutes.[23]   Major-General Thomas C. Hindman, commanding the Trans-Mississippi District, was reported to have ordered (June 2d) that substitutes should not in any case be accepted in his command.[24] Other officers apparently refused to receive them, for the Secretary of War ordered that any officer rejecting a substitute should report the reasons.  They generally took advantage of this opportunity to state their objections to the policy of substitution.[25]

The system of substitution had become pernicious when Congress assembled in extra session in August, 1862.  It had produced moral turpitude, popular discontent, and class animosity; and was greatly reducing the fighting strength of the army.  The Secretary of War informed Congress that the privilege of employing substitutes at pleasure had been greatly abused.  Substitutes were illegally obtained and were usually unfit for service, if they did not desert.  His department had improved the situation materially by prohibiting the employment of foreigners as substitutes, but "the evils of the system [were] still very great," and it would be necessary to institute other remedial measures.  He was of the opinion that substitution should be allowed only where the principal's services at home were as useful to the public as they would be in the field.[26]

The substitution system needed a severe purging, as the Secretary of War recommended, but Congress did

[23] There was one company of sharpshooters which had only one substitute and his comrades were always surprised after each engagement to find that their hireling had not deserted.

[24] O. R. ser. I, vol. XV, 780; *Ibid.*, ser. IV, vol. II, 73; *Journal of the Congress of the Confederate States*, vol. 5, 331.

[25] Richmond *Enquirer*, August 2, 1862.

[26] O. R. ser. IV, vol. II, 45.

not alter it.[27] Perhaps it was thought that the new conscription act which raised the age limit from 35 to 45 years would leave little substitute material and the system would automatically adjust itself. The orders published by the War Office for the enforcement of the new conscription act contained nothing pertaining to substitution which had not appeared in previous orders. Any able-bodied citizen over eighteen, of good moral character, and not subject to enrollment might be legally employed as a substitute.[28] The system continued to disgrace itself and to embarrass the Government in the usual ways.

The second conscription act (September 17, 1862) made substitutes between the ages of 35 and 45 liable for service on their own account and thereby raised the very important question of the status of their principals. The principals had employed these substitutes at a specified sum for the duration of the war or for three years, but Congress by this act took them from the principals and left the principals without proxies in the army. The War Department took the position that the principals became liable for service again the moment their substitutes were taken by the act.[29] The principals brought

[27] Senator Phelan of Mississippi said that "A bill nearly abolishing the whole system did pass the Senate" but the House "foolishly" refused to accept it. O. R. ser. I, vol. XVII, Pt. II, 791.

[28] Persons not domiciled were not eligible, it was repeated, for substitutes, and the content of "domicile" was defined as "residence with intention permanently to remain in [the Confederate] States and to abandon domicile elsewhere." O. R. ser. IV, vol. II, 164.

[29] By order of the Secretary of War, September 8th, when a substitute became liable to service his principal also became liable; so there was nothing left for the principal affected by the conscription act to do but seek relief in the courts, if he did not wish to go to the front. The Secretary held tenaciously to his position until substitution was abolished. The government of South Carolina took a similar position with regard to its principals as early as March. O. R. ser. IV, vol. I, 975.

suit in the courts to protect their rights. They claimed that since they had furnished substitutes upon the condition laid down by the Government, the Government was under contract with them to exempt them during the time for which they had engaged their substitutes. Even if the transaction were in the nature of a contract between them and their substitutes only, they maintained that the Government could not impair it since it was made under the authority of a public law.

Judicial opinion was divided but in most cases, of which reports have been found, it was held that substitution did not involve a contract with the Government. The contractual aspect of the subject was not generally stressed, however, until after Congress abolished substitution. The core of the few opinions adverse to the policy of the Government was the incompetency of the Secretary of War to give the second conscription act a retroactive application. Thus the judges chose to liberate the principals upon the basis of the unconstitutionality of the methods employed by the Government to draft them, rather than upon the more doubtful ground of the constitutional impotency of the Government to abrogate a contract.[30]

Although Congress was in session when the hair-splitting discussions about this particular class of principals were going on in the newpapers, upon the street corners, and in the court rooms, it did not register an opinion as to whether the Secretary of War had exceeded his discretionary authority or not. Nor did the opinion of prominent judges that the principals could be conscribed only by a retrospective act of Congress induce it to pass such act. It was said that Congress "dared

---

[30] See pages 178-181 below for a fuller discussion of the court decisions pertaining to substitution.

not go back and undo its blunders by a retroactive law. Accordingly the War Department with high-handed tyranny took it upon itself to remedy this by setting at naught the provisions of the act of Congress." [31] The Secretary of War evidently ignored the adverse opinions of some of the State judges, as he had done before, because he issued no orders countermanding those pertaining to the liability of principals. Orders reiterating the former orders as to principals were promulgated November 3, 1862, and February 27, 1863; and on July 20th an order was issued which introduced the new principle that when the service of a substitute was lost from any cause, other than the casualties of war, his principal became liable to service.[32] Presumably the Government did not bother the principals who were exonerated by the high State courts, since it was its policy to accept the findings of these courts in the cases before them.

By the end of the year there was general contempt and disdain among patriots for substitution, and Congress considered seriously various propositions for radically amending the system or abolishing it altogether. The strong currents of opposition that had set in against it betokened for it nothing better than a begrudged existence in 1863.[33]

At the opening of the new year the War Department

[31] *Southern Confederacy,* January 14, 1863.

[32] This order was the result of the wholesale desertion of substitutes, O. R. ser. IV, vol. II, 648. It was the logical result of the opinion of the Department that service was the debt of the principal and not of the substitute, so far as the Government was concerned. In the fall of 1862 Congress considered seriously amending the law so that the principal would become liable when his substitute deserted. House *Journal,* vol. V, 312.

[33] Congress continued to deliberate upon plans of revision and of abolition during the winter and spring of 1863. See the House and Senate *Journals,* Index, "Military Service."

devised new plans for preventing substitution frauds. Enrolling officers were instructed not to honor the certificate of exemption of a former soldier who claimed he had furnished a substitute unless his certificate was signed by a battalion or regimental commander.[34] Commandants of conscripts were instructed to accept no substitute unless they were sure that he had been employed in good faith, that he was reliable and of good character, and that "the interests of the Government [would] not suffer because of physical or moral inferiority of the substitute to the principal, or by the withdrawal of men from the service, who were interested in the country." [35]

Incisive investigations were instituted and they unearthed more substitute scandals. The Superintendent of the Bureau of Conscription said that "self-styled officers" were signing substitute papers "without commission or authority"; and company and regimental officers, whether "moved by corruption, complacence, or recklessness," had exhibited a criminal disregard of law and orders. He had abundant evidence of irregularities "grossly criminal and mischievous, in the conduct of the officers of the army respecting substitutes," but all remedies applied by his Bureau had, because it lacked authority, generally failed and guilty officers escaped with impunity. All limitations imposed upon recruiting officers or upon company and regimental officers as to the num-

[34] A month or two later it was ordered that all such certificates must bear the signature of the general commanding the army (O. R. ser. IV, vol. II, 412, 553). The Clarke County *Journal,* June 11th, observed that a panacea for the ills of substitution in the army had been found. Since generals did not care to have their commands encumbered with substitutes, the "substitute market may be hereafter quoted as dull, and few offering." Quoted in the *Examiner.*

[35] O. R. ser. IV, vol. II, 611. The Superintendent of the Bureau of Conscription recommended that substitutes should be received for examination at only one camp of instruction in each State. *Ibid.,* 583.

ber and qualifications of substitutes had generally proved "mere fetters of straw." It had been the policy of the Bureau and of the War Department, he said, not to make innocent persons suffer for the misdeeds of officers, but this leniency had inspired little gratitude. In all cases allegations of innocence by principals, the efforts of lawyers, public sympathy, and the active exertions of public functionaries and influential men were encountered.[36] He indorsed the use of expert detectives to ferret out all malefactors, especially the professional substitute agents and the self-willed and corrupt army officers who were wont to disregard law and orders.[37]

There were able-bodied young men at home with whom to replenish the wasted armies, and the demand for them had become so importunate by the summer of 1863 that thoughtful patriots everywhere tried to discover how they had escaped through the meshes of the law. The opinion was current that the poor had done and were doing their part and that most of those who were skulking behind were men of wealth for the security of whose rights and interests the war was begun.[38] Those who had a philosophical slant of mind tried to discern what manner of folk these derelicts were, who could with equanimity of mind and peace of soul enjoy the good things of life while their fellow-countrymen were enduring the worst of tortures for a common defense. They were discovered, it was thought, to be just ordinary men who had been unmanned by the possession of wealth. Indifference, selfishness, and sordid ideals had been infused

[36] The phrase "public sympathy" should be understood to embrace the friends and relatives of the party concerned.

[37] O. R. ser. IV, vol. II, 582.

[38] Superintendent Preston said that wealthy farmers, enterprising manufacturers, and mechanics furnished most of the substitutes. O. R. ser. III, vol. V, 696.

into them by wealth. Discussions appeared in the papers which purported to dissect this monster and to show how it degenerated the unfortunate possessors of it.[39]    A general overhauling of the military system so as to induct able-bodied delinquents became a popular demand.[40]

In the search for measures by which to induct men of means all eyes were focussed unavoidably upon substitution. The abolition of it became a noisy and portentous demand. There were those who believed that the armies would dissolve within a few months unless the substitute law was repealed and its beneficiaries were forced to take the field in person,—"so intense and growing [was] the dissatisfaction [with the] wholesale withdrawal of the slave-holding class as it engendered. The repeal of that law would be hailed with universal acclaims of joy by our gallant soldiery." [41]

The perilous condition of affairs led General Bragg and seventeen other generals of the Army of Tennessee to hazard a joint lecture (July 25th) to the President, through the War Office, on the woeful weakness of the armies numerically and on methods of renovating them. They were "thoroughly satisfied" that there were enough able-bodied young men to replenish the decimated ranks without injuring materially the great interests of the country; and they implored the President to lay hold upon them, (1) by resorting to the old expedient of calling

[39] The *Independent*, August 8, 1863.
[40] *Jones' Diary*, II, 30; O. R. ser. IV, vol. II, 656.  *Appleton's Annual Cyclopædia*, 1863, 231; The *Independent*, August 29, 1863.
[41] The *Eastern Clarion*, quoted in the *Independent*, August 1, 1863.  A Mississippi correspondent of President Davis' asked why extortioners and speculators should be allowed to furnish worthless men while they stayed at home and filched the public. The partiality and corruption shown in "the mysterious discharge of many able-bodied conscripts," he said, was causing discontent and dereliction. O. R. ser. vol. II, 856.

on the States for them, or (2) by assembling Congress in extra session at once to modify the conscription policy so as to reach them. Various discrepancies in the military system were touched upon, but they "especially" deplored that "unfortunate provision of the exemption bill which [had] allowed more than 150,000 soldiers to employ substitutes." [42]  And they expressed an honest conviction that not one in a hundred of these substitutes was then in the service.[43]  "In numerous instances fraudulent papers were employed, in others diseased men were presented and accepted but to be discharged; in still more cases vicious and unprincipled substitutes were bought up but to desert at the first favorable moment." [44]

It was the opinion of the War Department that it would be disastrous to assemble Congress and wait for it to revise the military system and for the new adminis-

[42] The Adjutant General was surprised at this statement, and since his office did not have the data with which to verify the figures presented he asked the generals to inform him how they ascertained their figures.  O. R. ser. IV, vol. II, 696.

The Assistant Secretary of War had a few days previously observed that more than 50,000 persons were said to have employed substitutes (O. R. ser. IV, vol. II, 656). In November, the Assistant Adjutant General regarded 50,000 as a "moderate estimate" (*Ibid.,* 947), and the Secretary of War reported to the President that the best conjectural computation would place the total number of substitutes "at not less, certainly, than 50,000" (*Ibid.,* 997). The *Sun,* November 11, 1863, observed: "It is said that the books in the War Department at Richmond show that over 74,000 substitutes have been put in the army since the war began."  The *Examiner* of August 4, 1863, and March 25, 1864, estimated the number at 60,000 to 70,000. In his volume, the *Third Year of the War* (p. 183), the editor of the *Examiner* estimated the total number of substitutes to be more than 70,000. The truth seems to be that no one knew just what the number of substitutes was, but all the facts point to a large figure.

[43] The *Independent* of August 29, 1863, asserted that three-fourths of the substitutes deserted, many of whom were foreigners.

[44] O. R. ser. IV, vol. II, 671. For corroboratory statements concerning the use of fraudulent papers see the reports from the Adjutant General's office, *Ibid.,* 808, 946.

trative mechanisms to swing into operation. The Adjutant General wrote to General Bragg and his associates that the only hope lay in promptitude of action with the means and powers already possessed.[45] And vigorous action was taken with regard to substitution.[46]

The rigid surveillance instituted revealed conditions that were intolerable. Among other things, fraudulent substitute papers were quite generally being used.[47] The Bureau of Conscription reported that there were probably 10,000 to 15,000 of these spurious papers, and all available data indicated that not more than five to ten per cent of the substitutes had been put into the army.[48] The Adjutant General informed the Secretary of War a few days later that "a fearful proportion of substitute papers [were] fraudulent." [49]

Some of the conscript officers became so impatient and disgusted that they adopted the high-handed scheme of making principals prove that their substitutes were in the army when there was no positive evidence that they were out.[50] Owing to the general delinquency of substitutes no principal could relish the onus of proving that his substitute was in the army.

The Richmond authorities shared the general impatience and disgust with the substitute system, and turned their attention to securing its abolition when Congress convened. Their indictment of it was trenchant. It was

[45] O. R. ser. IV, vol. II, 696.

[46] *Ibid.,* 801, 822, 823, 827.

[47] *Ibid.,* 808.

[48] The Assistant Adjutant General thought that not more than 3,000 or 4,000 substitutes over the age of conscription were in the field. *Ibid.,* 940, 947. See also *Appleton's Cyclopædia,* 1863, 17.

[49] O. R. ser. IV, vol. II, 946. The War Department called in all substitute papers in November to detect fraud. Columbus *Sun,* November 27, 1863.

[50] *Ibid.,* 911.

the opinion of the Adjutant General that it was a "most glaring error" to have permitted substitution at all, and the only way to retrieve it was to apply the ax to the root of the system. "I am persuaded," he said, "that the people would cheerfully submit to a law annulling the contract between the principal, substitute, and the Government upon refunding the substitute money. The number of men to be secured by such a measure is very large." [51] The Secretary of War observed: "The law allowing substitutes has proved a means for depleting the army, while it has done more than any single measure to excite discontent and impatience under service among the soldiers. The persons received as substitutes have proved, for the most part, wholly unreliable;—while the fact that the wealthy could . . . purchase liberation from the toils and dangers . . . naturally produced among the less fortunate and poorer classes repining and discontent. The men thus exonerated, too, were, from the advantages of position and learning they had enjoyed, among the most spirited and reliable of our soldiers. . . . The law is deservedly regretted and reprobated by all acquainted with its operation." He earnestly recommended to the President that it should be repealed at once and all those who enjoyed its benefits should be subjected again "to the sacred duty of defending in arms their property, their liberties, and their country." [52]

[51] O. R. ser. IV, vol. II, 947. One Robert S. Hudson of Benton, Miss., wrote President Davis that there was much dissatisfaction with substitution in Mississippi. He said that most of the principals had gone into speculation and extortion to reimburse themselves for the money they had expended for substitutes. With the exception of a few honest planters, he thought the principals hired substitutes in order that they might engage in speculation. O. R. ser. IV, vol. II, 857.
[52] Ibid., 996. President Davis indorsed the Secretary's recommendations. Ibid., 1041.

The proposition for abolishing substitution raised in a new form the question of the relation of the Government and the principals who had furnished bona fide substitutes. As we have seen, the principals whose substitutes were taken from them by the second conscription act were held to be liable for service. Now it was proposed to make the rest of them liable by the more positive method of abolishing the privilege of substitution. Would Congress violate a contract obligation to the principals by passing such an act?

The President and his Cabinet foresaw the legal question involved [53] but they believed that Congress had full authority to abolish substitution and to force the principals into service. The Secretary of War was of the opinion that Congress could "regularly and constitutionally" abolish substitution, which was not a compact between the Government and the principal but a privilege "which from grace or policy the Government has accorded to him." The principal, he contended, was exempted only from the call for which the substitute was furnished; after this call he fell back into the body of citizens and became "one of the militia of the country, liable like all others to be summoned on other exigencies and upon further calls to military service." He thought the obligation of service should not be evaded or bargained against longer.[54] The President concurred in the Secretary's opinion: "To accept a substitute," he observed, was "to confer a privilege, not to enter into a contract." [55]

When Congress convened, December 7th, the demand for the abolition of substitution was inexorable. Popular

[53] They anticipated some difficulty in enforcing a law abolishing substitution. O. R. ser. IV, vol. II, 947.

[54] O. R. ser. IV, vol. II, 997.

[55] *Ibid.*, 1041.

clamor against it was tumultuous: Congressmen-elect were pledged to repeal it;[56] generals in the field petitioned for the abolition of it;[57] some of the State legislatures expostulated Congress to abolish it;[58] the President and his Cabinet had committed themselves to its abolition and were prepared to meet any legal objections that might be raised; and the War Department had attempted to garner statistics concerning its operation, which were not anticipated to be of a complimentary character.

In evidence of the pressure that was brought to bear, Congress immediately directed its attention to substitution.[59]   It requested the President to inform it as to the number of substitutes in the army and what proportion of them were foreigners.[60]   But no satisfactory information could be given.   Authority was at this time dissipated between three bureaus of conscription and officers were dilatory in making reports.[61]   Not being able to get the statistical information sought, Congress proceeded to act upon the urgent recommendations [62] of the President and upon its own general information.   Before the end of the month a bill abolishing substitution passed both Houses by a large majority,[63] and it was

[56] Columbus *Sun,* November 11, 1863.

[57] *Jones' Diary,* vol. II, 123.

[58] The *Sun,* November 11, 1863; *Appleton's Annual Cyclopædia,* 1863, 230; *Journal,* vol. III, 496.   The *Sun* (November 10th) reported that Governor Brown had asked the legislature to petition Congress to abolish substitution.

[59] The deliberations of Congress on the subject of abolishing substitution may be found in the *Journal,* vols. III, 434*f,* and VI, 515*f.*

[60] O. R. ser. IV, vol. II, 1054.

[61] See pages 191-193 below.

[62] O. R. ser. IV, vol. II, 1040.

[63] The vote was 52 to 13 in the House and 17 to 4 in the Senate, according to *Appleton's Annual Cyclopædia,* 1863, 230, 232.   The *Journal* shows that the House passed the bill for the abolition of substitution and the

immediately followed by another one making all those who had furnished substitutes liable for service.[64] Thus did substitution receive its *coup de grace;* and thus did the army receive its "New Year's Gift," as some one put it.

The principals were ordered, January 9th, to report for service without delay, either as volunteers or conscripts; [65] but they challenged the constitutionality of the act on the ground that it annulled a contract which they had bona fide executed.[66] They met with indifferent success. The highest courts of the States and the Confederate district courts generally rejected the depositions of the principals [67] on the ground, first, that nothing more than a legislative contract existed and in every such contract there was an implied condition that any succeeding legislature might repeal it;[68] and, second, grant-

one for enrolling the principals by the vote of 52 to 13; but there is no record of the Senate's vote on the first bill, and its vote on the second one was 17 to 2. Vols. III, 499, and VI, 561.

[64] The President approved the first act December 28th, and the second the following January 5th (O. R. ser. IV, vol. III, 11 and 12). It is noteworthy that the Federal authorities refused to recognize that a contract existed between the Federal Government and the principals who had furnished substitutes for the Northern armies. O. R. ser. III, vol. V, 627.

[65] They were given the privilege of volunteering until February 1st. O. R. ser. IV, vol. III, 12.

[66] The Richmond *Whig* thought the discussions in Congress of substitution exhibited little regard for the Constitution; but suspected that the "little respect in which substitute men" were held would "influence a temporary acquiescence in them." Quoted in McPherson, *History of the Rebellion,* 1211. The *Examiner* opposed the act conscripting the principals (January 4th and February 6th). Editor Pollard called it an act of "unparalleled infamy." *Third Year of the War,* 185.

[67] O. R. ser. IV, vol. III, 201.

[68] The Texas court observed, in the case of Mayer, that the limitation imposed upon Congress as to *ex post facto* laws had generally been construed by the courts to relate to criminal legislation only. 27 Texas, 715.

ing the contention as to contract, there was nothing in the Constitution to prevent the Government from impairing a contract.

There were inferior judges and a few superior judges in all of the States who maintained that the act conscripting principals was unconstitutional. The Secretary of War complained that he had experienced much embarrassment from the eccentric decisions of these judges.[69]

The principals of North Carolina found an asylum in Chief Justice Pearson, at chambers, who took the position that the decisions made by the high courts of the other States were made *post litem motam*. His decisions at chambers did not possess the full force of an adjudicated case but they were by the statutes of the State, and the Secretary of War acquiesced, binding until overruled by the supreme court.[70] The supreme court, however, did not convene until June. Must the Government, then, stand by with folded arms and see all of the principals of North Carolina liberated for months by the towering stubbornness and dogmatism of Judge Pearson, sitting placidly at chambers in Salisbury?[71] Congress promptly answered the question by suspending the writ of habeas corpus, among other cases, in that of persons trying to avoid military service.[72] Thus it was proposed

[69] O. R. ser. IV, vol. III, 231. See page 180 below for a fuller discussion of the position of the courts.

[70] O. R. ser. IV, vol. III, 176, 197.

[71] It was said that he liberated from 115 to 120 persons. O. R. ser. IV, vol. III, 256. In the case of Gatlin *v.* Walton, the supreme court later overruled his decisions.

[72] O. R. ser. IV, vol. III, 203, 256. The probable necessity of this had been suggested by the Assistant Adjutant General in the preceding fall. O. R. ser. IV, vol. II, 947.

to deal with refractory judges by suspending civil authority.[73]

But civil authority did not yield gracefully to the military in North Carolina. Judge Pearson took the view that the act of February did not apply to the principals of substitutes, though it must have been generally known that the opposition of some of the courts to the drafting of principals was the immediate cause of the suspension of the writ of habeas corpus.[74] Governor Vance threatened to support his decisions with the armed forces of the State if necessary.[75] The President's reply was that the acts of Congress for recruiting the army would be enforced in the same manner and to the same extent in North Carolina as in the other States.[76] The Secretary of War informed Governor Vance that all temporary discharges granted by Judge Pearson before the writ of habeas corpus was suspended would be honored but any that he had made afterward would be ignored by the Confederate officers.[77] The firm stand of the President and the Secretary of War reduced the Judge and the Governor.[78]

The suspension of the writ of habeas corpus smothered the hopes of the principals for a legal exemption, unless they could secure a detail.[79] Some absented themselves

[73] The trouble with the courts in the Cis-Mississippi Department was duplicated in the Trans-Mississippi Department. See General Greer's complaint, O. R. ser. I, XXVI, Pt. II, 493-95; ser. IV, vol. III, 231.

[74] The Raleigh *Confederate*, March 24, 1864; Clarke County *Journal*, January 14, 1864.

[75] O. R. ser. IV vol. III, 176.

[76] *Ibid.*, 201.

[77] *Ibid.*, 198.

[78] See pages 187-188 and 286 below for a more complete statement of this episode of conflict.

[79] The Bureau of Conscription anticipated that they would advance new claims to exemption. It instructed enrolling officers to regard the fact

from the country. The *Whig* observed: "By what routes they have started we do not know, but it is certain that they have gone, fled, vamosed." [80] "Thousands will soon withdraw," the *Examiner* asserted cynically, "in virtuous indignation at the jesuitry of our legislators. The children of Israel will decamp in companies of fifties and hundreds, and hasten back to the flesh pots of Egypt, weary of the unsubstantial manna of Confederate notes, and frightened by the fiery serpents of conscript officers." [81] Millionaires had suddenly become "nautical in their tastes, and are bidding high for little cribs in Mallory's Department." [82]

It was freely talked among the principals that the Government's policy of inducting them would impair public confidence in its good faith and the consequence would be a rapid depreciation of Confederate currency. "Already, it is understood, holders of Confederate bonds are putting them before the market, to be disposed of

that they had furnished substitutes as *prima facie* evidence that they had no claim to exemption and to examine with care any claims advanced by them (O. R. ser. IV, vol. III, 25). Notwithstanding this caution, Preston complained in April that there seemed to have been "a general effort to keep principals of substitutes out of the army." Many of them had been detailed, he said. O. R. ser. III, vol. V, 696.

[80] Quoted in the Clarke County *Journal*, January 14, 1864. "The speculators and extortioners who hired substitutes are in consternation," Jones recorded in his *Diary* (vol. II, 123), "some flying the country since the passage of the bill putting them in the army, and the army is delighted with the measure."

[81] January 4, 1864. Two weeks later this paper stated that bids amounting to tens of thousands had been made for department clerkships by some of the "most atrocious speculators" in Richmond.

[82] January 18, 1864. The *Examiner* called attention (June 10th) to an extraordinary method of escape. One McClure, an embalmer, "ceased his regular business and turned his wagons and coffins to the more profitable business of smuggling fleeing Israelites and Yankee 'Southern citizens' across the lines." It repeatedly called the attention of the Government to this vicious practice and to the burden of supporting the families of the emigrés left behind.

at any price." [83]  There may have been a tendency, born
of pique, to depress the credit of the Government by
a concerted flooding of the market with Confederate
bonds, but there was no precipitous depreciation at this
time in money values.  After their wrath subsided and
sober reflection possessed them again, the principals
who held bonds, like other persons, submitted to the
all-pervading authority of their central Government.
What revelations of central authority the cruel Mo-
loch of war was making to the citizenry of the
Confederacy!

The evils flowing from the substitution system which
allowed men, who for any reason did not want to serve
in the army, to employ proxies were most serious and
far-reaching.  On the face of it there was a semblance
of fairness, but it furnished no relief for those in the
lower walks of life.  The masses could not avail themselves of the privilege proffered by it,[84] hence they were
impressed anew with the convenience and power of capital.  They must go into the ranks while their neighbors
who happened to be blessed with money could hire substitutes; they must give of their blood while men of
property must give only of their possessions.  The inequality produced gave much poignancy to the slogan of
the mountains: "the rich man's war and the poor man's
fight." [85]  It took the heart and nerve out of many poor
soldiers and they took to the dens and caves, where sometimes by concerted effort they prepared to fight the bat-

---

[83] Richmond *Whig*, quoted in the Clarke County *Journal*, January 14,
1864.

[84] O. R. ser. IV, vol. II, 7.

[85] Jones, *Diary*, II, 30; O. R. ser. IV, vol. III, 915, 1041; North, *Five
Years in Texas*, 167; *Independent*, August 29, 1863; Fleming, *Civil War
and Reconstruction in Alabama*, 102.

tles of self-defense against what seemed a wealth-sponsored Government, in preference to the battles of sacrifice for their wealthy compatriots against the Federal armies.

Substitution did more than reduce the *esprit de corps* of the poor and those of the wealthy who were doing their part; it tended to incline persons liable to service to be ever on the search for substitutes, and consequently they were not imbued with the spirit of the soldier and could not buckle on the armor of service. They thought so much in terms of service by proxy that they could not visualize the glamor of service *in persona*. A man snatched from the substitute chase was not psychologically equipped for service in the field. It had, too, a depressing effect upon soldiers in the field. Some of them never reconciled themselves to service because there was always a chance to get a substitute; they looked forward eagerly to the fruition of their dreams and were not inclined to expose themselves, for they wanted to be every whit whole when the happy day of delivery arrived. Soldiers generally, as we have seen, had immeasurable contempt for substitutes, and it was very distasteful to them to serve as patriots for $11 per month alongside of hirelings with good pay. Moreover, it took thousands of good soldiers to keep the substitutes with their commands, and most of them were of little value when present.

When the system was abolished there was a sigh of relief, but it had already produced irreparable loss. It reduced the numerical strength of the army, honeycombed it with sedition, broadened the hiatus between the rich and the poor, alienated the sympathy and support of many persons of means, and agitated once again the sensitive political conscience of ultra-States-rightists. All things considered it was the most lamentable feature of the conscription system.

# CHAPTER IV

## STATUTORY EXEMPTION (1862-1864)

No more serious problem confronts a nation at war than that of properly allocating its man power. During the World War we were sufficiently enlightened upon the difficulties involved to understand, in a measure at least, the endless vexation it caused the Confederacy where there was a scarcity of men and an industrial system that was extravagant in its demands upon labor. An ideal system of exemption would hold from the armies only the requisite numbers for effective production in each non-combatant field of service. But the accomplishment of this ideal is scarcely to be expected in any nation, least of all in a young nation that is not thoroughly orientated and stabilized.

The Confederate States had a large supply of un-skilled labor which could be utilized toward relieving the labor demands in the essential industries. The most productive portions were supplied with slave labor which under skillful direction would, when cotton had proved to be the Pretender and not the real King in the economic world, supply abundantly the agricultural needs of the army and of the public. By the careful development and direction of the reserve powers of its peculiar system of labor the Confederacy had an opportunity to relieve much of its fighting population from the obligations of production and manufacture.

Five days after the passage of the first conscription

act Congress made its initial attempt at an economical separation of the population into two groups, the fighters and the producers.[1]  The following classes were placed on the producers' side of the line: Confederate and State officers, and the clerks allowed them by law; mail carriers and ferrymen on post roads; pilots and persons engaged in the marine service; employees on railroads and river routes of transportation; telegraph operators; ministers in the regular discharge of their duties; employees in mines, furnaces, and foundries; printers; presidents and professors in colleges and academies; teachers of the deaf, dumb, and blind; teachers having 20 pupils or more; superintendents, nurses, and attendants in public hospitals and lunatic asylums; and one druggist in each drug-store.  Superintendents and operatives in wool and cotton factories could be exempted at the discretion of the Secretary of War.

The *raison d'être* of the exemption act, so far as Congress was concerned, was the necessity of exempting governmental officers and able-bodied men to keep in active operation agriculture, trade, mechanic arts, and the interests of education and religion as indispensable collaterals  to the war and the preservation of a healthy national life.  To the minds of many within the military age and possessed of good sound bodies, it offered an opportunity to escape the arduous duties, privations, and dangers of camp life and of service in the field.  Thousands of those who loved the good things of life, and who, because of a lack of interest in the war or through sheer cowardice were reluctant to go to the front, began to cast around for some way of sheltering themselves under the beneficent wings of the exemption act.  In this process

[1] O. R. ser. IV, vol. I, 1081.

of "agreeable adaptation" they exhibited a remarkable degree of resourcefulness. Those vocations which afforded exemption suddenly became popular, and were filled to the point of overflowing. When they could hold no more and a new school, a new postoffice, a new shop, a new drug-store, or a new office could not be created; or through the assistance of an influential friend or public representative a detail to some harmless service in some secure place could not be had, strange bodily afflictions and mental discrepancies were developed. It was said that in a few cases where the body did not respond properly to these attacks, an offending toe or finger was severed.[2]

It will be instructive as well as interesting to notice how some of the clauses of the exemption act were perverted and abused by the ingenuous devices of those for whom the peal of the cannon and the scent of gunpowder had no fascination.

The clause which exempted teachers in schools of twenty pupils or more made school teaching popular.[3] Indeed the public school system, which had not received wide extension in the South before the war, now had a spontaneous development in some localities. It would not strain one's credulity to believe, with the Columbus *Weekly Sun*, that many of these impromptu schoolmasters knew as little of the substantial and practical facts in the usual academic course as Don Quixote did of knight errantry. This paper August 26, 1862, said that

---

[2] Montgomery *Advertiser,* quoted in the Columbus *Sun,* May 8, 1862.

[3] There was good reason for exempting teachers since they were not at all plentiful. The census of 1860 showed that there were 18,819 teachers in the public schools and 4,606 in the academies and colleges of the seceded States; and according to the *Independent,* November 5, 1864, a large percentage of them returned to the North when hostilities broke out.

an inordinate number of little schools had sprung up all over the country, and that in almost every county in some of the States a captain's company of "professors" could be found.[4]   Since there were no qualifications laid down for teaching, the number of such schools might be increased *ad infinitum*.   Indeed, about the only conceivable limitations were the number of students and the indulgence of patrons, for it took little money to finance some of the schools in those days.   A very small salary would equal that paid to the private in the army, and some, we are told, who had other means of support, were generous enough to teach gratis, if they could only get twenty or more students.[5]

In each drug-store already established and doing business "one apothecary in good standing," who was a "practical druggist," was exempted from the operations of the conscript law.   This exemption by which drug-stores were to be maintained in the hands of practical pharmacists, was intended to meet a real public need.   Certainly Congress did not intend to give birth to the character of "apothecary shops" that soon sprang into being.   According to the *Sun* some proprietors and clerks "turned their establishments into large speculating concerns, dealing indiscriminately in everything, from strawberries and watermelons up to sugar, coffee, molasses, and spun cotton,

[4] The editor was pained that a good soldier was "frequently spoiled in making up an indifferent pedagogue"; and he lamented the character of teaching that was being foisted upon the schools.

[5] Many who felt keenly the need of these men at the front, and looked askance at the character of their instruction, urged Congress to amend the exemption act so as to meet this flagrant injustice and abuse. It was pointed out that women could meet all the demands of teaching; and even if they could not, elementary education might be interrupted temporarily for the sake of independence from an "implacable foe." See *Southern Confederacy*, September, 1862, and *The Weekly Sun*, August 26, 1862.

including cards at $15 a pair." Thus, it would appear, the establishments of some exempted "apothecaries" looked more like variety stores or produce depots than drug-stores, and we may imagine that the "apothecaries" themselves probably knew as "little of chemistry, either theoretical or practical, as a Patagonian does of Sunday." "Nearly every little village in the Confederate States has an exempt in the person of some 'apothecary' whose dealings are not confined to any particular branch of any particular trade, and who could not analyze the simplest compound or put up the plainest prescription in a satisfactory manner if his life depended upon it; a few empty jars, a cheap assortment of combs and brushes, a few bottles of 'hairdye' and 'wizard oil' and other Yankee nostrums, is about the only evidence of their being 'apothecaries in good standing'." [6]

The exemption of Confederate and State officers from military service was a fruitful source of escape for many young men who had no fancy for the tented fields. Many of them eagerly pushed and elbowed their way into little insignificant county and other offices to escape service in the army. They did not disdain the offices of constable, deputy bailiff, coroner, county clerk, and postmaster. It is said that some of these offices even went at a premium,

[6] September 2, 1862. The editor of the *Sun* said he was in Atlanta in the spring of 1862 and saw a couple of "apothecaries" from another State "buying up molasses, tobacco, brown domestic, cotton yarns, and writing paper for speculation, and when asked what connection there was between spun cotton and pharmacy, they replied that drugs could not be had and they were therefore investing in other articles that would 'pay' as well. These men were both exempt from military duty by reason of their being 'apothecaries in good standing.'" A "select" committee of the Senate reported (March 18, 1865) that no complaint had reached Congress of abuses of exemption by physicians and druggists (O. R. ser. IV, vol. III, 1150). This committee, however, held a brief for statutory as against executive exemption.

young men offering from $50 to $500 for positions in post offices as clerks, or for the procurement of an appointment as postmaster in some little remote country office.[7] These little offices became forums upon which all of the wickedness of the "Yankees" was canvassed and vigorously condemned, and feelings of fervent patriotism were expressed; though the full-chested young men in charge might have surrendered their positions to educated women or to disabled soldiers.

The militia also furnished a place of refuge for many young men, especially in Georgia. Governor Brown was so obsessed with the idea of the importance of the militia that he steadfastly refused to allow his militia officers to be conscribed. The War Department ruled at first that militia officers betwen 18 and 35 were embraced by the conscription act, but it soon gave way under the vigorous protests of Governor Brown and exempted all of them who were recognized by their States as in commission.[8] After Governor Brown had won his point apparently he did not hesitate to fill militia offices with young men who were subject to conscription. He was ridiculed throughout the war by the press of his own State, as well as of the other States, for protecting useless militia officers. Apropos of the situation in Georgia, the *Sun* observed: "Every little office with perhaps a few exceptions, from corporal up to Major General, has been sought and obtained by young gentlemen—who are *ex officio* the military teachers and superiors of the older men." Hundreds of young men, of conscript age, were "virtually appointed by his Excellency Jos. E. Brown, to drill

[7] Columbus *Weekly Sun*, September 22, 1862; Savannah *Republican*, January 20, 1863; Charleston *Daily Courier*, April 2, 1863; the *Examiner*, January 20, 1863, and February 6, 1864.

[8] O. R. ser. IV, vol. I, 1105, 1120, 1123, 1129, 1154, 1155, 1169.

and discipline the militia, a duty which they occasionally perform by having a Saturday evening 'muster' about fifteen minutes once a month." [9]

There was less objection to the exemption of ministers than any other class of persons, though there were those who would have all of them within the conscript age to shoulder their muskets and repair to the battlefield.[10] Many ministers volunteered for service, and little evidence of abuses in respect to their exemptions has been found. It was hard to turn preacher instantaneously and get a church, and only those ministers "in the regular discharge of their ministerial duties" were exempted by law. However, a few were "called" by the exemption act to spend their Sundays in the pulpit, and they spent the other six days out in the world. But there was no general inclination to cavil with the ministry, for Southerners were as a rule very religious and public opinion would frown upon any attempt to substitute the pulpit for the camp.

Congress touched a responsive chord in the hearts of the masses when it exempted their ministers. They could not indorse that degree of inconsistency involved in the dragging of God's chosen ministers from the altars and

---

[9] September 22, 1862. See also the *Confederacy*, July and August numbers, 1862. Savannah *Republican*, January 8, 1863; and the *Southern Recorder*, quoted in the *Republican*, April 30, 1863. These are typical examples of press criticism. It was said that there were from 2,700 to 3,000 militia officers exempted in Georgia. O. R. ser. IV, vol. III, 348, 384, 419.

[10] The *Enquirer*, August, 1862; the *Sun*, September 15, 1862. Representative Collier of Virginia thought they could do more good on the battlefield than "in preaching to empty meeting houses and old maids and grannies." The *Confederacy*, January 28, 1863. It was held, *in re* Cunningham, that a minister who engaged in another kind of work for self-support was not precluded thereby from claiming exemption as a minister. 60 N. C., 392.

forcing them into the ranks, after they had dedicated
their cause to Him and were fasting and praying for success, and appointing days of thanksgiving for each victory. They could not dispense with the aid and guidance
of the ministry in an hour of such temptation and tribula-
tion. The *Sun* was of the opinion that there was more
need for preaching than ever before, because "the very
devil appears to be stalking at large in every little village and city in the Confederacy." The preachers "should
remain at home and renew their efforts to civilize a people who have become terribly possessed with the demon
of extortion and other lesser spirits of a similar nature."
"The minister and the priest [should] remain at the
altars; continue their warfare against the Devil (who
is perhaps the strongest ally of the Yankees)," and labor
to build up the church.[11]

There was still a chance for some of those who could
not avail themselves of the various opportunities for
exemption already described; they could renew or pro-
claim their allegiance to some foreign power. The conscription act included able-bodied men between the ages
of 18 and 35 who were "residents" of the Confederate
States. The Secretary of War interpreted the act to
mean all persons who had acquired a domicile in the Confederate States. Since the question of domicile was a
question of law he ordered that it should be determined
by the facts in the case and not by the opinion or oath of
the party concerned.[12] Cases soon came before the courts
in which it was generally held that all persons not do-

[11] September 2 and 15, 1862.
[12] O. R. ser. IV, vol. I, 1127. At the beginning the Department was
lenient as to proof. The oath of the party, supported by the oath of one
credible witness, was deemed sufficient proof. *Ibid.*, vol. II, 70.

miciled, *e.g.,* not having permanent residence, in the Confederate States were exempt from service in the armies. However, at least two Confederate district judges held that all men residing and transacting business in a country were bound to turn out in defense of it when it was being invaded.[13] The War Department accepted the prevailing opinion of the jurists and instructed the enrolling officers to the effect that *domicile* meant residence with intention permanently to remain in the Confederate States. Long residence did not of itself constitute domicile. A person might acquire domicile within a few months or he might not acquire it within twenty years of residence. If there was a constant intention to return to the native country the alien did not acquire domicile.[14] This interpretation was thoroughly in accord with the practice of nations, but its susceptibility to abuse is obvious.

The position of the War Department and the courts encouraged many young men to lose their domicile by embracing new intentions with regard to the old country.[15] It was said that many of those who protested that they had never contemplated citizenship in the Confederacy had been accustomed to voting and scrambling for office.

[13] Judge Halyhorton of Virgina and Judge Jones of Alabama. *Daily Courier,* July 8, 1863, quoting the Mobile *Tribune;* the *Enquirer,* August 27, 1863. The decision of Judge Swayne of Memphis, Tennessee, was typical. Quoted in the *Sun,* May 16, 1862.

[14] O. R. ser. IV, vol. II, 164. It was suggested that declarations of the party, the exercise of the rights of citizenship, the acquisition of real estate, etc., might be taken as criteria for determining the fact of domicile.

[15] The *Republican,* April 22, 1863; the *Courier,* July 8, 1863, quoting the Mobile *Tribune; Examiner,* March 22, 1864. During the spring of 1862 nearly 500 young men in Mobile, Alabama, were reported to have received certificates of citizenship from consular agents, and Mobile had a white population of only 20,854. Appleton, *Annual Cyclopædia,* 1862, 245.

With disgust the *Sun*, August 26, 1862, remarked that, while before hostilities broke out foreigners could rarely be found, "now . . . it is astonishing to observe the great number of 'foreigners' in our midst and therefore exempt from the Conscript Act. . . . Nearly every town and city in the South is full of this class of persons— most of them able-bodied young men who voted at our elections two years ago, and who ought to be in the tented fields in defense of the government of their adoption. Instead of this, however, many of them are engaged in smuggling and amassing their private fortunes at the expense of our cause." [16]

There was much discontent throughout the war because aliens were not conscripted. In some towns practically all business was done by aliens, who charged extortionate prices and did their part in depreciating the currency. Leading newspapers crusaded for the conscription of them and Congress deliberated on various propositions for the same.[17] The hostility toward foreigners was great, and some of them who were entitled to exemption were rushed off to camp only to be released upon the protest of consuls to the War Department. The hope of foreign intervention probably held Congress to a liberal policy with regard to aliens.

Some who could neither affiliate themselves with any of the exempted classes nor lose their citizenship, developed the wanderlust. Under various pretexts they roamed from State to State and between the North and South, taking advantage of a weak spot in the law which made

[16] Apparently it was little trouble for them to avail themselves of consulate papers.

[17] For example, see the *Courier*, March 2, April 10, and July 8, 1863; the *Republican*, April 22, 1863; the *Enquirer*, April 7 and August 27, 1863; the *Examiner*, March 22, 1864; the *Journal*, vol. III, 236.

it impossible to draft men outside of the State in which they were domiciled.[18]  In all the cities and towns in the Confederacy, it was said these "padding gentry" could be found claiming exemption from enrollment because they lived in another State or owed allegiance to some other power, and representing themselves as sojourners or transient visitors.  This thing alone, in the opinion of the *Sun* September 2, 1862, caused the enrolling officers more trouble, perhaps, than all other obstacles combined and accounted in a large degree for the paucity of conscripts which was just then eliciting the deep concern of the Confederate Government.[19]  It doubted not that when peace came a large portion of these "citizens of other States" and "foreign subjects" would claim all of the privileges of full-fledged citizens.

In the summer and fall exemption was extended by the discretionary powers of the Secretary of War to new classes, and the opportunities for abuse of the law were correspondingly enlarged.  Manufacturers of ordnance, cotton goods, and other army supplies, complained that labor was so scarce they could not comply with their contracts.[20]  To meet this deficit of labor, persons were enrolled and detailed to work in Government plants and for Government contractors at the journeyman trader's price.[21]  Factories of various sorts, foundries, railroads,

[18] According to the Clarke County (Alabama) *Journal* of January 7, 1864, some wealthy parents sent their sons to Europe to avoid conscription.

[19] The provost-marshal of Atlanta, Georgia, complained to the Secretary of War (July 20th) that the Government was being most dexterously swindled by hordes of migratory persons (O. R. ser. IV, vol. II, 9).  The Secretary of War recommended that power should be given to enroll conscripts wherever found and Congress conferred the power by special act, October 8, 1862.  O. R. ser. IV, vol. II, 45, 162.

[20] O. R. ser. IV, vol. I, 1127; vol. II, 50.

[21] *In re Guyer,* 60 N. C., 66.

furnaces, and mines offered good employment and exemption from service in the field, and persons within the draft age flocked to them for employment.[22]

Salt making became a popular employment, we are told, because of its power to save young men from the despoiling business of war. Governor Milton informed the Florida legislature (September 11th) that many persons from other States had come to Florida to engage, along with Floridians, in making salt to avoid conscription. He knew of ten of them who had been engaged in salt making for six weeks but had not produced a bushel of salt.[23]

The exemption system had not worked as advantageously as it was hoped it might and there was much dissatisfaction with it. Although intended to subserve the interests of the public at war, persons had shown a painful tendency to translate it into considerations of private interests. In the summer there was considerable complaint that many more men were employed in factories and in the railroad service than were necessary to supply the wants and needs of the people.[24] There was even a feeling of hostility toward the manufacturers of the prime necessities of life who sold their surplus at exorbitant prices, in utter ingratitude for the favor conferred upon them by the exemption act. Their conduct made the exemption act, as applied to them, seem like class legislation. The manufacturers of cotton and woolen goods

[22] The *Confederacy*, September 24, 1862. I. M. St. John, Superintendent of the Niter Bureau, said that many attempts had been "made by designing men to avoid military service through niter as well as through commissary, ordnance, and other contracts of the service." O. R. ser. IV, vol. II, 223.

[23] O. R. ser. IV, vol. II, 94.

[24] The *Sun*, September 22, 1862; the *Confederacy*, September 24, 1862; O. R. ser. IV, vol. II, 670.

became special targets of criticism. These industries were accorded exemption privileges to secure a supply of clothing for the army and people independent of the contingency of raising the blockade. It was soon claimed that the Government was not purchasing nearly all the output of the mills and the remainder was being put upon the market at extortionate prices. Instead of operating the mills to ameliorate the inconveniences of the blockade, they were being used primarily as a means of accumulating enormous wealth. Self-enrichment, it was claimed, had become the *génie dirigeant*. A manufacturing aristocracy was being built up by the accident of war and the privilege of exemption from service. Mill operators had lost sight of the purpose of their favored position and were identifying their whole resources and opportunities with their own interests, and serving themselves in lion-like fashion.

The planters, especially, felt that their plantations, which were of prime importance to the sustenance of the army and the public, had received scant consideration at the hands of Congress; and they launched a propaganda early in the spring to secure equality with the industrial groups before the law.[25] An effort was made to have persons who had been enrolled detailed as overseers, but the Secretary of War refused them relief and suggested that they should carry their case before Congress in August.[26] It was reported that Governor Moore of Louisiana uniformly ordered his colonels to leave one white man on every plantation,[27] but the President in-

[25] O. R. ser. IV, vol. I, 1106, 1138; the *Sun,* May 1, 1862,

[26] O. R. ser. IV, vol. I, 1138.

[27] The *Sun,* May 12, 1862,

formed Governor Pettus of Mississippi that there was no authority under the existing law to exempt overseers.[28] By persistent effort they established their cause before Congress and were given relief by the exemption act of October 11th.

Other classes, like tanners, millers, salt-makers, and physicians strove for exemption, and they had the support of the President, the Secretary of War, and several of the Governors.[29] President Davis instructed Governor Pettus (May 1st) to exempt tanners and gunsmiths, since they were so clearly comprehended by the spirit of the law, until the pleasure of Congress could be ascertained.[30] Governor Milton thought it would be wise to exempt only such artisans as the State authorities would recommend after a prudent and impartial investigation; and that exemption should be valid only so long as the exempted person sold his products at a reasonable price. He was in favor of fixing a maximum price upon all the products of their labor.[31]

No account of the efforts of classes to secure exemption would be complete without mention of newspapermen. The press had on the whole scrupulously followed the course of conscription and ably bolstered up the Richmond authorities in the administration of the law, by pointing out weaknesses in the enforcement of it and trying to stimulate a public sentiment against all forms of "slackerism," but when it seemed certain that newspaper employees would be conscripted it turned to vitri-

[28] O. R. ser. IV, vol. I, 1110.

[29] *Ibid.*, 110; vol. II, 17, 45, 94; the *Journal,* vol. V, 331, 343, 361, 379.

[30] O. R. ser. IV, vol. I, 1110.

[31] *Ibid.,* vol. II, 94.

olic criticism of Congress.[32]   Their vantage ground in getting their case before the public was fully utilized; deluges of rhetoric poured forth in eulogy of the accomplishment of newspapers in the war and of their indispensability as educational factors.   Persons not fully satisfied as to the *raison d'être* of newspapers in civilized society would do well to consult the editorials of this time.   Some claimed that the conscription of newspapermen would be an unconstitutional interference with the freedom of the press, while others stigmatized the movement as an effort to sever the only medium of communication between the Government and the people, and to "blot out the light of civilization and religious liberty, and to envelop the community in darkness and confusion." The "wise Senate" was warned that if the press should be suppressed it would be "as voiceless as the grave." [33] Some editors took a more liberal and elevated view, and expressed a willingness to have their cases disposed of upon the principle that every individual should operate where he could render his maximum service.   Even these, however, sustained a wounded pride at the thought that Congress and the President should regard the toil of the humble tanner, miller, and miner of greater public utility than all of the information and enlightenment gleaned and spread abroad by themselves.[34]

It is clear that the first exemption act was susceptible

[32] The *Enquirer's* correspondent was excluded from the Senate chamber in March of 1863 because of some caustic remarks he made about Senator Albert G. Brown of Mississippi, who had opposed the exemption of newspaper men.  Unfortunately this frustrated the ambitious plan of the editor to keep a complete record of the debates in Congress.  *Southern Hist. Ass. Pubs.*, vol. 4, p. 84, note 2.  See also *Enquirer*, March 19, 1863.

[33] The *Sun*, September 30, 1862; Macon *Telegraph*, quoted in the *Confederacy*, September 2, 1862.

[34] The *Confederacy* September 16, 1862; the *Sun*, October 7, 1862.

of egregious abuse, and as it functioned it was a serious handicap to conscription. The practical inequality of its operation and the blatant transgression of the spirit and purpose of it brought down upon it the odium of public hatred. It needed to comprehend other professional classes and to be judiciously restricted in its application in all classes.

An amendatory act was passed early in October which greatly increased the number of exempted classes.[35] The earnest efforts made by overseers, millers, tanners, salt-makers, physicians, and others to secure exemption adver-tised the value of their services at home and induced Congress to exempt them.[36] The new act was more ex-plicit and detailed than the original act, in order, doubt-less, that questions of interpretation might not arise and confuse the public understanding.

In addition to those included by the original act the following classes were exempted: railway employees, ex-cept "laborers, porters, and messengers"; telegraphers, not to exceed four in any locality; employees of river and canal navigation companies; factory owners; tanners; shoe-makers; blacksmiths; wagon-makers; millers and their engineers; Government artisans, mechanics and employees for the manufacture of war munitions;[37] ship-

[35] O. R. ser. IV, vol. II, 160. It was passed by substantial majorities (*Journal*, vols. II and V). The President endorsed it October 11th.

[36] It was announced in the regulations for enforcing the new law that it would be construed prospectively and hence could not operate to dis-charge persons in the service prior to October 11th. O. R. ser. IV, vol. II, 165.

[37] *In re* Barfield it was held that the trade on which the claim of a mechanic to exemption was based must be his regular occupation and not one which he might pursue at odd times. 60 N. C., 73. Again, an indi-vidual whose liability to service was once fixed could not evade it by voluntarily engaging in a new employment which would exempt one bona fide pursuing it. Camfield *v*. Patterson, 33 Ga., 562.

builders; salt-makers producing twenty bushels or more per day; miners of lead and iron; charcoal and coke burners; one white man who was engaged exclusively in raising stock, for every 500 head of cattle, 250 head of horses or mules, or 500 head of sheep; one white man on each plantation where the State law required one to be kept, and in States having no such law, one white man on each plantation of twenty or more negroes [38]; the public printer and his employees; one editor and necessary printers for each paper; members of the Friends, Nazarenes, Dunkards, and Mennonites, who might furnish a substitute or pay a tax of $500 into the public treasury; [39] physicians who had practised for five years or more; superintendents and operatives in wool and cotton factories, paper mills, and wool-carding machines, at the discretion of the Secretary of War; and other persons whom the President might designate because of justice or equity.

As if to deter the speculative impulse, artisans and manufacturers were granted exemption upon the condition that they should not sell the products of their labor at prices exceeding 75 per cent upon the cost of production.[40]

While exempting new classes, Congress made an earn-

[38] This was popularly known as the "twenty-nigger law." If each of two or more plantations within five miles of each other had less than 20 negroes, but all aggregated 20 or more, one white man might be exempted to oversee them.

[39] Some persons professed conscientious scruples against bearing arms and tried to secure exemption under the provision concerning these creeds. A test case of this (In re Stringer) was carried to the supreme court of Alabama. The court held that only those creeds denominated by the act were legally exempt. 38 Ala., 457.

[40] Governor Milton had predicted a few weeks earlier that there would be "heartless villains who would barter the liberties of the country for a 'mess of pottage,'" and he was in favor of fixing maximum prices for their products. O. R. ser. IV, vol. II, 94.

est effort to prevent the repetition and extension of abuses which had become notorious. Affidavits attesting to the facts of employment, of skill, and of indispensability to the work pursued were required of persons engaged in any of the industrial activities embraced by the act.[41]    It was generally provided, in order that there might not be more of the practice of changing professions to secure exemption, that no one could claim exemption because of his profession unless he had pursued it continuously for a number of years immediately preceding the enactment of the law.    For example, a teacher must have been engaged in teaching for two years,[42] and a physician in the practice of medicine for five years before they could lay claim upon exemption.[43]

The War Department supported the efforts of Congress to prevent the evasion of the conscript law by issuing drastic instructions to examining surgeons.[44]    The principle was laid down that any conscript who could perform the duties of the various occupations of life was able to do military service; and surgeons were warned not to allow themselves to be deceived by the practice of simulating diseases.

[41] Affidavits concerning the utility of laborers in their respective industries were intended to check the vicious practice of packing and over-crowding industries favored with exemption.  Details for Government shops and for those in contract with the Government could be made for sixty-day periods only.

[42] *In re* Dollahite it was held that a schoolteacher whose occupation had been suspended was not entitled to exemption.  Dollahite had been teaching for 10 or 12 years but his school had been suspended 12 to 18 months as a result of the troubled conditions of the country.  Notwithstanding he was teaching again at the time of his enrollment, his claim was rejected because of the few months of forced interruption.  60 N. C., 74.

[43] *In the matter* of Hunter, a dentist was held to be a physician in the meaning of the act of Congress.  60 N. C., 373.

[44] O. R. ser. IV, vol. II, 408.

The act of October 11th and the determination of the Administration to secure a scrupulous enforcement of it did not lay to rest the question of exemption. If the masses, in and out of the army, were still unable to appreciate the necessity of exempting persons skilled in the various trades, professions, and mechanical pursuits, they were less inclined to accept the policy of exempting owners, agents, or overseers of large plantations. Heartburnings were freely voiced, flagrant violations of the law continued, and classes strove to get on the enumerated exemption list.[45]

Under the pressure of public necessity and planter influence Congress exempted overseers on large plantations, but it soon discovered that in so doing it had turned over a Pandora's box of trouble and embarrassment. Of course agriculture and the lives of families could not be entrusted to slaves unrestrained by overseers. They had as a rule been managed by overseers and had neither the will nor knowledge of their own to farm successfully; and without the awe-inspiring presence of the overseer the social and economic order of the Confederacy would be endangered.[46] But the public refused to believe that the exemption of overseers was a necessary collateral to successful farming and to the preservation of civil order. The "twenty-nigger" law, as it was commonly called, seemed like pure class legislation, and it "caused great dissatisfaction, both with the country

[45] Numerous special requests were made for exemption. See citations under "Military Service" in the index of vols. III and VI of the *Journal*.

[46] Governor Milton was of the opinion that there could be no more effectual auxiliary to Lincoln's emancipation scheme and to the subjugation of the South than that of taking the overseers from the plantations. O. R. ser. IV, vol. II, 401.

and the army." [47] Were not the planters, to whom this concession was made when men were paying their part of a common obligation in travail and in blood, the same men who in the pre-war times had appropriated to themselves the benefits of social and political leadership? "Never did a law meet with more universal odium than the exemption of slave-owners. . . . Its influence upon the poor is most calamitous, and has awakened a spirit and elicited a discussion of which we may safely predicate the most unfortunate results." [48]

The attitude in army circles toward the law and its beneficiaries was probably well expressed by General D. H. Hill, who spoke to his troops of the masters of slaves thus: "Some exempts claim to own twenty negroes, and with justice might claim to be masters of an infinite amount of cowardice." [49] A soldier from Jonesboro, Georgia, wrote: "I have seen the soldier in pleasure and in melancholy, in prosperity and in adversity, but

[47] Chief Justice Walker in the State *ex rel.* Dawson, *in re* Strawbridge & Mays, 30 Ala., 377. The Clark County *Journal,* January 29, 1863, said the law had been denounced as an unjust discrimination; it had to some extent demoralized portions of the army and had been used as an excuse for evading the conscription law.

[48] Senator James Phelan to President Davis, December 9, 1862. He said that even some of the beneficiaries of the law denounced the injustice of it, and bodies of men were being banded together to resist it. O. R. ser. I, vol. XVII, pt. II, 790.

[49] Quoted in Clark County *Journal,* May 14, 1863. The General went on to pay his compliments to other exempts: "Others are stuffy squires, bless their dignified souls! Others are warlike militia officers, and their regiments cannot dispense with such models of military skill and valor. And such noble regiments they have!—3 field officers, 4 staff officers, 10 captains, 30 lieutenants, and 1 private with a misery in his bowels. Some are pill and syringe gentlemen, and have done their amount of killing at home. Some are kindly making shoes for the army and generously give them to the poor soldiers, only asking two months' pay. Some are too sweet and delicate for anything but fancy duty—the sight of blood is unpleasant and the roar of cannon shocks their sensibilities."

the source of most trouble and anxiety to his mind is the ill treatment of his family by the very men who are, by the clause referred to, exempt from duty." The soldier had no fear of the enemy, but the thought that his family was suffering at the hands of the rich, "for whom he [was] fighting" unnerved the "strongest arm" and sickened the "stoutest heart." [50] Undoubtedly many soldiers felt that they could not entrust their families to the care of planters left behind and to the scanty charities of extortion and speculation.

The dicta of the courts concerning the equity and the merits of the law had little effect, as did the President's swing around the circle in defense of it.[51] Congressmen became alarmed at the preparation of political guillotines back home and busied themselves early in January with making the law more palatable to the poor.

Rumors of gigantic preparations in the North and unrest at home caused Congress to consider seriously the making of radical changes in the exemption system in the early part of 1863. From January to May it pondered over exemption. Propositions for abolishing statutory exemptions, restricting class exemptions, preventing fraud, etc., were debated at length, while the press expostulated with Congress and the people to drive young men from their places of safety at home into the ranks.[52]

[50] The *Confederacy*, October 30, 1862.

[51] The *Republican*, January 14, 1863; the *Confederacy*, January 7, 1863.

[52] The *Journal*, vols. III and VI, citations in the index under the caption of "Military Service"; the *Confederacy*, January 21, 27, 28 and 29, 1863; the *Republican*, January 22 and 23, 1863; the *Sun*, February 14 and 24, 1863; the *Mercury*, January 26 and February 16, 1863; the *Courier*, January 21 and April 2, 1863; and other numbers of these papers and the *Examiner*. The *Courier* hit upon a popular note when it demanded that the law for putting extortioners in the ranks should be enforced against the "greedy rogues" among the exempts, who were growing "fat upon the public privations and distress."

The opposition in Congress to exemption as it stood was strong, but it was not able to push through its program of revision.[53]   Three amendments represent the total results of four months of hard work.   Exemption was extended, with certain reservations, to contractors for carrying the mails and drivers of post coaches and hacks; an equitable system of exempting State officers was instituted; and the "twenty-nigger" law was changed.

The law exempting mail contractors caused division in the President's Cabinet.   The Post Office Department interpreted it to be retroactive, albeit the Bureau of Conscription, under instructions from the War Department, had ruled that previous exemption acts were not retroactive.[54]   It advertised for carriers, representing exemption, including a discharge from the army, as one of the benefits attaching to a contract to carry the mails.   The inevitable result was more or less competition between officers and men to obtain contracts at nominal prices to carry the mails, even in obscure districts and upon insignificant routes.[55]   Some of them established in the State courts their legal right to a discharge from the army[56]

On May 1st the "twenty-nigger" law was modified so

[53] See vols. III and VI of the *Journal,* citations in index under "Military Service."

[54] O. R. ser. IV, vol. II, 127, 128, 165, 231; *in re* Hine, 60 N. C., 165. Since Congress was in session it might have interpreted the act but it did not.   The House of Representatives called upon the Secretary of War to give his reasons for denying men in the service the privilege of the act, but he continued to act upon the theory that the cause for exemption must have existed at the time military service was claimed.

[55] The Secretary of War knew of three men in one company who accepted mail contracts for one mill, one cent, and ten cents respectively, and were discharged by the order of a State judge. O. R. ser. IV, vol. II, 1056.

[56] *Ibid.,* 1056; *In re* Bradshaw, 60 N. C., 379; *In re* Sowers, 60 N. C., 384; *In re* Russell, 60 N. C., 388, *Ex parte* Lockhart, *in re* Mitchell, 39 Ala., 452; Hunt *v.* Finnegan, 11, Fla., 105.

as to embrace only the plantations of dependents, minors, imbeciles, *femmes soles,* and men in the field.[57]   On each of such plantations, having twenty negroes or more, one white man was exempted, provided he had served in the capacity of overseer prior to April 16, 1862, and that the owner or agent of the plantation would pay $500 into the Confederate treasury.[58]   In order to make the law still less offensive to the poor, and to allow communities already depleted of most of their man power to retain their small residue of labor, it was further provided that the President might exempt laborers whenever and wherever it seemed necessary to do so.[59]

Great pressure was brought to bear by some of the planters, and by disinterested men who could see the public necessity for a rigid control of the negroes, to stay the operations of the act for a few months.   Popular clamor had moved Congress to adopt the hazardous experiment of modifying materially the "overseer" law after all plans for crops had been laid and all the agricultural agencies had been in operation for many weeks. Agricultural production for the year would have been jeopardized but for the fact that the War Department relieved the situation by applying the law cautiously.   The full momentum of it was stayed till autumn by the expedient of granting temporary exemption to the overseers, who were on plantations employed in the production of crops likely to be appropriated to the use of the

[57] O. R. ser. IV, vol. II, 553; *Public and Private Laws,* 1862-1864, p. 158.
[58] The law required the owner to make affidavit that it was impossible to get an overseer not liable to service.
[59] A sop was also handed to some of the recalcitrant governors by exempting all State officers in any State, whom the governor would claim to have exempted for the administration of the Government, until the next meeting of its legislature.   This was probably intended, also, to introduce uniformity and equity in the practice of exempting State officers.

army and the public.[60]    The policy was rewarded by the production of large crops of grain.[61]

The cycle of agriculture for the year was not complete, however, until the crops had been harvested; so with solicitude and logic some of the planters launched a virile propaganda in the early fall for a few more weeks of grace in order that they might gather what they had made.[62]    But their requests fell upon deaf ears.

The concessory character of the act of May 1st did not placate the partisan sensibilities of the common folk; and, of course, any leniency in the enforcement of it was odious to them.    Ominous mutterings reverberated through the Confederacy and men began to talk lightly of their obligations to a Government which would so distribute its most painful burdens as to relieve in large

---

[60] O. R. ser. IV, vol. II, 573, 728, 838, 850, 865, 874.    June 8th it was ordered that the overseers should be regularly enrolled and then detailed to their plantation duties whenever necessary.    For some reason the order miscarried, temporary exemptions were still granted.

[61] Governor Milton commended it because it enabled the planters to produce "abundant crops of grain."    O. R. ser. IV, vol. II, 838.

[62] O. R. ser. IV, vol. II, 838, 850, 864.    Some of the planters, like other persons, welcomed and utilized every opportunity to secure exemption. The act of May 1st did not extend to any plantation on which negroes had been "placed by division" since October 11, 1862, indicating that the owners of some farms had augmented the number of their slaves to the blessed number of *twenty* by drawing from neighboring farms or plantations.    Such devices, of course, made the cause of the planters the more unpopular.

The deep solicitude some of the planters had for their exemption is manifested by the following story:

One Black Belt farmer in Alabama who had 19 negroes did not want to go to war.    He rummaged the country round about in the quest of another negro, however small.    But his neighbors thought he ought to go to war and would not sell him even a tiny slave.    So, steeped in disappointment, he began to make preparations to leave when one morning he was rejoiced by the announcement that one of the negro women had given birth to a fine boy.    Darling little slave!—"the tale of twenty negroes was [now] complete, and the master remained at home."    Fleming, *Civil War and Reconstruction in Alabama*, p. 93, note 5.

measure the upper social structure. Cognizant of these facts, the Secretary of War recommended (September 23d) that exemptions or details should be granted to the planters very sparingly. He thought that persons with such large means should be able to secure some assistance in the management of their estates, and their exemption was causing "great dissatisfaction." [63] The Bureau went a step further on October 1st and ordered all overseers and plantation owners, holding certificates of exemption under the act of October, 1862, to report and be enrolled for service.[64]

The detailing of men from the army to do special kinds of skilled labor was in effect an exemption to them and thus may appropriately receive attention in the narrative of exemption. The Secretary of War, acting upon his discretionary power, began the practice in the summer and fall of 1862 to meet the pressing needs for skilled labor in the production of war munitions.[65] Persons were enrolled and detailed to work in Government plants and for Government contractors at the journeyman trader's price.[66] Factories, foundries, furnaces, railroads, and mines offered good employment and exemption from service in the field to thousands, and persons of draft age turned their attention to these industrial pursuits.[67]

On October 9, 1862, Congress detailed men from the army for the purpose of manufacturing shoes for the

---

[63] He thought that wherever concessions were made they should be made in the form of details. O. R. ser. IV, vol. II, 848. See also page 856.

[64] O. R. ser. IV, vol. II, 865.

[65] *Ibid.,* vol. I, 1127.

[66] *In re* Guyer, 60 N. C., 66. These men really were soldiers detailed for special duties and were subject to army rules as regards furloughs, desertion, etc. O. R. ser. IV, vol. I, 1139; vol. II, 78.

[67] The Confederacy, September 24, 1862; O. R. ser. IV, vol. II, 223.

soldiers;[68] and by the exemption act of the 11th the whole policy of the War Department with regard to details for skilled labor was translated into law. All necessary employees in plants engaged in the manufacture of army supplies and in mining activities were exempted, as we have seen, but they had to be enrolled and detailed to their special duties.[69]  This opened the floodgates to new fields of exemption and the "deadheads," so called, poured in.  According to General Bragg and his lieutenants the aggregate loss to the army from details alone was "most enormous."[70]  Complaints were frequently made that details were excessive and in many cases illegally granted.[71]  Reports of this kind caused the Bureau of Conscription to make a thorough investigation of the whole detail system in the summer and fall of 1863.[72]  Commandants were ordered to report with particularity on the "great abuse" of details in Government workshops and in the shops of Government contractors.  They were instructed to make correct returns, also, of all persons detailed or employed in the quartermaster, commissary, medical, and ordnance departments, and of persons employed by railroad, telegraph, and express companies.[73]  Upon the basis of the meager reports

[68] Public Laws, C-S-A, 1st Cong., 2d Sess.  These details were carried on the rolls of the companies.

[69] O. R. ser. IV, vol. II, 167.

[70] Ibid., 670.

[71] Ibid., 781.  Some of the courts allowed managers of plantations who were denied exemption to qualify as skilled mechanics for the purpose of securing exemption.  Example, Gates v. McManus, 33 Ga., 67.

[72] O. R. ser. IV, vol. II, 709, 792, 1070.

[73] The Alabama legislature (August 29th) by a joint resolution submitted to the President, among other things, that details of soldiers from the army to workshops, foundries, railroads, etc., had been entirely too numerous and in many cases even useless.  O. R. ser. IV, vol. II, 767.

received the Bureau estimated that the number of details outside of the army amounted to 13,000.[74] It was the opinion of the War Department that the number of details constituted "a serious abstraction from the army" and would have to be reduced.[75]

The desire to secure exemption had become so inordinate, and the law had been so circumvented by the cunning of those who did not have the sacrificial spirit, that the thought of exemption was odious to patriots. It was coming to be bad social form to be an exempt. Many persons no longer differentiated between the exempt and the derelict. Soldiers in the field aired freely their deep disgust for the "miserable creatures" (exempts) who were "only concerned about screening their worthless carcasses from Yankee bullets."[76] Quite generally the theory of the social and economic necessity of retaining skilled laborers at home was rejected, and exemption was discredited by the moral principle that it was incumbent alike upon all men to serve on the battlefield. From this premise they easily deduced the fact that it was "unfair, unjust, to exempt a man from the service of his country because he happens to be a shoemaker." With impatience and indignation they dubbed the system "grossly invidious."

The unscrupulous methods by which exemptions were frequently obtained were highly unworthy, and the conduct of some of the exempts was galling. Being none too good to compromise their honor for exemption, they were bad enough, of course, to use the privilege and

[74] O. R. ser. IV, vol. II, 1070.

[75] *Ibid.*, 945, 998.

[76] See General Hill's address on taking command of General Hardee's corps, quoted in the *Sun*, August 11, 1863; also, O. R. ser. IV, vol. II, 670.

their trades in such a way as to make most of the acute demands created by the war for the prime necessities of life. The people remonstrated that these extortioners were sapping their life's blood, and that they were responsible for the depreciation of the currency and for other woes that were encompassing the country; and they pointed a warning finger at the Government for making contracts with persons of conscript age "at the most extraordinary prices" instead of conscripting them.[77]

There was not only widespread discontent with the exemption system by the fall of 1863, but it was operating so as seriously to impair the conscription law.[78] Professor J. M. Richardson of the Georgia Military Institute estimated, August, 1863, that the number of exempts in Georgia amounted to about 29 per cent of the total number of troops sent to the field.[79] Upon the basis of meager reports received up to November from Virginia, North Carolina, South Carolina, and Georgia, the Bureau

[77] O. R. ser. IV, vol. II, 856. One Robert S. Hudson, of Benton, Miss., wrote President Davis October 5th: "Many of the exempts make themselves and their trades engines of oppression to all classes, and especially to the poor. Doctors, blacksmiths, tanners, shoemakers, and artisans generally, together with all speculators, constitute the main body of extortioners. They are the men who are depreciating our currency and shaking our Army and country from center to circumference." O. R. ser. IV, vol. II, 857. The *Courier* (April 2, 1863) said of the exempts: "Avarice has taken possession of their craven spirits, and truth and honor they account foolishness." It was in favor of putting these "heartless paltroons" in the ranks.

[78] "Had the exemption act been entitled an act to aid the enemy in diminishing the number of men in the Army and answered its nomenclature, it could not more thoroughly have effected its purpose." Col. John S. Preston, Superintendent of Bureau of Conscription, to the Secretary of War, August 17, 1863. O. R. ser. IV, vol. II, 725. Representative Henry S. Foote said that the spirit and purpose of the act had been ignored. The *Journal*, vol. VI, 524.

[79] O. R. ser. IV, vol. II, 740.

of Conscription computed the number of exempts in those States at 50 per cent of the total sent to the front.[80]

A few weeks earlier the Superintendent of the Bureau wrote the Secretary of War that there were "many, very many, more persons between the ages of eighteen and forty-five years exempted from service by the act of October 11, 1862, than [were] sent into the service by all the acts calling for men between those ages." The Bureau "is called to let drop," he complained in disgust, "ninety-nine through the expanded and broken meshes of the law while it takes insecure hold of one and lands him in the Army, unless he be snatched away by a railroad factory or some other supposed benefactor of the Confederacy." [81] The estimates of the Bureau exceeded the very liberal allowance made for exemptions by the Secretary of War in October, 1862.[82]

The Bureau of Conscription tried to improve upon the exemption situation. An effort was made, as has been shown, to enforce the law as to the planters, and the expedient of substituting men fit for "limited service" only for the able-bodied young men in the non-combatant departments was tried again.[83] Meanwhile, a plan of revision of the exemption system was being developed.

[80] O. R. ser. IV, vol. II, 939.

[81] *Ibid.*, 725. The Alabama legislature by a joint resolution, August 29th, asked Congress to reduce the number of exempts (*Ibid.*, 767). See O. R. ser. I, vol. XXVI, Pt. II, 126, for another complaint about the large number of exempts.

[82] O. R. ser. IV, vol. II, 132. He estimated that about 43 per cent of those between 18 and 35 would be exempted. The actual percentage must have been very much larger, for with only 43 per cent exempted he was afraid the army could not assimilate the remainder, and no evidence has been found of the assimilative powers of the army having been over-exercised. General Bragg and his seventeen lieutenants believed that the number of detailed and exempted men exceeded a quarter of a million. *Ibid.*, 670.

[83] The practice of accepting men for limited service was begun in the summer of 1862 but it was so unpopular Congress abolished it. O. R Ser.

When Congress assembled in December the Administration had a plan of radical revision to lay before it. It was proposed, first, that all persons within the draft age should be enrolled and the Executive department should be given authority to detail for special duty such of them as were necessary to meet the industrial needs of the country, and, second, that persons unfit for field duty should be used in the non-fighting collaterals of the service. It was suggested that the ranks of the latter might be augmented to meet the fullest needs by drafting able-bodied men over 45 years of age and by the use of slaves.[84]

The significant part of the plan was that it proposed to put exemption under the discretionary powers of the President. A similar proposition had been voted down by Congress the preceding winter because it was thought that it would be too great a delegation of power to the department which had already grown robust out of the exigencies of war.[85] It would be difficult still for the Administration and its leaders in Congress to force this project over the opposition, which had some misgivings about an all-pervading executive authority, but more, perhaps, about the Executive.

The Administration planned to furnish Congress a vast deal of information concerning the workings of the exemption system. Commandants of conscripts were instructed to report the number of details and exempts and

IV, vol. II, 92, 731; the *Confederacy,* September, 1862; the *Sun,* September 7, 1862; Lovingwood *v.* Bruce, reported in the *Confederacy,* September 26, 1862; *In re* Bryan, 60 N. C., 11. It was intended that persons qualified for limited service only should be placed in factories and on plantations as overseers, as well as in other non-combatant activities.

[84] O. R. ser. IV, II, 946, 997, 1041; Richardson, *Messages and Papers,* 370.

[85] The *Journal,* vol. VI, 36, 525.

the cause for same by November first. Those of Virginia, North Carolina, South Carolina, and Georgia were required to make full and minute reports as to the status of conscription. To the chagrin of the Administration only a few "extremely meager" reports had filtered in when Congress convened.[86]

While Congress pondered on exemption new reports of "cases of fraudulent, irregular, and improper exemptions" came to the Bureau of Conscription.

It was claimed that certificates of exemption were being counterfeited and some officers were thought to be "not free from liability to grave charges in granting exemptions." The Bureau ordered (January 9, 1864) an examination of all exemptions previously granted. Because of "the great increase in special applications for exemptions and the facilities with which signatures" were obtained, it became necessary to adopt some method of preventing exemption "in cases specially presented and supported by many signers, with some show of testimony, but without real merit." Accordingly commandants of conscripts were instructed to require affidavits from two reliable persons in support of each application, and wherever possible to push their inquiries behind the affidavits.[87]

[86] O. R. ser. IV, vol. II, 830.

[87] *Ibid.*, vol. III, 12, 24, and 36 contain the authority for the statements in this paragraph.

# CHAPTER V

## STATUTORY-EXECUTIVE EXEMPTION

A NEW exemption act was passed February 17, 1864, but it did not carry all of the President's recommendations.[1] Congress was not willing to abolish all class exemptions and to commit all individuals and vocations to the exclusive control of the Executive department.[2] It did, however, reduce the number of exempted classes by more than half; and the President and Secretary of War were given authority, within certain limitations, to exempt or detail men in these classes. The class exemptions retained were of the professional and public service type, while those abolished pertained to classes that were engaged in agricultural and industrial production. Thus the President and the Secretary of War were given

[1] O. R. ser. IV, vol. III, 178; *Public and Private Laws*, vol. II, 213, *et seq.* Some papers like the Tallahassee *Floridian* (quoted in the *Republican*, February 11, 1864) thought that exemption should have been abolished altogether and a system of details for industrial pursuits set up in its stead. Details would be more industrious than exempts it was claimed. There was some propaganda for abolishing details as well as exemptions, but leading papers attacked this as "egregious folly." The *Examiner*, January 2 and February 6, 1864; the *Republican*, January 18, 1864; the Montgomery *Mail*, quoted in the Nashville *Dispatch*, January 29, 1864. The *Examiner* favored the detail system but was opposed to placing it in the hands of one man; especially in the hands of the President who seemed to be *au fait* only in regard to officers and office-holders. January 14, 1864.

[2] Justice Phelan of Alabama said, *ex parte* McCants, that Congress preferred to grant exemptions rather than to authorize details for the reason that exempts would be liable to service in the militia and details would not. 39 Ala., 38.

authority to exempt or detail men for promoting production. This enlargement of the power of Executive exemption,[3] and the modification of the policy of blanket exemption in the classes retained, mark a turning point in the history of exemption. It was probable that, owing to the ever-increasing pressure for men, the number of exempts would be diminished and the President's power to detail would be expanded, if he exhibited strength and efficiency in directing the details for mechanical and agricultural production.

The "overseer" clause was materially changed as regards its commutative feature.[4] Instead of the $500 required by the act of May, 1863, overseers were now compelled to give bond with good security to furnish the Government 100 pounds of bacon, or 100 pounds each of pork and beef, for each able-bodied slave, at prices fixed by the impressment commissioners.[5] Any marketable surplus they had on hand or might produce they were pledged by their bond to sell to the Government or to the families of soldiers at prices fixed by the commissioners.[6] The Bureau of Conscription adopted the

[3] The President had had power from the beginning to exempt or detail persons in special cases of necessity, but this scarcely affected the exemption system.

[4] It was required also that the fifteen negroes should be able-bodied field hands between the ages of 16 and 50, whereas formerly there were no age limits imposed.

[5] If the planter could not, for good reason, furnish the full amount of meat he might with the consent of the Secretary of War commute two-thirds of it in grain or other provisions. The money obligation was transmuted to a food supply obligation probably because of the depreciated currency, and to have, if possible, a food supply and surplus in each locality as the transportation system broke down.

[6] The Bureau of Conscription allowed one person to be detailed to two farms, that were contiguous or within five miles of each other, having an aggregate of 15 or more slaves. If these farms were owned by different persons they had to execute a joint bond on the terms prescribed

policy of requiring other overseers, planters, and farmers, specially detailed, to meet the above conditions, only the amount of provisions to be furnished was less in their case.

If Congress by the act of February 17th made a conscientious effort to augment the field forces, the War Office and the Bureau were none the less diligent.[7] Enrolling officers were instructed to exercise the utmost caution in exempting or detailing able-bodied men between the ages of 18 and 45. The pertinent circumstances, *e.g.*, fitness for field service, private or public necessity, aptitude for the purposes of the detail, conditions of family, justice or equity, in every case must be carefully examined. A patriotic appeal was made to them to perform diligently their sacred duties as to maintaining an invigorating industrial productivity and supplying the armies with men. A board of investigation, consisting of "reliable and intelligent citizens" between the ages of 45 and 50, was established in each county for their aid. Its duty was to ferret out all the facts pertaining to applications for exemption and detail for the guidance of the enrolling officers, and to furnish all other information needed by them in the performance of their labors. Unfitness and delinquency were guarded against by placing it under the supervision and control of the enrolling officer.[8]

The Bureau promptly recast the system of medical examinations according to the mandate of the new law. No physician was allowed to sit on the medical board in his Congressional district, and the commandants of conscripts

for the owner of 15 slaves, except that they could not commute their meat obligation into that of other provisions. O. R. ser. IV, vol. III, 221.

[7] O. R. ser. IV, vol. III, 217, 224.

[8] Authority to establish these boards was conferred by the exemption act. O. R. ser. IV, vol. III, 181.

were required to report promptly any well ascertained irregularities or delinquencies of the boards. The new boards had power, with the indorsement of the Congressional district enrolling officer, to grant certificates of exemption to persons who were permanently incapacitated; and it was made their duty to report to the enrolling officers all persons capable of only a limited service, indicating specifically the kind of service they might do.

Manifestly the system of exemption was improved by the act of February 17th and by the executive orders issued in the promulgation of it. Certainly something was to be gained by instituting a system of executive detail with regard to the agricultural and industrial classes, and by restricting exemptions in the other classes; by requiring that details should be made from the ranks of the senior reserves and from the ranks of those between 18 and 45 who were not able to do active field service, and that all details and exempts should apply themselves diligently to their tasks.[9]

The enrolling officers had an unusual opportunity to press the advantages of the new system by reason of the fact that the writ of habeas corpus had been suspended in cases of "attempts to avoid military service." They need no longer be vexed and perplexed by the eccentric decisions and dicta of the inferior judges who had been prodigal in the bestowal of the writ of habeas

[9] The President had an opportunity to exercise discretion in the making of details, for he could ascertain through the sworn testimony of the neighbors of men and through the local inquisitorial-presenting boards the pertinent facts in each application for a detail. O. R. ser. IV, vol. III, 181, 218-220. Pollard lauded the fact that exemptions and details were to be permitted on the principle of promoting public service. *Third Year of the War*, 239.

corpus upon those seeking asylum from the conscript law. Persons could no longer look to the courts to be discharged upon *ex parte* hearings and at chambers, even when the courts were in session and without the knowledge of the counsel for the Government.[10]

The law was not rigidly enforced for several months in order that industrial enterprises might have time to adjust themselves to the new conditions.[11]    It was Superintendent Preston's opinion that few more small farmers and mechanics could be spared to the army. It had become necessary for every manufacturer and mechanic to keep to his trade, and since the army and the people were dependent upon the toil of the small farmers for supplies it would be ruinous to conscript them extensively. He thought that all necessary labor, except that of the agriculturists and mechanical experts, could be done by the exempt classes, reserves, light-duty conscripts, and the "invalid corps"; and he was sure that there was not an "absolute necessity" for cne detail in every ten of the able-bodied men between 18 and 45.[12]

Every department of the Government and every sort of enterprise expected a lenient enforcement of the law. Besides, there were the multitudinous requests of laborers for exemptions and details, which requests passed slowly along the tedious and circuitous route from the local enrolling officer to the Bureau of Conscription.

[10] A few judges like Chief Justice Pearson of North Carolina were not willing to be reduced to innocuous desuetude in the matter of exemption, and persisted in the use of the writ until forced to yield. See pages 181, 187-188 below.

[11] Details of persons who were necessary to the departments and bureaus were allowed till April 10th. Meanwhile, persons who were unfit for service in the field were to be substituted wherever possible. O. R. ser. IV, vol. III, 182.

[12] O. R. ser. III, vol. V, 696-8; ser. IV, vol. III, 356-8.

The Government bureaus asked for 12,000 able-bodied men, the railroads for a brigade more than the allowance of exempts, the express companies for a regiment, and the State authorities for at least 10,000.[13] The allegation of public necessity, of course, accompanied every application or request.

The landowners were also quick to accept the opportunities offered them. Jones complained to his *Diary* that "nearly every landed proprietor has given bonds to furnish meal, etc., to obtain exemption."[14] Superintendent Preston said that the large planters did not as a rule produce more than they consumed; the real surplus producers were the classes having much less than " 'fifteen hands,' and down to single laborers on farms."[15] Some of those who had fifteen negroes or more, and produced a surplus, asserted the right to exchange such part of it as they pleased for provisions, clothing, and the like for the comfort of their families, and to sell what then remained to the Government or to the families of soldiers. Adjutant General Cooper said that it had been

[13] Preston sarcastically remarked that "Wherever a contract is made with the Government in which a large profit is provided, the Government is immediately called upon to do the work for which it pays. Thus a railroad, an express, telegraph, or manufacturing company contracts with the Government and lays its profits; it then asks the Government to detail from the Army or abstain from the military use of all the labor necessary to fulfill the contract. The evil is an enormous one. The authority of the Bureau is not competent to the remedy." O. R. ser. III, vol. V, 698; ser. IV, vol. III, 358.

[14] O. R. ser. IV, vol. II, 271, 272. "Arithmetic," a correspondent of the *Republican,* said (October 21, 1864) that there were 114,000 exempts each bonded to furnish not less than 1,500 pounds of bacon and 1,500 pounds of fresh beef, and many others were obligated to give two to four times that much. The minimum production would be 342,000,000 pounds, or enough to feed 400,000 men till 1867. If these 114,000 men were put in the army the next spring it would not be necessary to conscript the slaves.

[15] O. R. ser. IV, vol. III, 356; ser. III, vol. V, 696. He said that a large majority of the farmers were in the service.

reported to his office that some of the planters had little respect for their contractual obligations; and that they had become speculators in food and provisions, were "negligent and careless as to the extent of their productions," and openly affirmed that they did not intend to have a surplus.[16]   Such contumacious disregard for their moral and legal obligations irritated the impetuous Preston and he ordered that they should be arrested and transferred to the camps of instruction where their cases would be disposed of.[17]

The exemption law was amended again (June 4th) so as to revive the stipulations of the act of the preceding October with regard to certain religious denominations [18]; and a joint resolution was passed extending the exemption accorded to newspapermen to the publishers of magazines and periodicals.   With evident surprise and

[16] General Orders, August 27, 1864.   O. R. ser. IV, vol. III, 608.

[17] O. R. ser. IV, vol. III, 515.   The question arose as to whether the bonded agriculturists were liable to duty in the militia.   Most of the States forced them into their service at critical moments.   The courts in these States denied that these agriculturists had been detailed by the Confederate Government; they were no more agents or instruments of the Government "than private individuals are of private persons to whom they have contracted to sell the products of their plantations on specified terms."   Some of the State judges strongly dissented from this view, and there were several conflicts between the Confederate and State governments over the matter.

[18] The amendment extended only to persons who belonged to the denominations at the time of the passage of the act of October.   The Assistant Secretary of War said that the membership of these denominations had been largely augmented since October from families not previously connected with them.   "This has been a cause for distrust and probably led to the adoption of the precise language of the act.   The Department has exercised a liberal indulgence in favor of those who held or were supposed to hold conscientious scruples upon the subject of bearing arms, but there is no reason for affording any countenance to efforts to avoid the performance of public duty by hypocritical pretenses of a religious belief, which has no root in the conscience or influence upon the conduct."   O. R. ser. IV, vol. III, 515.

impatience President Davis promptly vetoed the resolution. He saw "no reason for exempting these citizens from the duty of defending their country which would not apply to all authors, publishers, book-sellers, printers, and other persons connected with the publication of books, pamphlets, religious tracts, and other reading matter. At a moment when our lives, our liberty, and our independence are threatened by the utmost power of our enemies, when every citizen capable of bearing arms ought to be found in the ranks, I cannot but deem it impolitic to add to the list of exemptions without the most urgent necessity. Seeing no such necessity, and believing the precedent set by this resolution, if passed, to be productive of evil effect, I am constrained to return it without my approval." [19]

By early autumn it was clear that the new exemption system was not producing the results hoped for by its supporters. Time was demonstrating the difficulty of separating the non-producers from the producers. The detail system, which had been in a large measure substituted for exemption proper, was a disappointment. There were several things that militated against the success of it. First, the mass of laborers were not apt to substitute the rifle for their tools as the war became increasingly painful; indeed, they were strongly inclined to use every method, foul if fair would not avail, to keep off of the battlefield.[20] Second, details were made solely upon the

[19] O. R. ser. IV, vol. III, 472.
[20] According to General J. L. Kemper there were 8,000 details in Virginia by July, and at least 25,000 applications were pending. Judge Magrath wrote President Davis (September 15, 1864) that it was the opinion of the best authority that from 20,000 to 30,000 men could be put in the field from S. C., N. C., and Ga., by modifying the detail system. O. R. ser. IV, vol. III, 558, 652.

recommendations of the heads of the noncombatant and civil arms of the service, some of whom did not scruple at protecting friends by false testimony and implications, and all of whom had an interest in maintaining a copious and efficient labor supply with which to make their mark. Third, the right of appeal from the decision of the local enrolling officers through a long chain of officials, some unscrupulous, some out of sympathy with, if not hostile to their superiors, and many ignorant and indifferent, gave the candidate for detail an opportunity to defeat the purpose of the law for a period of months.

The Bureau of Conscription started out on the principle that all able-bodied laborers except "skilled artisans, experts, and men of science, and a few others actually indispensable for the maintenance and supply of the armies" should be drafted into field service. The plan was broad enough to give every laborer reason to hope for a detail, for if he were impersonal and critical enough to realize that he was not possessed of super skill and a vast store of scientific information, he could at least induce himself to believe that he could qualify with the class of "indispensables."

Those who were not sure of the validity of their claims were encouraged to make application for a detail by the system of appeals which allowed the applicant to continue his work during the pendency of his case.[21]    A flood of applications moved slowly along their circuitous channel, many of which were intended "merely to obtain delay." [22]    The Assistant Adjutant General said that the

[21] The demand for labor, the incompetency of enrolling officers, and the difficulty of discriminating accurately between the various war necessities were the chief reasons for allowing the appellate system.

[22] O. R. ser. IV, vol. III, 732.

testimony of the most judicious enrolling officers showed that "almost every man puts in a petition as soon as he is enrolled, for the sake of delay." The effect was that numbers of conscripts who should have been taking part in the campaign before Richmond were spending a "quiet summer at home by means of a sham petition." Officers reported that invariably when they rejected a man's claim for a detail, as of no merit, and sent him to camp he returned in a few days with liberty to stay at home until his appeal to Richmond was heard from.[23] This was an intolerable situation. The enrolling officers were ordered (July 8th) to transfer all whose appeals were pending to the camps of instruction so that they might be assigned promptly to active duty.[24] This attempt to crush the evil produced another quite as ominous. The wheels of industry began to stop for a want of labor and the common carriers to do a languishing business.[25] A quick effort was made to mollify the rigor of the July circular.[26] The new status, however, was not satisfactory. Superintendent Preston observed: "When the cases are gotten into this routine it seems to be the hardest of all possible things to get the men into the Army, for while

[23] O. R. ser. IV, vol. III, 539.

[24] They were entitled to be discharged if their appeals were sustained. *Ibid.*, 534.

[25] The evidence indicates that railroads suffered because of a deficit of labor. The law allowed only one man per mile of track on even the roads used for military purposes. This was not enough labor to keep up a roadbed heavily trafficked for any length of time. Railway officials protested vigorously against the substitution of disabled soldiers for trained railway men. O. R. ser. IV, vol. III, 598. The *Republican,* January 19, 1864.

[26] *Ibid.*, 578, 732. The new policy allowed persons whose applications were approved by the district enrolling officer a sixty-day furlough. If rejected by him the application could be sent up to the Bureau of Conscription, but the applicant must be immediately inducted into service.

the cases are dragging their slow length along the applicants often change their residence or occupation, or somehow their States, or appear to be buried beneath the accumulated office matter." [27]

Some who could not secure a detail through the law, through the corruption of officials, through the misrepresentations of the heads of departments and employers,[28] or protect themselves by indefinite delay, sought and apparently obtained relief from the medical boards. It was reported that the quartermaster, commissary, ordnance, medical, and post departments in Alabama, Mississippi, and Georgia were full of healthy young men. Inspector Walter said that he could not send them to the army because when he approached a detail, however sound, he had a certificate of disability thrust into his face. "The disease is occult, the name scarcely known to me." The detail "looks strong enough to brain an ox with his knuckles and eat him afterward. I have the prima facie evidence of my senses against the prima facie evidence furnished by the certificates." [29] He thought it unwise to force the question of fitness of details upon the surgeons at any post because of their

[27] Communication to the Secretary of War, November 24, 1864. O. R. ser. IV, vol. III, 861. The ignorance and indifference of many officers and the precarious mail service made delay inevitable. *Ibid.*, 868.

[28] Inspector Walter of Mississippi said that in repeated instances the district enrolling officers in Mississippi, Alabama, and Georgia, made details which they did not report to the commandant of conscripts. Every post, he said, was filled with skulkers under the name of details. *Ibid.*, 976.

[29] *Ibid.*, 977. The sources indicate that conditions as to details were as bad in the other States as in Alabama, Georgia, and Mississippi. Walter thought the medical officers were as free from corruption as any other class of officers; and the improvement in the medical department had been "wonderful."

dependence upon the quartermaster for their houses, offices, transportation, food, and clothing.

If the detail system needed anything other than the factors already mentioned to guarantee its defeat, it was furnished by the unwillingness of officers and employers to accept disabled soldiers in lieu of their trained men, and by the unsympathetic attitude of the authorities in many of the States.[30]

State authorities quite often did not comply in good spirit with the purpose of the law as to State officers. All officers certified by the governors to be necessary for the administration of affairs in their respective States were exempted. Some of the legislatures multiplied the local offices and the governors certified their incumbents, however nominal their functions. Nor did the claims of some of the governors stop there; they boldly certified all industrial laborers employed in State enterprises. The conduct of the governors and the exemption acts of some of the legislatures led to sharp conflicts between State and Confederate authority.[31]

The governors east of the Mississippi in conference jointly requested the Confederate authorities to send every able-bodied conscript to the front whose place could be filled by a disabled soldier, a senior reserve, or a negro; and to dispense with most of the provost and post guards and passport agents, since they were an "unnecessary annoyance to good citizens and of no possible benefit to the country." [32] These things they earnestly requested

[30] The departments, bureaus, factories, and railroads did their utmost to retain their trained men. As labor became scarce they were reluctant to exchange their able men for untrained and disabled soldiers, and the records show that they quite generally did not give them up.

[31] O. R. ser. IV, vol. III, 754, 817, 818, 867, 909. See pages 249-253, 265-270, 301-302 below for a full account of this controversy.

[32] O. R. ser. IV, vol. III, 735; ser. I, vol. XLII, Pt. III, 1150.

of the President; as regards themselves, they pledged their "best exertions to increase the effective force of the armies." [33] While the governors thus were giving a *carte blanche* to their zeal, the records of the Bureau showed that they were carrying 25,892 men on their certified lists. Governor Vance of North Carolina was carrying 14,675 names on his list of certified officers and Governor Brown of Georgia 8,229, and each was daring the Confederate authorities to touch them. Virginia was said to have had 1,422, Alabama 1,223, South Carolina 233, Mississippi 110, and Florida 109. Obviously the records were charitable to some of the governors, though Governor Vance's list was probably overstated.[34] Inspector Walter said that there were at least 4,000 officers exempted in Mississippi; and President Davis rejected the report of the Bureau because of its manifest inaccuracy as to South Carolina, Mississippi, and Florida, and because he believed that it exaggerated the number certified in North Carolina.[35]

The report of February, 1865, showed slight increases in all the States except Georgia, Mississippi, and North Carolina. In Georgia and Mississippi the number remained unchanged, while in North Carolina it was decreased from 14,675 to 5,589.[36] According to the records the conspicuous decrease in numbers in North Carolina

[33] O. R. ser. IV, vol. III, 735.

[34] The commandant of conscripts in North Carolina thought that the number of certified officers in that State had been exaggerated. O. R. ser. IV, vol. III, 868. For other evidence of the unreliability of reports see pages 866, 868, 869, 976, 1101.

[35] When the report was rejected Superintendent Preston ordered a special inspection. The new report that came from Georgia corroborated the earlier report, and such data as came in from North Carolina before the end of the year indicated, so Preston said, that the first estimate for that State was approximately correct. O. R. ser. IV, vol. III, 866

[36] *Ibid.*, 1102.

was due in large measure to faulty reports. It is a safe assumption that there were fully as many persons certified in North Carolina as in Georgia, and the general impression prevailed that there were more. Georgia may have had more local officers, owing to her large number of counties, but Governor Vance more than made up for this by certifying all persons engaged in making supplies for the State troops.[37]

While it is impossible to speak with exactness concerning the numbers of officers and employees certified by the governors, the sources plainly show that it was out of all proportion to the needs of the civil service. The courtesy extended to the governors was quite generally abused.[38]

The success of the overpowering Federal armies in the early fall produced widespread consternation and a serious effort was made to put an end to the abuses of exemption and detail. The conscription machinery was simplified so as to give it celerity of operation.[39] All able-bodied officers and men engaged in the enrolling business were ordered to be sent to the field as soon as practicable, and those holding furloughs or temporary exemptions because of pending applications for detail were ordered to report at once to the camps of instruction.[40] The Secretary of War said that considerable numbers of able-bodied men between 18 and 45 had been granted details, but the critical condition of affairs made it neces-

[37] See pages 394-400 below for an account of the conflict between the Government and Governor Vance over the matter.

[38] O. R. ser. IV, vol. III, 345, 348, 530, 869, 906, 976, 1102. It is said that some of the local offices which had not functioned for years were revived and supplied with able-bodied young men. The reports show that most of the officers were between 18 and 45.

[39] Ibid., 859-63.

[40] Ibid., 712, 715.

sary to revoke such details and to enforce rigidly the conscription laws, "limiting to men capable only of light duty and to reserves employment in the departments of the public service." Exception was made of "skilled artisans, experts, and men of science, and a few others actually indispensable for the maintenance and supply of the armies." [41] Also, the medical department was given another overhauling in the hope of reducing the number of physical exempts. The medical boards created the preceding spring apparently had not justified their existence.

General Lee thought that if re-examinations could be made by select medical boards many additional recruits might be obtained. Major-General Kemper informed him that there were 19,000 men in Virginia and 32,000 in North Carolina reported to be physically unfit. Of the Virginians he thought that 10,000 would be found by a rigorous examination to be effective.[42] Inspector Walter of the Mississippi department said the board at Brookhaven, Mississippi, examined from April to October 1,125 men and discharged 807 (over 70 per cent) of them.[43] Superintendent Preston said that the medical boards in the several districts were "subject to the suspicion of local and personal influence,

[41] O. R. ser. IV, vol. III, 760. Assistant Secretary of War, Judge Campbell, thought that this sweeping order of revocation "evinced extreme weakness; it carried despondency and dismay among the people." Letter to Judge Curtis, July, 1865, *Century Magazine,* October, 1889, p. 951. It probably did carry dismay and despondency to the details, but I have found no evidence to show that it affected others this way. It emphasized, no doubt, the intensity of the struggle at that time, but it did not produce a panic in the minds of those, at least, who were in the field and their relatives and friends at home.

[42] O. R. ser. I, vol. XLII, Pt. III, 1144.

[43] O. R. ser. IV, vol. III, 976.

and being charged with favoritism and other abuses, and the system being, at best, an unwieldy and dilatory one," he deemed it wise to send an experienced surgeon to each district with power to decide preliminarily what men were fit to be sent to the medical boards in the field.[44] Thus, after nearly three years of experiment with medical boards in an effort to secure fair examinations, the extreme expedient of throwing the examinations to the field medical corps was adopted. Inferentially, however, the leakage did not cease for Inspector Walter complained, December 29th, that there were still many able-bodied young men in the detail service with certificates of disability.[45]

No doubt there was just ground for the complaints against some of the medical officers, but the examining boards were in a real dilemma and much of the criticism was inevitable. If they exempted too many men they were liable to censure from their superiors; if they exempted only a few the community accused them of forcing cripples and weaklings into the army. Try as they might, they could not give general satisfaction, and those who were baffled in their purpose to evade service were always ready to malign and asperse them. Much of the complaint undoubtedly should be regarded simply as complaint.

Because of the serious conditions in the late fall the

[44] O. R. ser. IV, vol. III, 860. He had already sent out these surgeons to round up all persons holding certificates of disability. See page 734.

[45] *Ibid.*, 977. The boards were restored in modified form in March, 1865. From the beginning to the end of the war complaints were made against the medical boards. As early as March, 1862, Governor Letcher of Virginia complained of the indulgence of the medical examiners, and said that cases were reported of applicants who paid a fee of $5 or $10 and were not required to appear before the boards for examination. *Ibid.*, vol. I, 1022.

President determined, even at the expense of temporarily impairing some of the industrial activities, to put every available man in the field, but he was not allowed to succeed. The unavoidable exceptions made to the absolute enforcement of the law gave just so many opportunities for escaping field service; and the weariness produced by the strenuous campaigns of 1864 caused many to employ the full momentum of their wits to find an easy and safe place in the service, if a place at all.[46]   Complaints were made at the end of the year that through official incompetency and corruption many able-bodied young men were still sheltered in the non-combatant branches of the service.[47]

The House committee on military affairs reported, March 16, 1865: "experience has demonstrated that the power of detail as heretofore exercised has afforded more unnecessary immunity from military service than the well-guarded legislation upon the subject of exemptions"; and the "select" Senate committee frankly stated

[46] The detail situation at the end of the year was about like that of the preceding spring, as described by Preston. In "no department of the Government," he said, "has the law been rigidly complied with in the matter of details. The plea of public necessity has been so strenuously urged and so distinctly proved that continuations have been allowed beyond the contemplation of the law." O. R. ser. III, vol. V, 697; ser. IV, vol. III, 356.

[47] Fleming says that before the enrolling officers reached those employed in the non-fighting branches "nearly all of them had secured a fresh exemption, and from a large district in middle Alabama, I have been informed by the agent who revoked the contracts, not one recruit for the armies was secured. Often the exemption was only a detail, and large numbers of men were carried on the rolls of companies who never saw their commands." Frequently when men of influence were conscripted they secured a detail at once and never joined their companies. If a new way of securing exemption were discovered the whole fraternity of "deadheads" soon knew it. *Civil War and Reconstruction in Alabama*, p. 101, note 3.

that the power of detail had been so greatly abused that it was necessary to divest the Administration of it.[48]

Some idea of the general course of exemption between January and August of 1864 may be had by consulting the report of Colonel Wm. M. Browne, the commandant of conscripts in Georgia,[49] though such reports, as suggested before, cannot be implicitly trusted. It should be borne in mind, moreover, that conditions in Georgia were probably worse than elsewhere, except in North Carolina. Unfortunately, no statistical reports have been found concerning the operation of the conscription laws for the remainder of the year, when a more drastic policy was pursued. According to Colonel Browne's report 7,542 men between the ages of 18 and 45 were conscribed in Georgia between January and August and 5,588 were exempted. There were 3,910 detailed or given limited service, making a total of 9,498 men between 18 and 45 exempted from service in the field, as against the 7,542 who were inducted.[50] In all of the exempted and detailed classes the men between 18 and 45 were far in excess of those of other ages.

After three years of experience the Richmond authorities were firm in the belief that the only way to put the able-bodied derelicts in the army was to abolish class exemptions. It was the opinion of the Secretary of War, "more than once expressed in former reports," that the policy of exempting those able to do military service was unwise, and that all able-bodied men between the ages of 18 and 45 should, "without distinction of occupation

---

[48] O. R. ser. IV, vol. III, 1145, 1149. The select committee of the Senate reported that 22,035 men east of the Mississippi had been detailed by Executive authority.

[49] *Ibid.*, 871.

[50] The medical boards exempted 2,053 of this number.

or profession," be placed in the field. The few "indispensable exceptions" for the home needs might be provided readily and more conveniently by details. "Exemptions by classes necessarily cover many not actually demanded by society for the needs that, on the average, may have given plausibility to the exceptions, and such exceptions, besides inducing invidious feelings and dissatisfaction, compel a discrimination in the call for service which both delays and measurably defeats its full accomplishment." He believed that the time had come when by the aid of slaves those above and below the prescribed age limits and those fit for light duty only "would suffice adequately to maintain necessary production and supply, both for the armies and the people." [51]

Superintendent Preston reiterated, upon the basis of his thirty months' experience, "that for the uniform, impartial, and thoroughly efficient administration of conscription, first, all exemptions by classes should be absolutely abolished; second, conscription should be made independent of the regular military authorities." [52] Preston's views were supported by many of the soldiers and conscription officers. [53]

In his message to Congress, November 7th, President Davis renewed with emphasis his former request that

[51] O. R. ser. IV, vol. III, 761. He favored, of course, the exemption of Confederate and State officers actually essential to the conduct of those governments.

[52] *Ibid.,* 854. But there were those who thought that exemption could not be dispensed with without involving the country in irretrievable ruin. See the *Independent,* November 5, 1864, and the Montgomery *Advertiser,* quoted in the Clarke County *Journal,* November 17, 1864.

[53] O. R. sev. IV, vol. III, 978. Inspector Walter believed that in Mississippi alone that there were enough deserters, skulkers, idle officers, improper details, and useless exempts to give victory to any army to which they might be added.

class exemptions should be abolished. With dignified and well chosen phrases he pointed out the weaknesses of class exemptions. The exemption of all persons engaged in specified pursuits "is shown by experience," he averred, "to be unwise, nor is it believed to be defensible in theory. The defense of home, family, and country is universally recognized as the paramount political duty of every member of society, and in a form of government like ours, . . . nothing can be more invidious than an unequal distribution of duties and obligations." No individual should be exempted unless his services were more useful to the defense of his country in another sphere. "But it is manifest that this could not be the case with entire classes." All persons in the numerous exempted classes could not be equally useful in their "several professions nor distributed through the country in such proportion that only the exact numbers required" could be found in each locality. Moreover, he was sure that it was not everywhere impossible to replace those of conscript age by men older and less capable of service in the field. Exemption "of entire classes should be wholly abandoned. It affords great facility for abuses, offers the temptation as well as the ready means of escaping service by fraudulent devices, and is one of the principal obstructions to the efficient operation of the conscript laws." [54]

Amid perilous surroundings Congress settled down with apparent imperturbation to deliberate upon and to debate *in extenso* the recommendations of the President for strengthening the army. After about four months' consideration it passed a bill, March 11, 1865, revoking practically all details made by the President and the Secretary of War and placing exemption back on the old

[54] O. R. ser. IV, vol. III, 796.

class basis.[55]    The "fifteen negro" clause and a few minor ones were repealed but the advantages that might have resulted from these changes were counterbalanced by the exemption again of all skilled artisans and mechanics in the employment of the Government.[56]    The President vetoed the bill because he thought the wholesale exemption of skilled artisans and mechanics and the revocation of all details and exemptions made by himself and the Secretary of War would "in practice so impair the efficiency of the service as to counter-balance if not outweigh the advantages that would result from the other clauses contained in it."    "There is little hazard," he observed, "in saying that such a provision could not be executed without so disorganizing the public service as to produce very injurious results."    To withdraw the experts at once would be to "throw the whole machinery of Government into confusion and disorder, at a period when none who are not engaged in executive duties can have an adequate idea of the difficulties by which they are already embarrassed."    He assured Congress that nothing but an "imperative public necessity" could induce him or the Secretary of War to keep men out of the army, and he earnestly indulged the hope that it would so amend the bill as to eliminate the objectionable features which he had specified.[57]

[55] President Davis said that it revoked all details made by him and the Secretary of War, but it did not revoke details of persons over 40 years of age and those working for the Confederate and State governments. The exception made was probably of little consequence and the President ignored it.    The *Journal*, vol. VII, 686, 697.    The act is given in Mc-Pherson's *History of the Rebellion*, p. 612.    See also O. R. ser. IV, vol. III, 1128.

[56] O. R. ser. IV, vol. III, 1128, 1144.    Overseers could still be detailed from the senior reserves.

[57] *Ibid.*, 1128.

On the same day the exemption bill was returned the President submitted a long message explaining why he had a few days previously requested Congress to postpone its adjournment. The events of the past four months made it necessary to pass "further and more energetic legislation than was contemplated in November last." He was "impelled by a profound conviction of duty" to urge again the indispensability of revising the exemption system along the lines laid down by him the preceding fall. "A law of a few lines repealing all class exemptions," he submitted, "would not only strengthen the forces in the field, but be still more beneficial by abating the natural discontent and jealousy created in the army by the existence of classes and privileged by law to remain in places of safety while their fellow-citizens are exposed in the trenches and the field." He tried to spur Congress into action by referring to some of the embarrassments produced already by its tardiness. Some of the measures, he said, passed by it in pursuance of his recommendations in November were passed so late that they lost much of their value, or had to be abandoned altogether because of altered conditions, while others had not been considered at all.[58]

By amendments (March 14th, 16th, and 17th) Congress repealed that part of the new exemption act which provided for the exemption of the mechanics and artisans, and modified the system of medical examina-

---

[58] He conceded that protracted debate and delay were natural phenomena in representative assemblies and he thought they were laudable under normal circumstances; but in moments of danger delay was itself a new source of peril. O. R. ser. IV, vol. III, 1131. He was reminded by the Senate in turn that "promptitude is a great virtue in Executive action." *Ibid.*, 1152.

tions.[59]   Congress informed the President that it exempted mechanics and artisans in consequence of certain suggestions contained in the Secretary of War's report.   According to the report of the "select committee" the Secretary had complained that the military bureaus had been constrained by the "stringent legislation of Congress, to relinquish their most active and experienced agents and employés and substitute them from more infirm and aged classes," and expressed a hope that a permanent "system of providing and retaining in continuous employment a sufficient number of artisans, experts, and laborers for all essential operations" might be adopted.   And then the strange information was exhumated that the "bill originally introduced into the Senate exempting skilled artisans and mechanics was actually prepared in one of the bureaus of the War Department." [60]

Congress refused to be stampeded into adopting a system of executive details.   Instead, it restored the class exemption system that obtained in February, 1864, only the number of classes was reduced.   The President and Congress concurred in the opinion that the number of exempts needed to be reduced, but they could not agree on how best to accomplish it.

Under conflicting demands Congress had made and unmade exemption laws.   And the subject had a tumultuous *finale*.   As the Confederacy tottered to its fall

[59] The *Journal,* vol. IV, 686, 697, 725, 735, 739, 741; O. R. ser. IV, vol. III, 1149, 1176.

[60] O. R. ser. IV, vol. III, 1150.   This information, given out by the special committee of the Senate appointed to defend Congress against the depreciating imputations and admonitions of the President, seems extraordinary in view of the fact that President Davis concerned himself a great deal about the affairs of the War Department.

the President and Congress were in sharp conflict over the revision of exemption, and there was serious friction between the Confederate and State authorities over the enforcement of it as it stood. Friction with the State authorities was particularly acute at this time because of the incompatibility between the Confederate and State exemption laws, and because some of the States refused to give up the bonded agriculturists whom they had inducted into their militia at a time when, according to their court decisions, they were not in the Confederate service.[61]

The testimony is cumulative that many persons were exempted in the Cis-Mississippi Department,[62] but the dearth of statistical data makes it impossible to speak with exactness concerning their numbers. Several reports have been discovered but they are so incomplete and so obviously inaccurate it is believed that nothing could be gained by using them.[63] Moreover the general report of Superintendent Preston in February, 1865, included all reliable data that the earlier reports may have contained.[64] One cannot claim more for this report than Preston did; namely, that it was "as accurate as the im-

[61] O. R. ser. IV, vol. III, 1138. See pages 275-6, 293, and 301-2 below for a fuller account of this episode.

[62] The Bureau of Conscription exercised no jurisdiction over the Trans-Mississippi Department, and very little material has been found concerning exemption in that area. It is reasonable to suppose, and such evidence as is available indicates, that exemption in this Department proceeded along the usual lines. O. R. ser. I, vol. XXVI, pt. II, 494.

[63] The Bureau had great difficulty in getting reports from the enrolling officers, especially after generals in the field were given authority to conscribe. In the offices of some of these generals few records were kept; "exemption and details were granted or refused on the back of the applicant's letter and no memorandum made of it." O. R. ser. IV, vol. III, 95.

[64] O. R. ser. IV, vol. III, 1099. The only other effort made at a general estimation of the results of the conscription laws was that of the Superintendent of Special Registration, January 25, 1864. *Ibid.*, 95 *et seq.*

perfect agencies allowed to the enrolling service would admit," but it is presented with the thought that it may give some idea of the course of exemption.

Number of Exempts and Conscripts from April 16, 1862, to February, 1865:[65]

|  | Exempts | Conscripts | Percentage of Exempts |
|---|---|---|---|
| Virginia ................. | 13,439 | 13,933 | 49.9 |
| North Carolina ........... | 16,564 | 21,348 | 43.7 |
| South Carolina ........... | 5,839 | 9,120 | 39.3 |
| Georgia [66] ................. | 15,346 | 8,993 | 63.5 |
| Alabama ................. | 10,218 | 14,875 | 40.7 |
| Mississippi ............... | 4,108 | 8,061 | 33.7 |
| Florida .................. | 748 | 362 | 67.3 |
| East Louisiana ............ | 219 | 81 | 73.9 |
| East Tennessee ........... | 573 | 5,220 | 0.9 |
| TOTAL ................. | 67,054 | 81,993 | 44.9 |

There are some obvious discrepancies in this report. For example, Florida and East Louisiana furnished more men through conscription than they are accredited with, and in all probability exempted more than is indicated; while in Mississippi there were more than 4,000 State officers exempted, not to mention the other classes of exempts.   Moreover, the list of those pardoned by President Johnson shows that men were exempted for many occupations not mentioned in the report.

There is every reason to believe that the total number of exempts was much larger than indicated by this report. The Superintendent of Special Registration reported in January, 1864, that there were 96,578 exempts in the first six States listed in the above report,[67] and

[65] O. R. ser. IV, vol. III, 1101; ser. III, vol. V, 700. McPherson gives the number of exempts at 66, 586 (p. 612).

[66] The Atlanta *Intelligencer* placed the number of exempts in Georgia up to 1864 at 7,772, according to the Columbus *Sun,* January 12, 1864.

[67] O. R. ser. IV, vol. III, 103.

General Lee, on the authority of General J. L. Kemper, asserted (the following September) that there were no less than 40,000 exempts in Virginia.[68] Schwab estimates, without telling us the source of his information, that the total number of exempts east of the Mississippi was 100,000,—61,167 physically unfit, 18,785 State officers, 3,086 ministers, 4,982 railroad employees, and more than 4,000 overseers.[69] The sources indicate that Schwab's estimate is too conservative; he does not allow enough for the exempted classes not mentioned by him, and his figures for the physically unfit and the State officers are too small. There were probably more than 100,000 men exempted outright, and from 25,000 to 40,000 detailed to duty in the civil and noncombatant arms of the service.[70]

Some light may be thrown upon the Confederate exemption system by comparing Preston's report with the reports concerning exemption in the North and in the first selective draft of the World War. In the Confederacy 39.6 per cent of those examined were exempted from active service because of physical weakness, in the

[68] Freeman, D. S., *Lee's Dispatches to Davis,* p. 298; O. R. ser. I, vol. XXXIX, Pt. III, 1144.

[69] *The Confederate States of America,* p. 198.

[70] For a rough estimate of the number of details see O. R. ser. IV, vol. III, 1104-1110. This tabulation is apparently unreliable. General Kemper said there were 8,000 details in Virginia in the summer of 1864 and 25,000 applications were pending (*Ibid.,* 558). Judge A. G. Magrath estimated, "upon the best of authority," that from 8,000 to 10,000 men could be added to the army from South Carolina, and from 20,000 to 30,000 from the Carolinas and Georgia by a modification of the detail system (652). General Pillow said that the commandants of conscripts exercised the power to detail, and, of course, made no reports of it. He thought about one-third of the conscripts in his department were detailed in this way (vol. II, 850). General Pillow's estimates, however, should always be accepted with caution because he held a very strong brief against conscription as conducted by the Bureau.

North 25.7 per cent, and in the first draft of the World War 29.1 per cent.[71] The relatively large number exempted in the Confederacy may be partially accounted for by the fact that an older class of persons was examined, especially toward the end of the war, than in either of the other cases. The contrast between the ages of the men called out in the Confederacy in 1863 and 1864 and those called out in the fall of 1917 is especially striking.

According to the incomplete reports, the Confederate Government exempted 44.9 per cent of the total number of men called out by conscription, while the Federal Government up to 1865 exempted about 57 per cent and the United States Government in the World War 37.6 per cent of its first draft.[72] If the details in the Confederacy should be counted as exempts, which is fair in this comparison, and due allowance should be made for the inaccuracy of official returns, the number of exempts would exceed 50 per cent. Thus the number of persons exempted from field duty in the Confederacy compared to the total number conscribed was high, but the proportion would have been much less if conscription had been accredited with all those it forced into the service. The many persons who volunteered through fear of conscription were not included in the final estimate of the total number of conscripts.

The system of extensive exemptions in the Confederacy

[71] The sources indicate that in some of the Confederate States nearly half of those examined were rejected.

[72] In the draft of July, 1863, the Federal Government allowed 50 per cent for exempts, and 100 per cent in the draft of July, 1864. It is significant that 100 per cent was allowed for exempts in the latter draft when commutation was allowed only in the case of a few religious creeds. O. R. ser. III, vol. V, 717, 719, 731-739. Richard Barry, *World's Work,* 36: 562 f.

bore a direct relation to the industrial barrenness of the country. Perhaps no civilized country ever espoused war with such meager industrial resources. Few articles of clothing or mechanical production were supplied in the Southern States at the outbreak of hostilities, and the masses in the cotton belt were dependent in large measure upon the farms of the West for their bread and meat supplies.[73] Consequently when the Southerners were girdled by the blockade they were forced to attempt the impossible task of readjusting their agriculture and industry, of organizing them on a self-sustaining basis, while fighting against tremendous odds. With little surplus capital, poor equipment, and a limited supply of skilled labor the factory system could not be expanded to supply all the demands of the war. Recourse was made to household and shop production, and this resulted in extravagant demands upon the labor resources of the country. Much to the undoing of the Confederacy, there was no chance to use the technical labor-saving machinery that was giving the North its phenomenal industrial expansion.

The acute demands for skilled labor led the Government into a policy of indulgence, which in turn led conscripts and their employers to hope and plead for their exemption. Farmers asked for exemption; Government bureaus and contractors, factories and railroads demanded able-bodied and skilled laborers; towns and cities asked for able-bodied men for policemen and firemen; banks and brokers for clerks; charitable institutions for wardens; editors for the maintenance of their publications; public functionaries for subalterns; and no author-

---

[73] The South produced only about 11 per cent of the total manufactures of the country in 1860, and much of this was of the extractive type.

ity, association, or individual offered, so Superintendent Preston said, a man to the military service. Under such conditions it is not strange that large numbers of able-bodied young men, in spite of the effort to substitute disabled soldiers and limited-service conscripts for them, were kept in the non-fighting branches. Throughout the war conscription officers, generals in the field, governors, and patriots everywhere complained of this condition. Purchasing agents, sub-purchasing agents, sub-sub-agents, provost guardsmen, passport agents, tithe gatherers, cattle drivers, agents of the Niter Bureau, agents to examine prisoners, agents for distributing goods to soldiers' families, financial agents, and various other Confederate and State agents without distinct nomenclature could be found everywhere.[74]

The evidence is irrefutable that there was much fraud connected with exemption, and that many persons secured exemption who had no legal or moral right to it. Men bestirred their wits to graft themselves on to some of the exempted classes, even at the expense of deserting their accustomed vocations. They turned to teaching, preaching, selling drugs, mining, manufacturing, milling, blacksmithing, wagonmaking, tanning, shoemaking, harnessmaking, salt-prospecting, charcoal burning, railroading, carpentering, cattle-driving, etc. Amorphous drugstores, county schools, mills, salt pits, impromptu shops, and backyard tanneries spontaneously sprang into being. The South only a short while before was lacking in skilled labor, now it was overstocked with mechanical adepts. Some, who could not by their own ingenuity and the con-

---

[74] Governor Bonham of South Carolina complained that many of the purchasing agents were more concerned about buying for themselves than for the Government. O. R. ser. IV, vol. II, 709.

nivance of officers qualify in any of the exempted classes, developed physical disabilities. There was a tendency in some localities for the general health to break down. Those were days of strange and malignant physical and mental disorders.[75]

The opinion was prevalent that official corruption was in large part responsible for the omnipresence of robust young men in the non-fighting enterprises. The dishonesty and favoritism of some of the surgeons generously indulged the extraordinary ailments of the times; and there is evidence of considerable official corruption in various forms,[76] but there is little doubt that the popular imagination overemphasized it. Jones believed that there was much corruption even in the Bureau of Conscription, and went so far as to charge that employees of the Southern Express Company were exempted because that company brought "sugar, partridges, and turkeys to the potential functionaries." He thought that some of the high conscription officials were possessed of genuine Falstaffian qualities.[77]

The exemption system failed to make a proper allo-

[75] O. R. ser. IV, vol. III, 977.

[76] *Ibid.*, vol. II, 670, 850, 856; vol. III, 977.

[77] *Diary*, vol. I, 258, 260, 286; vol. II, 257, 271, 307, 314, 328, 349. He paid his respect to the conscription staff by the following parody on the fickle and dissolute knight, Sir John Falstaff, of King Henry IV's entourage:

"*Bardolph.* Sir, a word with you: I have three pound to free Mouldy and Bullcalf.

"*Falstaff.* Mouldy and Bullcalf: for you Mouldy stay at home till you are past service: and for your part Bullcalf grow till you come unto it: I will none of you.

"*Shallow.* Sir John, Sir John do not yourself wrong: they are your likeliest men and I would have you served with the best.

"*Falstaff.* Will you tell me Master Shallow how to choose a man? Care I for the limbs, the thews, the stature, bulk and big assemblance of man! Give me the spirit, Master Shallow." Second part *King Henry IV*, Act III, scene 2.

cation of the man power of the Confederacy.   It was, in the opinion of the President and high officials around him, "one of the principal obstructions to the efficient operation of the draft law"; and they might have added, one of the contributing factors to the wholesale desertions toward the end of the war.   The system of class exemption released whole classes in some pursuits when a few persons, selected by some fair and judicious means, would have sufficed.   Some sort of selective system administered by the President and the Secretary of War should have been much more effective.

# CHAPTER VI

## THE FRUITS OF THE FIRST ACT

THE creation of machinery for the enrollment of conscripts was confided in large measure to the President and the Secretary of War. Promptly after the passage of the law the Secretary issued an order containing general instructions for the enrollment, transportation, training, and disposition of conscripts. It was provided that from one to two [1] "camps of instruction" should be established in each State in which the conscripts were to be collected and trained. Each camp, supplied with a commissariat and a hospital, was placed in charge of an officer of the rank of major or above. This officer, the so-called "commandant of the camp of instruction" (or simply the "commandant of conscripts"), was authorized to call upon the commandant of the department in which his camp was situated for competent officers to drill the conscripts and to direct the camp activities. The commandant of the camp was under the commandant of the department.

The commandant of the camp of instruction controlled the enrolling officers of the State. The enrolling machinery as completed consisted of a commissioned officer for each Congressional district and a non-commissioned officer or private for each county, city, or town.[2] If State

[1] There could not be more than two established in any State without a special permit from the War Department. The order is published in the *Official Records*, ser. IV, vol. I, 1097, *et seq.*

[2] O. R. ser. IV, vol. II, 44, 164.

officers were employed as enrolling officers the State regulations as to enrollment were to be adopted whenever practicable.

When the conscripts were ready for the field it was the duty of the commandant of the camp to apportion them among the corps requesting recruits according to the deficiency of each. The conscripts were allowed to select their arm of the service, and whenever possible they were to be assigned to units raised in their respective localities. By allowing conscripts to select their arm of the service and putting them in organizations from their homes it was hoped that some enthusiasm might be aroused and the temptation to desert, or "leak," as the soldiers were wont to call it, might be removed. This system with slight variations was maintained throughout the war.

The actual process of conscription was fairly simple and direct. The time and place for enrollment were announced by the local enrolling officer and all within the conscript age who had not volunteered were expected to report promptly. When squads of six, eight, or ten were enrolled they were sent to the camp of instruction.[3] Those who did not report were subject to arrest and imprisonment and to be transferred under guard to the camp of instruction. The civil authorities were expected to coöperate with the military in the arrest of the derelicts.[4] Upon arriving at camp the conscript was examined by the surgeon. If found able he was interned, vaccinated, and perhaps allowed to contract some of the

[3] Columbus *Sun,* June 24, 1862; Savannah *Republican,* June 19, 1862.

[4] The Augusta *Constitutionalist* (August 6th) said that General Heth had ordered all conscripts in West Virginia who did not report at camp to be shot. It was sorry for this "extraordinary display of military power and harshness." Due allowance should be made for the fact that this paper was hostile to conscription; however, the order was reported to the *Examiner* as early as June 28th.

lighter camp diseases. After having been made immune to the ordinary camp diseases and having had a few weeks of training in the elementary principles of military science, he was sent on to the front.[5] This was the process contemplated by the law, but in actual practice it was not rigidly pursued. At times the need for men was so importunate that the camps of instruction were little more than places of rendezvous from which conscripts were rushed to the field with no training and with no seasoning for the soldier's life.[6] The bloody battlefields and crowded hospitals tell the gruesome story of this unfortunate condition.[7]

There was much misunderstanding about the twelve-months' troops and the three-year troops who were under 18 and over 35 years of age.[8] The Secretary of War asked Attorney-General Watts for an opinion as to whether the "90 days" clause of the act affected these classes or not. He explained that in Virginia most of those who had reënlisted for the war had entered the twelve-months' regiments and therefore might come within the letter of the provisions granting the discharge of all persons under 18 and over 35 years, while most of the same class to the South were in the war regiments and not entitled to their discharge. As Congress could not have intended to make such a discrimination it was

[6] O. R. ser. IV, vol. I, 1096; vol. II, 77.

[6] *Ibid.,* vol. II, 78.

[7] Some persons recommended the use of the camps of instruction for rendezvous purposes only. They believed that recruits could be more quickly and more thoroughly trained in the field, and desertions which had resulted from the dull, monotonous life of the training camp could be eliminated by sending them direct to the field. See Governor Pickens' letter to the Secretary of War, July 24, 1862. O. R. ser. IV, vol. II, 16.

[8] Clarke County (Ala.) *Democrat,* July 10, 1862.

"questionable whether the letter of the act in this particular should be observed." [9]

The Attorney-General replied, July 24th, that he did
not "suppose that any over the age of thirty-five or under
the age of eighteen [could] under this law, be discharged
on account of age until the expiration of their stipulated
term, although some might be retained longer than ninety
days after the passage of the act." He thought that all
not of conscript age whose terms of service should expire
on or before the end of 90 days from the passage of the
act were entitled to discharges at the end of 90 days.[10]
This opinion was adopted by the Administration; so all
men not of conscript age who were already in the service
had to serve until the expiration of their terms of enlistment, or even longer in the case of those whose terms
expired before the end of 90 days after the passage of
the conscription act.

The enrollment of conscripts began immediately in
some of the States, but by the middle of June camps of
instruction had been established in only four States, while
in two or three others the commandants for the camps
had not been appointed.[11] Soldiers who were already
in the field, and especially those, perhaps, who had volunteered under the apprehension that they would be conscribed, complained of the law's delay; and the press felt
it necessary to explain by way of warning that conscription was a reality and the law would soon be put into

[9] O. R. ser. IV, vol. I, 1123.

[10] *Ibid.,* vol. II, 15. Adjutant and Inspector General Cooper had given
a similar order to the army on June 17th. *Ibid.,* I, 1155.

[11] Camps had been established in Virginia, North Carolina, South Caro-
lina, and Louisiana. O. R. ser. IV, vol. I, 1152. According to Governor
Moore the camp in Louisiana existed only on paper. *Ibid.,* ser. I, vol.
LIII, 812.

full operation.[12]    It was pointed out that conscription was being stayed only temporarily to discover the designs and full scope of the law by correspondence with the War Department, and to perfect the machinery for the execution of it.    Young men were admonished to volunteer before they were collected in the camps of instruction and summarily disposed of.    If they would do this before May 17th they would be allowed a bounty and the privilege of electing their officers, not to mention escape from the odium of being forced into the ranks.[13]

It took much time to establish and set in motion all of the agencies of conscription.    There were the usual difficulties of selecting officers and establishing them in their headquarters, and of locating, constructing, and equipping the camps of instruction.    Besides, there were the hindrances which inhered in the Confederate system.    The stubborn opposition of some of the State officers and public leaders to conscription, and the conflict between Confederate and State exemption laws in some of the States constituted impediments which required time to overcome.    It may be, too, that the Richmond authorities did not think it necessary to act precipitately since men were volunteering rapidly under the threat of conscription, and the immediate purpose of the act, namely, the retention of the twelve-months' men, had been accomplished.    Moreover, the need for agricultural production by the small farmers, who were not embraced by the exemption act, may have inclined the Government not to pursue conscription aggressively until their crops

[12] Clarke County (Ala.) *Democrat,* June 3, 1862, quoting the Montgomery *Advertiser.* The Columbus *Sun,* May 20, warned the young men who had begun to believe the law would not be enforced that they had better not "lay this flattering unction to their souls."

[13] Columbus *Sun,* April 18th, 28th, and May 13th.

had been planted and made. There was considerable agitation for leaving the farmers at home to make another crop, since there were no available arms with which to equip them.[14] It is notable that the Confederate Government, despite some very serious obstacles, was conscripting in a few States within a month after the conscript law was passed; while the United States Government during the World War, under conditions much more favorable, spent four months in preparation for drafting men after the first draft law was enacted.

While conscription was going through the preliminaries of organization thousands of young men of conscript age volunteered. They enlisted especially in those incipient units that were given thirty days of grace in which to complete their organization for field service.[15] The officers of these organizations campaigned vigorously to secure the required number of men within the allotted time; and they were supported by newspaper editors and contributors who eulogized the volunteer and excoriated the man who would not serve until forced,—holding out to the latter the never-to-be-forgotten taint that the draft would leave upon him.[16] These campaigns were effective.

[14] *Southern Confederacy* (May 9th), quoting the Milledgeville *Union* of May 6th and the *Southern Republican* of April 26th. O. R. ser. I, vol. LIII, 812.

[15] Congress, whether intentionally or not, made an adroit move when it permitted volunteering in these units. Many would volunteer into them because they were being raised at home and by so doing they could escape the odium of a draft, but they could not be recruited by those of draft age, hence sooner or later they would have to be disbanded and incorporated in the old organizations. Meanwhile, they would have made a valuable contribution to the service and received training of the highest order. The Secretary of War said this consideration probably prompted Congress to give the voluntary units which were in process of formation 30 days in which to complete their organizations. O. R. ser. IV, vol. II, 44.

[16] Romantic and fear-inspiring names were given to the companies that

Colonel Dunwoody complained to the Adjutant and Inspector General, May 26th, that "The multiplicity of permissions granted to individuals to organize regiments, battalions, and companies has in effect destroyed the main feature of the conscript act—the enrollment of men to fill up regiments now in the field, increasing them up to the maximum number allowed in said act, most of the conscripts having joined these new organizations, most of which are full or up to the maximum number."[17]   Ten days later he reiterated the complaint.  He was of the opinion that the number of conscripts would not exceed 5,000, or 6,000, because of the "authorities granted to individuals to organize regiments, &c., and the various constructions placed by them upon the decisions of the Department regarding their power to continue to enlist volunteers. . . ." [18]

were being raised,—Dixie Eagles, Dixie Sledge Guard, Columbus Rebels, Lula Guards, etc.  The following example shows the manner of advertisement carried by the papers, though some of them were more alluring:

"Attention!

Fifty Dollars Bounty!

"Fifty dollars bounty will be paid as soon as the company is mustered into service.  Arms of the first class will be furnished.  Call at Cook's Hotel and enroll your names, and save the Bounty and not be a Conscript."  Columbus *Sun,* May 9, 1862.

[17] O. R. ser. IV, vol. I, 1130.  The adjutant and inspector general of Alabama said (May 28th) that there had been 19 regiments recently organized in the State and a legion of 23 companies (O. R. ser. IV, vol. I, 1131).  Other evidence of enlistment in the voluntary units is carried in the *Southern Confederacy,* May 28, 1862; Columbus *Weekly Sun,* August 5, 1862; O. R. ser. IV, vol. I, 1142.

The Marshall *Republican* observed that men even furnished substitutes in these new organizations and were given certificates of exemption, which by law could only be granted at camps of instruction.  Quoted in the *Sun,* June 2, 1862.

[18] O. R. ser. IV, vol. I, 1142.

The conscription officers were further embarrassed by enlistments in the "Partisan Ranger" service. Along with the conscription act Congress passed an act authorizing the President to detail officers to form bands of "partisan rangers." These special troops were to be used primarily on detached duty to meet emergencies as they arose. The bands were usually mounted, though the law permitted the organization of infantry rangers. The thought of being in a mounted company, independent and upon detached service with little prospect of steady fighting, except in a few peculiar localities, appealed strongly to adventurous horsemen. Governor Clark said that the idea of being mounted was very agreeable to the habits of his fellow-North Carolinians and that it had attractions which would carry every one into the cavalry or rangers if no deterrent were interposed.[19] He had observed that substitutes, particularly, had a preference for the ranger service. This was not strange for the substitute was likely to be a venturesome spirit, hence the saddle, the guerilla existence of the rangers with its air of romance and outlawry, and the prospect of receiving the full money value of all property taken from the enemy appealed strongly to him. He was to become a real knight, neither better nor worse, perhaps, than those of old.

By the middle of the summer there were more partisan-ranger units than were necessary. When they could no longer organize upon the recommendation of the district commander and the approval of the War Department, they did so without authority. According to Governor Clark the records of the War Department did not contain one-third of the companies that claimed to have organized under the Secretary, and Generals Holmes,

[19] O. R. ser. IV, vol. II, 4, 31.

Hill, and Smith. Many of them, he observed: "are un-equipped, unarmed, and have only a paper organization to keep them from an enrollment as conscripts." [20] The Secretary of War issued an order on July 31st prohibiting the future enrollment of conscripts in the ranger service.[21]

From the outset evasion of the law became widespread. Young men enlisted in the militia, sought petty offices and clerkships, vowed fealty to foreign powers,[22] turned to teaching school and selling drugs, and entered freely the exempted trades. Some who could not find lodgment with these exempted classes escaped through the kindly indulgence of family physicians.[23] Considerations of friendship and sometimes the purchasing power of a few dollars, it was said, influenced some of these physicians to grant exemptions for trivial defects, or no defects at all.[24]

[20] O. R. ser. IV, vol. II, 4, 31, 72, 82.

[21] Ibid., 26.

[22] The exemption of foreigners was a constant source of abuse, and their ever swelling ranks and heartless speculation wore public patience threadbare as the days went by. Impatient conscript officers frequently enrolled foreigners (O. R. ser. IV, vol. II, 67, 70, 84, 85, 95), and soon there was a demand that all foreigners dwelling and transacting business in the Confederacy should be drafted. O. R. ser. IV, vol. II, 95; Columbus *Weekly Sun,* August 26, 1862; Charleston *Mercury,* September 20, 1862.

[23] Enrolling officers frequently allowed local physicians to examine conscripts, although they had instructions to send them to the camp of instruction unless they were obviously unfit for service. Apparently in some cases the local medical boards used by the States before the conscript act was passed were allowed to examine conscripts. O. R. ser. IV, vol. I, 1141. The *Daily Courier* (March 4, 1863) declared that these boards exempted large numbers of able-bodied young men as "unfit for service" without mentioning the disease. They were a class of "hardy, robust, double-jointed exempts."

[24] Columbus *Sun,* June 24, 1862. The lax examinations led the Surgeon-General to issue an order that examinations should be more rigid,

Conflicts with State conscription laws and with some of the governors over the use of State officers in the enrollment service added something to the confusion and delay of conscription. Before the act was passed four States had enacted draft laws as a means of furnishing their quotas for Confederate service, and these acts were accompanied by exemption acts. A question of precedency as between the Confederate and State laws was involved when the two exemption systems did not coincide. In South Carolina there was serious friction for several months, the Governor and Council going so far as to threaten to countermand a Confederate order to enroll persons exempted by the State law.[25] The President's tactful but firm stand reduced this opposition, and, except for a modified recrudescence of it in the fall of 1863, there were no more conflicts of this kind in South Carolina until toward the end of the war.[26]

The persistent opposition of influential leaders was an important factor in the weakness of conscription. The eternal challenge of the constitutionality of the conscription act, whether by men like Governor Letcher and Honorable H. V. Johnson, who merely wished to protest against the principle of it while yielding to the enforcement of it for the public good, or by men like Governor Brown and Congressman Foote, who would not surrender one tittle of States' rights to considerations of public weal, tended to throw a nimbus of doubt around the legality and justice of it which encouraged the eva-

that all who were "capable of bearing arms" should be accepted.  O. R. ser. IV, vol. II, 2.

[25] O. R. ser. IV, vol. I, 1140; II, 73.

[26] See pp. 298-300 below for a fuller statement of this affair.

sion of it, and desertion among those who had rushed into the army through fear when it was passed.[27]

Unfortunately there was not an opportunity to present the question through test cases to the high State tribunals, as most of them did not convene until the following winter. There was no way to silence speculative discussions, although there was great danger of wrecking the Confederacy with debate. The decisions rendered in the early summer by Confederate Judge A. G. Magrath and by the Texas court in support of conscription tended to dignify it and to give it prestige before the people.[28]

But the salutary results of these decisions were neutralized to some extent by the adverse decisions of some lower court judges as the test cases made their way up to the highest courts of appeal.[29]

The adverse results of the hindrances to conscription were beginning to be felt by the early summer. The administration, the army, and persons, generally, who were deeply concerned about the issues of the war, complained of the inefficiency of the system.[30]   The War De-

[27] President Davis thought these discussions prompted popular discontent. O. R. ser. IV, vol. II, 52; vol. III, 1049.

[28] See pages 168-169 below for a discussion of these cases.

[29] A good example of this sort of decision is that of Judge Thomas of the superior court of Gordon County, Georgia, in the case of Jeffers v. Fair. He declared the law and all proceedings under it to be null and void. Reported in the Columbus *Weekly Sun*, September 30, 1862.

[30] *Southern Literary Messenger*, vol. 34, Nos. 6 and 7, 582; O. R. ser. IV, vol. II, 95; Columbus *Weekly Sun*, September 2, 1862; Augusta *Constitutionalist*, August 20, 1862. The *Mercury* and the *Examiner* also were displeased with the net results of conscription (June and July numbers).

A military catechism by one Colonel T. C. J. probably represented the army viewpoint. It ran in part as follows:

(To a class in military affairs)

"Q.  What is the first duty of the Southern people?

"A.  To keep out of the army.

partment urged the conscript officers to be diligent and circumspect in the performance of their duties.[31]    A more rigid system of physical examinations was ordered; the practice of allowing examinations by family physicians was abandoned and the certificates of exemption which they had granted were invalidated; and the practice of accepting for limited service those who did not have sufficient physical stamina to do field service was begun. Special surgeons were appointed to conduct the examinations and the Surgeon-General ordered them to accept all men who were able to perform the common avocations and "whose disability was not so great as to make them useless as farmers and daily laborers." [32]

The departure by the medical staff from the regulations governing examinations in times of peace resulted in the conscription of a class of men whom the people were unaccustomed to seeing in the military, and gave the discontented an opportunity to complain.    Pathetic stories were told of physical weaklings hobbling off, under orders of hard-hearted and arbitrary officers, to distant towns or camps of instruction for examinations by army surgeons.[33]    One who visited Camp Watts (Alabama) reported that examinations there were a farce.    He gave the following picture of physical infirmities in support of his contention: "One man is minus two fingers, and

"Q.  What is the second duty?

"A.  To make all the money they can out of the government and the soldiers, as wars come seldom."  *Southern Literary Messenger,* vol. 34, Nos. 7-8, 576-8.

[31] Their orders were to enforce the law "with the utmost activity, and without fear, favor, or affection."  O. R. ser. IV, vol. II, 6.

[32] The *Constitutionalist,* August 5 and 20, 1862.

[33] The *Sun,* June 24th; the *Constitutionalist,* August 6th; *Southern Confederacy,* November 2d.  Commandant Dunwoody ordered that those who did not report for reëxamination should be brought to camp under guard and in irons if necessary.

has two more that he cannot use; another has very little use of his right hand,—another has rheumatism or paralysis, and drags his feet when he walks—one of his messmates says he cannot step over his arm if it were placed on the ground; another is an ordained minister—his chest is sunken over the region of the left lung, and is utterly unable to do the duties of a soldier." [34]   Even the conservative and self-poised Governor of Florida wrote President Davis that the camp of instruction in his State had "more the appearance of a camp provided for those afflicted with lameness and diseases than a military camp," and he assured the President that the driving of invalids into the camps was having a "most unhappy effect." [35] Judge T. W. Thomas, of one of the superior courts of Georgia, declared in an animated dictum that the use of the halt, lame, and blind for clerks, messengers, nurses, cooks, waiters, etc., was illegal.   Neither the Commander-in-Chief nor any of his subordinates had "any more power to press the free people of this country for such purposes than to hire them for grooms for his horses or scullions for his kitchen. The purpose to do such shows ignorance of the spirit of the people and of free government." [36]   These reports of the conscription of cripples,

[34] The *Weekly Sun*, Oct. 7, 1862.

[35] O. R. ser. IV, vol. II, 92. See also the *Weekly Sun*, October 7th. Representative Dargan of Alabama told a pathetic story in the House (January, 1864) of a man who had been conscribed, although he had never been able to walk a quarter of a mile in one day. All of his efforts with the Secretary of War to secure this man's release failed, yet the officer who conscribed him gave a secret exemption to another man because he professed to be writing a history of the war in which, it was assumed, Secretary Seddon would have a notable place. Pollard, *Third Year of the War*, 183.

[36] Levingood *v.* Bruce, reported in the *Confederacy*, September 26th. Justice Moore observed at a later time, *in re* Bryan, that the practice of considering those not bedridden fit for service had "driven thousands of individuals to substitution to save themselves from death by the hard-

whether true or not,—and no doubt some persons did suffer, because criticisms for leniency tended to drive the medical examiners to rigidity, and their charity was exhausted by impositions upon their credulity by the would-be infirm—produced a popular indignation that caused the abandonment of the limited service practice.[37]

In the absence of complete statistical data it is impossible to say how many conscripts were enrolled during the spring and summer; and no satisfactory estimate can be made of the net results of the efforts to improve the system. Early reports from the various States indicated that the number would be small, owing to volunteering and to the multifarious methods of evading the law. The adjutant general of Alabama reported (July 29th) that unless the enemy could be expelled from the northern part of the State the number of conscripts would probably not exceed 10,000. If the enemy could be ejected, 3,000 more might be furnished.[38] Reports from Georgia showed that it had furnished only 2,718 conscripts by September 26th, or an average of about twenty-four and a half per county.[39] In North Carolina, according to Governor Clark, only 5,066 conscripts had

ships of the service." 60 N. C., 1. Even the temperate *Confederacy* could not approve of the practice of using men for limited service. It observed that no officer had "authority to create chemical corps, messenger battalions, or hospital nursery companies out of the sick and infirm of the conscript age." September 7th.

[37] The *Weekly Sun* made the extreme suggestion that it would be better to have the conscript law include all between the ages of 10 and 90 and to draft the able-bodied between these extreme points of juvenescence and longevity than to take invalids between 18 and 35. September 7, 1862.

[38] O. R. ser. IV, vol. II, 21.

[39] Secretary of War's report to the President, O. R. ser. IV, vol. II, 95. The Department was so dissatisfied with this result that it appointed Colonel John B. Weems to supersede Major Dunwoody as commandant of conscripts in Georgia.

reported to the camps of instruction up to August 22d.[40] Governor Pettus of Mississippi reported to the War Department, July 26th, that the commandants of the camps were calling out the conscripts and would soon have all of them in the service.[41]

Such evidence as has been found indicates that the condition of conscription in the Trans-Mississippi Department was by no means better than east of the Mississippi. In this Department the commander was given practically complete control over conscription, and a regular correspondence was not maintained with the Secretary of War.

Governor Rector of Arkansas was disposed to ignore the conscription law and to defy the Richmond authorities when the Government began to withdraw troops from the Trans-Mississippi Department. He threatened secession and called upon all able-bodied men between the ages of 18 and 45 to volunteer in the militia.[42]

According to General Blanchard no conscripts had reported for enlistment by June 2d. He said that he had issued orders for them to come in but it would be weeks before they would arrive. No arms were to be had and the people made no attempt to resist the marauding parties of the enemy.[43] It was reported that General Hindman, commander of the Department, ordered all men between the ages of 18 and 35 to enroll themselves as members of volunteer infantry companies by June

[40] O. R. ser. IV, vol. II, 68. The Secretary of War said that 400 men were being conscripted daily, but Governor Clark informed him that the work was progressing slowly.

[41] *Ibid.*, 17. The report of the Secretary of War, September 8th, indicated that the number of conscripts was much less generally than had been expected. *Ibid.*, 77.

[42] Harper's *Pictorial History of the Civil War,* vol. I, 218; the *Examiner,* June 26, 1862.

[43] O. R. ser. I, vol. XV, 780.

20th.[44]   Substitution was prohibited, and the exemption act was extended so as to include persons actually engaged in the manufacture of wool, cotton, arms, powder, salt, breadstuffs, leather, army equipments, and overseers upon plantations owned by widows, minors, officers, or soldiers in the field, provided that the plantations had been planted largely in grain, and had not less than ten negro men on them.[45]   If the report was true the General was acting in high-handed fashion.   The House of Representatives became sufficiently interested to request the President to inform it whether General Hindman had refused to receive substitutes, and whether he had organized conscripts into new companies and regiments or not; and if so, upon what authority and instructions he had acted.[46]

Not only do the available records show that the increments to the army by purely conscription methods were small, but that within a month or two desertion had become so common that it attracted the attention of the War Department.   Various orders were sent out for the arrest and return of deserters.[47]   Chief among these deserters were the mountain yeomen, the "hill-billies," so-called, who had not learned to relish the mandates of distant governors, and who had an innate dislike for war for the perpetuation of slavery which they knew was the bed-rock of the power and prestige of their proud neighbors of the lowlands.   This natural opposition was fanned into a burning passion when they were led to be-

[44] O. R. ser. I, vol. XV, 780.

[45] Ibid., 781.

[46] O. R. ser. IV, vol. II, 73.

[47] Ibid., vol. I, 1120, 1151; vol. II, 5, 14, 186; Appleton's Annual Cyclopædia, 1862, 246; the Examiner, June 21st.   The Whig observed (July 23d): "The evil is great and not abating."

lieve that the wealthy were skulking, and when they observed that the mere pittance paid them could never save their large families from abject misery against prices ever soaring because of war and speculation. Their exaggerated impression of the dereliction of the wealthy and the needs of their families justified desertion in their own minds, and the powerful opposition to the conscript law encouraged them to believe that the public would not frown upon their stroke for justice.[48] In some communities these mountain folk banded together and defied the Confederate authorities.[49]

When Congress assembled in extra session in August the Secretary of War did not have a good conscription record to present. The law, however, had by no means been a failure. It accomplished its immediate and primary purpose,—that of retaining the twelve-months' men. In the next place, while the forces actually added as conscripts were not numerous, it should be borne in mind that the conscription law was the real stimulus to volunteering in the spring and summer.[50] Many of these volunteers might have gone into the service of their own volition later, but the conscription act gave them to the service just at the moment when they were absolutely necessary to check the onrush of the enemy toward Richmond. In a series of brilliant victories they gave a distinct check to the powerful Federal armies, and impressed President Lincoln with the necessity of calling

[48] Because of serious opposition, the conscript law was temporarily suspended in East Tennessee early in June. O. R. ser. IV, vol. I, 1153.

[49] O. R. ser. IV, vol. I, 1149; vol. II, 87.

[50] *Ibid.*, vol. II, 34. Richmond *Enquirer*, June 20, 1862. The *Examiner* observed that volunteering had failed before the law was enacted. But for conscription the twelve-months' men would have gone home and nobody would have taken their place. September 12th.

for 600,000 more men. Any system that could produce such great results in so short a time was entitled to further consideration and trial. It promised splendid results for the future if its weaknesses, some of which had clearly exhibited themselves, could be amended.

The total results of conscription justified it to the minds of the Richmond authorities, of the army, and of many well-informed persons in all of the walks of life.[51] The Secretary of War warmly indorsed the accomplishments of it.[52] He had no misgivings about recruiting the army in the future if the conscript law and its complement, the exemption law, could be amended in certain lame places and then energetically enforced. Experience and observation had shown to him the indispensability of certain changes in the law. First, State officers should no longer be accepted as enrolling officers; the experiment of using State officers had proved a failure because the military systems of many of the States had so greatly deteriorated that either no enrolling officers could be found, or none could be had who were trustworthy.[53] Second, conscripts should be enrolled wherever found. The fact that persons could acquire immunity from the conscript law by absenting themselves from their States had impeded the enforcement of it. Third, exemption should be extended to a few other classes of producers,

[51] *Weekly Sun,* September 10th; Richmond *Examiner,* June 24th; Mobile *Tribune* (quoted in Clarke County *Democrat,* June 26th) ; O. R. ser. IV, vol. II, 42, 53, 56. Congressman Chas. F. Collier of Virginia and Senator W. E. Simms of Kentucky warmly commended the results of the conscript law. *Enquirer* September 12th, October 1st and 6th.

[52] O. R. ser. IV, vol. II, 42 *et seq.*

[53] He suggested that recruits might continue to be enrolled by a certain number of enrolling officers for each Congressional District, or by supernumeraries given to each corps to act as enrolling officers for that corps. He was inclined to the latter because a more direct and rigid military supervision would be established.

like millers, tanners, and salt-makers, and the opportunities for substitution should be restricted. The privilege of substitution had been greatly abused; many persons who were really not needed at home had employed worthless substitutes. He thought that those, and only those, whose activities at home were as productive as they would be in the field should be allowed to employ substitutes, as, for example, experts in the useful trades and overseers in localities where there were few white men and large numbers of slaves. Substitution based upon considerations of private interest should no longer be tolerated.

President Davis commended the results of it to Congress, though he admitted that there were weak features in the system and asked that favorable consideration be given to the recommendations of the Secretary of War for improving it. He recommended that the age limit should be extended to 45, and that he should be given authority to call out those between 35 and 45 at any time to meet an emergency. This he thought should be done in order to vouchsafe a force large enough to cope with the large forces just called out by President Lincoln. He entertained no doubt that the Confederate armies were strong enough to do successful battle with the Federal troops already in the field. With keen appreciation of the popular States' rights feeling, and mindful of recent tilts with State authorities, he cautioned Congress when it was legislating upon conscription, as upon every other military measure, to yield as much to the "most scrupulous susceptibilities of the State authorities" as was consistent with a just consideration for the public defense.[54]

There were many who did not share the optimism of

[54] O. R. ser. IV, vol. II, 54.

the President and the Secretary of War for the conscript law. Some of them admitted that it had accomplished two splendid results, in the retention of the twelve-months' men and the forcing of thousands of others into the depleted regiments in the field; but they were of the opinion that it could not be calculated upon any longer as a means of recruiting the army.[55] Senator Yancey thought that since the "hard necessity" for conscription no longer existed Congress should adopt some method of raising armies that would be generally more agreeable. He thought it wise to act as far as possible in harmony with the State authorities. There was danger of making State sovereignty,—in some respects the strongest feature— the weakest feature in the Confederate system.[56] General Howell Cobb, who was in the confidence of the Administration, wrote Secretary Randolph that the law could not be counted upon to add many more conscripts in Georgia; this, he said, was the common opinion of many persons of influence with whom he had conversed. The law was "unpopular—almost odious—and the officers charged with its execution young and inefficient." Like Yancey, he thought conscription could safely be abolished. It had served the master problem of the Confederacy; namely, the building of a powerful military machine. The task of maintaining it would be much less and could be done through the instrumentality of the States. Any inconveniences encountered by calling upon

[55] Athens *Banner,* quoted in the *Confederacy,* September 26th, 1862.

[56] Speech in Senate September 4th, reported in the *Enquirer,* September 10th. Yancey strenuously opposed Senator Hill's proposition to conscript justices of the peace. Senator Simms of Kentucky called Yancey's eloquent appeal on behalf of States' rights "sham-acting." He said Yancey knew that there was no intention of conscripting high State officers, and that there was no danger of Congress conscripting itself. *Ibid.,* October 6th.

the States would be more than offset by the harmony produced and the awakening of a healthy public spirit. It would silence the implacable oppositionists and assuage the internal quakes set in motion by them.[57] He believed that the abolition of the law would give a new impulse to volunteering; if not the States could use compulsory methods. Perhaps the President and his Cabinet did not share the confidence which the recent successes of the Confederate arms inspired in the Senator and the General; anyhow, their opinions found no place in the recommendations to Congress.

Although there was a difference of opinion among leaders as to the proper way of recruiting the army in the future, all were agreed that large forces must be speedily raised to meet the large contingents being added to the Union armies. The majority inclined to conscription, either by the Confederate Government or by the States, as the only available method of securing large numbers of recruits. The press launched a propaganda for an immediate extension of conscription so as to include all men between the ages of 18 and 50.[58] This was calculated to direct the minds of the masses, who were inclined to relax after the predominance of their arms in the second battle of Bull Run, to the seriousness of President Lincoln's call for 600,000 recruits, and also,

[57] He suggested the plan of authorizing the formation of companies, regiments, and even brigades and divisions, to be accepted and officered by the President as an alternative to calling upon the States. O. R. ser. IV, vol. II, 34.

[58] Some advocated the enrollment of boys between the ages of 16 and 18. The editor of the *Weekly Sun* (August 26th) said that some of his exchanges were advocating this, while others believed that all persons who were able to bear arms, irrespective of age, should be required to do so. Ex-Governor Brown of Tennessee, for example, championed this idea. *Weekly Sun*, September 4, 1862.

perhaps, to instruct Congress concerning the same thing.[59]

The moment was thought to be a critical one, and so it was. The reversal of McClellan's army upon the peninsula and of the combined armies of Pope and McClellan at Bull Run produced a feeling that the Confederate Capital was impregnable, and that the task of finally annihilating the Union forces was an easy one. Yet it was a stern and plain fact that the rapid increase of numbers in the Union army was a grave menace to the Confederate cause, and thoughtful patriots labored feverishly to produce a feeling of deep solicitude.[60] Everything was done to inspire the people to give the enemy a *coup de main* while he was visibly stunned. Some went so far as to suggest that all of the able-bodied should be called out, and even those who were physically unfit to be enrolled as regulars might be called upon to serve for a month or two when the campaign reached the critical stage.[61] Others who had opposed conscription because

[59] Columbus *Weekly Sun*, August 26 and September 4, 1862; the *Mercury*, August 30th; the *Confederacy*, August 22d, 29th, and September 17th; the *Enquirer*, September 2, 1862; Richmond *Dispatch*, September 4 and 24, 1862; the *Independent*, August 2, 1862; the *Examiner*, July 31st, August 5th, 13th, 18th, 22d, and September 12th. The Tailahassee *Sentinel* thought the extension to 45 would not add more than 100,000 men.

[60] An effort was made to spur the people into action by telling them that another victory or two would secure the recognition of the Confederacy, for the movements and combinations upon the great chessboard of European diplomacy already indicated that the Confederate cause was gaining much favor there. The Derby party seemed destined to overthrow the Palmerston cabinet because of labor unrest. Charleston *Mercury*, December 8, 1862.

[61] The *Independent* quoting the *Enquirer*, August 23, 1862. This paper suggested that the Confederate and State governments should mobilize all their strength to meet the new onset of the enemy. It preferred using men fit to serve for only a month or two to employing the militia. The militia organizations had been almost broken up by volunteering and conscription and the militia officers were generally incompetent to command.

it seemed to them to be subversive of State rights, waived this scruple and expressed a hope that Congress would conscript all between the ages of 18 and 50.[62] The right to have States now seemed more important to them than State rights.

Congress had much first-hand information concerning the conditions and needs of the conscription service, and it must have been pretty thoroughly imbued with the feelings and sentiments of the people. It had also the observations of the President and Secretary of War laid before it, and was favored with endless lectures by the press and with letters from observant persons everywhere. All of this information had to be molded by the discretionary powers of Congress into a policy which would determine the complexion of events during the next few months. These were momentous months, too, in the history of America and of the world. Another victory or two for the Confederacy and France and England might recognize her independence, and President Davis could announce the success of the Secessionists and the birth of a new nation; one more decisive victory for the Union arms and President Lincoln would promulgate a proclamation of emancipation, with the twofold purpose of committing the United States to a policy of freedom and of holding England and France steadfastly to their policy of non-interposition by appealing to their philanthropic impulses.

Through the long and sultry days of August and September Congress deliberated upon conscription.[63] The

[62] The *Southern Confederacy*, August 22d; the *Enquirer*, September 5th.

[63] Early in the session reports were requested concerning the numerical strength of the armies, the number of troops furnished by each State, and the progress of conscription in places where irregularities had been noted.

members of both Houses were generally agreed that the
age limit of service should be extended and that substitution and exemption should be modified.[64]   But there
was a divided opinion as to whether conscription should
be retained, or the old system of calling upon the States
for troops should be revived.

The debates were often intense and long-winded. Congressman C. C. Herbert of Texas affirmed that a majority of the people of Texas believed that the conscription
act was unconstitutional and would oppose an extension
of it.[65]   Senator Oldham favored the Senate with a message of defiance.   He said that a certain regiment, raised
to guard the frontier against Indians and jayhawkers,
might as well be exempted for the Government did not
have enough men to take it.[66]   Meanwhile the press got
impatient with the tardiness of Congress.   For example,

It is unfortunate for the historical investigator that considerations of
military expediency caused the Secretary of War to decline to give the
Senate the number of troops furnished by each State. O. R. ser. IV, vol.
II, 80.

[64] There were some heated discussions on the exemption question.
Some, like Senator Simms, wanted to exempt, so far as the civil service
was concerned, only the high officials of the Confederate and State governments; while others for the protection of States' rights would not
allow even a justice of the peace to be conscripted. Senator Yancey
made a powerful argument against conscripting local State officers and,
contrary to the practice of the Senate, it was said, gave his speech to the
press for publication. Senator Simms, who was ready to vote the last
man and the last dollar to the cause, ridiculed Yancey. He said that
Yancey by refusing to vote all aid and resources stood forth as an accom-
plice of the Greeleys and the Bennetts. *Journal* of the Confederate Congress, vol. II, 225-321; vol. V, 343-443; the *Enquirer,* September 10th,
12th, and October 6th.

[65] The *Enquirer,* October 28th.   One of Herbert's supporters expressed
"profound astonishment and mortification" that he should have so grossly
misrepresented the sentiments of his people (*Ibid.*).

[66] This challenge brought his colleague, Senator Wigfall, to his feet and
he defended the Government with his usual vigor and abruptness. The
*Mercury,* August 30th.

the peppery little Athens *Banner* observed: "Congress is fooling away its time now on the extension of the conscription bill. It was criminal dillydallying that caused the conscription law to be absolutely necessary last spring. Soon we will be in another such dilemma." It wished that Congress would give the President authority to call upon the States for troops and then "Adjourn, never again to assemble, until the war is over," since the statesmen were all in the field.[67]

Finally the House, by the combination of the enemies of conscription and those who were willing to relinquish it as a "peace offering" to certain State authorities, passed a bill by a vote of 49 to 39 providing for a revival of the old system of calling upon the States.[68]   Six days afterward the Senate passed a bill, 21 to 3, providing for retaining and extending conscription.[69]   A conference bill, which was fundamentally the same as the Senate bill, was then reported and promptly adopted by a large vote in both houses.[70]

The President was now in a strong position.  He had won a complete victory over his personal adversaries and the enemies of conscription in Congress, and conscription was being upheld by the leading papers of the country.

---

[67] Quoted in the *Confederacy*, September 26th.   The *Examiner*, the *Mercury*, the *Enquirer*, and the *Dispatch* were impatient, but, unlike the *Banner*, they supported conscription.   See files of these papers for August and September.

[68] The *Journal*, vol. V, 400.

[69] *Ibid.*, vol. II, 321.

[70] The House vote was 54 to 30 for the bill.   The Senate vote was not recorded since the opposition was not strong enough to require a yea and nay vote (*Journal*, vol. II, 320, 321, 335, 336; vol. V, 443).   It is interesting to note that Senator Yancey after his bill for a call upon the States was rejected (*Ibid.*, vol. II, 260, 261) voted for the Senate bill and served with Sparrow and Wigfall on the Senate Conference Committee (*Ibid.*, vol. V, 437).

Even the pungent *Mercury* had become almost cordial with him and the catapultic Pollard had been striking through the editorial columns of the *Examiner* for an extension of conscription.

# CHAPTER VII

THE second conscription act came none too soon. Ten days previously Lee's invading army was repulsed at Sharpsburg and hope vanished of relieving Virginia from another attack before winter; of spreading dismay in the North; of liberating Maryland from Federal control and adding it to the Confederate cause; and of creating a favorable impression in Europe.

The new act extended the age limit to 45 and authorized the President to call out all or a part of those within the draft age at any time he thought necessary, provided that if he called out only a part of those between 35 and 45 he must call out the younger men first.[1] Substitution was continued, and exemption was expanded by the act of October 11th so as to include many new classes.[2] The administrative machinery was essentially the same as before, and the practice of using State enrolling officers was continued over the protest of the Secretary of War. The original practices with regard to the rights of conscripts to volunteer [3] and to select their organization and the distribution of conscripts from the camps of instruction were continued. In furtherance of the custom of associating conscripts from the same local-

[1] O. R. ser. IV, vol. II, 160.

[2] See page 67 above.

[3] By an act, October 2d, conscripts were allowed to enlist in the Marine Corps or the Navy, if they expressed a wish to do so before being assigned to a company. *Ibid.,* 191.

ities, it was provided that separate hospitals should be maintained for the troops from each State. Thus the system made it possible for State troops to live, fight, suffer, and die together.[4]

In order that the system might be elastic enough to to meet special contingencies, the President was given power to suspend conscription in any locality where he found it impracticable to execute it, and to receive during the period of suspension troops under any of the acts passed prior to the enactment of the first conscription act. By the act of October 11th he was authorized to receive troops organized before December 1st in middle and west Tennessee, and in the counties of North Carolina that lay east of the Wilmington and Weldon Railroad and beyond the lines of the army.[5] This act of legislative suspension and the potential power of the President to confer the immunity bestowed by it encouraged requests for special privileges in organizing local defense troops, and the Administration was besieged with them.[6]

The amendatory acts of September and October exhibit very clearly the dilemma in which Congress and the Administration labored as regards conscription. The system had to be extended and made more thoroughgoing, while the opponents of it should be antagonized less, if possible. How well the revised system struck a balance between these two divergent, if not irreconcilable demands, will appear in succeeding pages.

[4] O. R. ser. IV, vol. II, 200.

[5] He was also authorized to receive troops organized out of conscripts in the States west of the Mississippi prior to the act, and all such units east of the River as had been organized prior to October 1st, in "good faith" with the consent of the Secretary of War or any "general officer of the Government." O. R. ser. IV, vol. II, 204.

[6] O. R. ser. IV, vol. II, 206 *et passim*.

The Secretary of War estimated roughly that the act would add 105,000 men, and recommended that only those between the ages of 35 and 40 should be called out immediately. This contingent would bring the available number of men up to about a half million.[7] Since it was doubtful if a greater number could be maintained in the field, he thought more would be gained if the remainder were left at home to produce supplies and munitions. President Davis endorsed this opinion and called out those between the ages of 35 and 40.[8]

Many things militated against the free operation of the law. Some of the difficulties inhered in the system set up by the law; some in the developments of the war; while others resulted unavoidably from social, political, and economic conditions.

It was unfortunate that the new act continued the practice of using State militia officers as enrolling officers; that substitution was not abolished; and that the system of blanket class exemption was continued and extended. The substitute system had become iniquitous,[9] and the disadvantages of employing State officers had been clearly demonstrated, but conditions seemed to make it, on the whole, advisable to continue them.[10] Experience had shown that other artisans would have to be exempted

---

[7] He allowed three-sevenths for exempts, but did not make allowance for those who had been killed or incapacitated. O. R. ser. IV, vol. II, 132. A few weeks later the Richmond *Dispatch* estimated that the conscription acts should yield 700,000 men between the ages of 18 and 40, and was very hopeful of victory with this large body of troops at the disposal of the new Secretary of War, James A. Seddon. Quoted in Clarke County (Ala.) *Journal*, January 15, 1863.

[8] O. R. ser. IV, vol. II, 132.

[9] See page 33 above.

[10] Concerning the unfitness of State officers for conscription service see O. R. ser. IV, vol. II, 215, 723.

to meet the needs of production, and President Lincoln's preliminary emancipation proclamation emphasized the need of exempting overseers for the purpose of policing the slaves. But a carefully classified system of exemption, or a system of executive detail, should have served the needs of production as well as unrestricted class exemption, and would have furnished more men to the armies.

The inadequacy of the new exemption act soon appeared. War was no longer a romance, it had become a bloody and awful business. It had produced conditions throughout the Confederacy in the presence of which ephemeral patriotism could not sustain men.[11] Those who were not prepared by stern devotion to make the supreme sacrifice, and those—doubtless there were many of them—who feared for their homes because of the approach of the enemy and the breakdown of civil authority utilized every available resource to secure exemption. The system was very susceptible to abuse and reports came in from all sides that large numbers were evading conscription by means of it.

The exemption of overseers caused much dissatisfaction among the masses and in the ranks. It was regarded as pure class legislation. In vain did the press attempt to explain that it was not intended to benefit the rich, that a poor man might be employed as an overseer, that it was only an incident of the law that a rich man was exempted here and there, and that the army was full of wealthy men fighting the common battle of freedom. In vain did the President in his swing around the circle in

[11] Assistant Secretary of War, J. A. Campbell, said there was homesickness in the army and the spirit at home was failing. O. R. ser. IV, vol. II, 242.

December tell the people and the people's representatives that men of property were bearing more than a fair proportion of the war burdens, and that men of the largest fortunes were serving as privates in the army. He asked them to verify his assertions by observing the crippled among them, but they could not do it to their satisfaction.[12]   Though he denied with fervor that the law was class legislation and explained patiently its purposes, it remained to the average man unmistakable evidence that the war had become the poor man's fight.

There was every reason to believe that the slaves would under the new conditions need to be more carefully policed.   As more and more white men were drawn from the farms it became increasingly necessary to supervise slave labor in such a way as to make it yield its fullest productivity.   The leaders saw their opportunity and had hoped to make the most of it.   If the plantations were converted into well managed food producing units and the agencies of distribution were at all adequate, there was no doubt that most of the farmers could be sent to the front without sacrificing their families.[13]   Slavery would then be a real war asset and President Lincoln's emancipation proclamation would be mere *brutum fulmen*, as he at one time predicted it would be.

The poor as a rule could not see the wisdom of the new policy since it seemed to be a special consideration for the plantations and incidentally the planters.   The fact that while the poor man could barely support his large family, a plantation of twenty field slaves, if prop-

---

[12] See *Southern Confederacy,* October 30, 1862, and January 16, 1863.

[13] Some of the States fell in line with the new policy by creating relief committees for distributing supplies among the families of non-slaveholders. Dubose, *Life and Times of William Lowndes Yancey,* 671; *Southern Recorder,* February 3, 1863.

erly managed, might make several thousand bushels of corn and meat, potatoes, vegetables, fowls, and butter in proportion, was usually not material to him. The question in last analysis was one of leaving one's family and enduring hardships, and the rich man's family needed him less than the poor man's family needed its head.[14]

So great was the discontent that some of the newspaper editors felt it necessary to give the poor a little preachment upon the advantages of slavery to the poor. But for slavery, they were told, "the poor would occupy the position in society that the slaves do—as the poor in the North and in Europe do," for there must be a menial class in society and in "every civilized country on the globe, besides the Confederate States, the poor are the inferiors and menials of the rich." Slavery was a greater blessing to the non-slaveholding poor than to the owners of slaves, and since it gave the poor a start in society that it would take them generations to work out, they should thank God for it and fight and die for it as they would for their "own liberty and the dearest birthright of freemen." [15]

The character of the Federal attack had become exasperating. Not only was there fighting in the main theaters of war, but slashing attacks were made on isolated seacoast communities and communities of the interior. Every seacoast town of any importance from Norfolk to Galveston, and the whole interior line from the eastern border of Virginia to the Panhandle of Texas had been invaded or was threatened with invasion. The entire Confederacy was like a besieged city; the most vulnerable points on the outskirts of it had been carried;

[14] The *Recorder*, February 3, 1863.
[15] *Southern Confederacy*, October 25, 1862.

other points were threatened, and there was tension, smarting, and anxiety all along the line. The fatal task of adequately defending the localities while recruiting and enlarging the armies on the main battle-grounds was imposed upon the Government. The outlying positions, some of which contained union or neutral sentiment, must be protected if the Government would command support from them, but in the nature of things this was impossible, and therein lies a fact that is significant to one who would understand the military history of the war.[16] It is clear that the processes of the war had by the late fall of 1862 set into operation forces that aided the accomplishment in the summer of 1863 of such definite Federal objectives as the capture of Vicksburg and Port Hudson, and ultimately the overthrow of the Confederacy.

When the men between the ages of 35 and 45 were drafted to check the enemy on the main battle-fronts there was anxiety in the sections not in the immediate theater of war. The taking of these men to distant battle-fields left not much defense against the enemy or servile insurrections in these areas. Visions of property destroyed and homes outraged caused sleepless nights and tortuous days. Some of the States requested the suspension of conscription until the following spring, while others requested special privileges as to the use of conscripts in the local defense organizations.[17] The

[16] The Secretary of War thought the true policy with regard to the defense of places not in the main theater of war was to maintain forces strong enough to prevent plundering by detached units of the enemy but not so large as to invite an attack in force. O. R. ser. I, vol. XIV, 738; vol. LIII, 272.

[17] O. R. ser. I, vol. XIII, 879; vol. XV, 848; vol. LIII, 263-272, 817, 818, 822, 834, 838; ser. IV, vol. II, 129, 178, 225, 247.

President was accused of being indifferent to the sufferings of the people in the Trans-Mississippi Department;
and when troops could not be spared from the hard-
pressed armies of the East and West for local defense
there were seditious mutterings among high officials in a
few of the States.[18]   Seaports and interior localities requested relief, and panic-stricken women begged generals in the field for aid with a pathos that must
have penetrated the heart of the hardest West
Pointer.[19]

The Administration did all it could legally and feasibly
to strengthen the local defense.[20]   It furnished arms
whenever possible and reduced conscription to the minimum in some States, while in others special arrangements
were made for the use of conscripts for local defense
during the winter.[21]   In furtherance of the same purpose
new military divisions were created in the lower South

[18] O. R. ser. I, vol. LIII, 816, 837. Governor Thomas O. Moore accused
the President of using Louisiana troops in States less exposed and less
valuable to the cause than Louisiana. His people were sore and bitter,
he said, and were sorry they did not strike independently for their liberty. A few months earlier secession had been threatened, and General
Beauregard was importuned to lead in Garabaldi fashion an army of
deliverance against General Butler at New Orleans. *Ibid.*, vol. XV, 792.
The Governor of Arkansas was in his former ugly mood (*Harper's
Pictorial History*, vol. I, 218), and Governor Brown warned of the
danger of rebellion if any more troops were taken from Georgia (*Ibid.*,
ser. IV, vol. II, 128).

[19] O. R. ser. I, vol. LIII, 246, 842; vol. XV, 848. The *Enquirer* (December 19th) pointed out the fact that local suffering could not be prevented. The Confederacy must be defended as a whole, and it hoped
that the States that were jealous of Virginia might not suffer the evils of
being 'fought for.' "

[20] It coöperated with the States in organizing local defense troops under
the act of October 13, 1862. O. R. ser. IV, vol. II, 206.

[21] O. R. ser. I, vol. XIV, 703, 738; vol. LIII, 838, 263, 269; ser. IV,
vol. II, 178, 225, 247.

and able and reputed generals were transferred to them.[22] The most that could be done was insufficient and President Davis became increasingly unpopular.[23]

There was much opposition to conscription in the hill counties of all the States, and by the end of 1862 it had become especially acute in East Tennessee and in portions of North Carolina, Alabama, and Mississippi.[24] Union or neutral sentiment; intense individualism; the increasing difficulty to support their generally large families in the face of soaring prices; the insecurity of families before hostile neighbors and the invading forces; missionary work for the Union by officers detailed from the Federal army and by civilian agents from the North; and the persistence of the pre-war feuds, prejudices, and political rivalries of the most malignant type; these were the chief causes of opposition among those unhappy people.[25]    It was a disadvantage to the South that much of the fighting had to be done in the communities least capacitated from every standpoint to endure the shocks of it.  Bragg in East Tennessee, like Washington before Philadelphia, was as much in the land of enemies as of

[22] General Howell Cobb was placed in command of the new Central Florida district, General E. K. Smith the new department of Louisiana and Texas, and General T. H. Holmes the Trans-Mississippi department.

[23] Senator Clark of Missouri said that by the middle of the preceding summer President Davis was the most unpopular man in the Confederacy, but his judgment is hardly to be trusted since he said that his indignation at the President was "inexpressible."  O. R. ser. I, vol. LIII, 817.

[24] O. R. ser. I, vol. XV, 872; vol. XX, Pt. II, 405, 407, 450; vol. XVII, Pt. II, 788; vol. LIII, 834; ser. IV, vol. II, 138, 140, 142, 146, 155, 207, 247, 254, 258; Knoxville *Register,* October 17, 1862, quoted in O. R. ser. I, vol. XVI, Pt. II, 955; *Southern Confederacy,* October 4, 1862; *Mercury,* November 22 and December 13, 1862.

[25] The mischievous effects of the work of Andrew Johnson and William G. Brownlow in Tennessee were especially emphasized. The *Confederacy,* August 3, 1862; the *Mercury,* December 13, 1862.

friends, and there were spies and tale-tellers on every side. To invade the South through the Mississippi Valley and occupy at the earliest moment the great food-producing areas of that section was military strategy of the first order, but there was doubtless besides a set purpose to carry aid to the Unionists of the hills, to hold the neutrals there to neutrality at least, to fight some of the decisive battles among friends, and to lay the foundations for a peace movement that would ultimately prove the undoing of the secessionists.

The relation of the high cost of living to recruitment among the poor deserves a word in this connection. By the fall of 1862 the full effect of the depreciation of Confederate paper money resulting from the military reverses of the preceding spring was felt. Prices soared far above the ability of the poor to pay.[26]  The inflation of prices is clearly illustrated by the following tabulation from the *Southern Confederacy*, September 24th:

|  | Former Prices | Prices on September 24th |
|---|---|---|
| Salt, per sack | $2.00 | $80.00 |
| Coffee, per lb. | .12 to .15 | 2.50 |
| Sugar, per lb. | .08 | 1.00 |
| Milk Cows | 20.00 | 100.00 |
| Butter, per lb. | .12½ | .75 |
| Chickens, per lb. | .10 | 1.00 |
| Eggs, per doz. | .05 | .60 to .75 |
| Brown Jeans, per yd. | .50 | 5.00 |
| Com. Cotton Cloth, per yd. | .10 to .15 | 1.00 [27] |

[26] Although prices were much lower in the preceding spring, the *Southern Confederacy*, April 22d, lamented the fact that they were so high that men of large families and small means could not afford to volunteer.

[27] Eight days earlier the *Confederacy* observed that tanners and shoemakers had increased their prices 500 to 1,000 per cent. For an account of the swift rise in prices in the upper South see Schwab, *Pol. Sci. Quar.,* vol. 14: 287.

The factors that naturally operated to depreciate Confederate treasury notes and to inflate prices were aided by rampant speculation and discrimination by brokers and money changers against the notes in favor of "shinplasters," which one paper observed had become "as thick as the frogs and lice of Egypt, and . . . almost as great a nuisance."

The derangement of prices was generally attributed to speculation, and speculators were denounced with vehemence by the press and public officials. It was the opinion of the *Weekly Sun* (September 2d) that speculators had done the people more harm since the blockade than all of the enemy's artilley. "We have in fact two wars upon our hands at once. Whilst our brave soldiers are off battling the Abolitionists . . . a conscienceless set of vampires are at home warring upon their indigent families and threatening them with immediate starvation." President Davis urged the Governors to recommend some means "to suppress the shameful extortions now practiced upon the people by men . . . who are worse enemies of the Confederacy than it found in arms among the invading force." [28] Some of the governors complied with the request and the legislatures passed acts for punishing extortioners.[29] Price conventions were held and obnoxious speculators were threatened with violence. Governor Vance said flour had become a luxury

[28] O. R. ser. IV, vol. II, 211. He recognized the fact, however, as he wrote to General Holmes, that extortion could not be entirely suppressed since prices "must always be regulated by the relation of supplies and demand." Ser. I, vol. LIII, 846.

[29] O. R. ser. IV, vol. II, 180, 191, 214, 251; Schwab, *Pol. Sci. Quar.*, vol. 14:294.

of the rich and leather and textile products were rapidly becoming so.[30]

Whatever the causes of the extremely high prices current in the fall of 1862, men who had large families solely dependent upon their labor, and there were thousands of them in the hills, could scarcely begin to support them on the paltry sum of $11.00 per month in treasury notes, which were reported to have been discounted heavily in competition with "shinplasters." The situation would have been intolerable enough had it been the fault of no one, but when the poor seemed to see that extortion was the work of those for whom they were fighting it was more than they could bear. The public agencies of relief being totally inadequate, there was no relief in sight and desertion, skulking, and violence became alarmingly prevalent.

The President's assertion that the affairs in East Tennessee "present a very difficult question" [31] is amply supported by the evidence, and it might have been said of certain counties in several of the other States. As the Federal troops invaded Tennessee and the northern parts of Alabama and Mississippi, "Toryism" became rampant, and in the vicinity of the Union pockets there was "cutting up high shines, shooting, yelling, hurrahing for Lincoln," and offending and killing of loyal citizens.[32]   Reports came in from all the States, except

[30] O. R. ser. IV, vol. II, 181.  The papers throughout the war were full of denunciation of speculators.  The observations of the *Enquirer*, December 13, 1862, were typical.  It thought that the producers and distributors of goods should be allowed only a fair price.  The eloquent denunciation of speculators by Judge Gholson was "meek and gentle" compared to what they deserved.  The evidence is copious that speculation injured the conscription service throughout the war.

[31] October 23d, O. R. ser. IV, vol. II, 140.

[32] Written to the *Confederacy* and reported in the *Weekly Sun*, September 23d.  The *Sun* called attention to the fact that it was the same

Florida, of passive resistance to conscription by hiding in the caves of the mountains or in the impenetrable swamps; and in some of the States armed bands of conscripts and deserters defied the authorities and plundered the communities round about.[33]   In East Tennessee and the hills of Georgia there were shotgun squads prepared to pepper conscript officers, while in Alabama and Mississippi, according to Governor Shorter and Senator James Phelan,[34] conscription was a "humbug and a farce."   Senator Phelan noticed men everywhere, "on cars, boats, in the streets, stores, etc.," who were subject to duty.   "You cannot imagine," he observed further, "the open, bold, unblushing attempts to avoid getting in and to keep out of the army.   All shame has fled and no subterfuge is pretended, but a reckless confession of an unwillingness to go or to remain."   Governor Shorter observed, "a large number of persons subject to conscription are shrinking from the toils and perils which those of like age are

class of persons that South Carolina hanged to dogwoods and blackjacks during the revolution and hoped that hanging had not become obsolete. A Yankee correspondent to the Louisville *Journal* said of the class, it "is composed—according to careful analysis made by an eminent chemist on the spot—of ten parts of unadulterated Andy Johnson Union men, ten of good lord and good devilites—five of spuss, and seventy-five of scallawags, too lazy to run, and, therefore, disqualified for service in the sesesh army, and too cowardly to steal of their own responsibility, but willing to be enrolled as 'Home Guards,' so as to plunder their neighbors under the Union flag."   The *Mercury*, August 9, 1862.

[33] O. R. ser. I, vol. XV, 872, Pt. II, 953, 955, 956; vol. XVII, Pt. II, 788; vol. XX, Pt. II, 405, 450; vol. LIII, 834; ser. IV, vol. II, 138, 140, 142, 146, 258, 301, 309, 369; *Weekly Sun*, September 23d; *Confederacy*, October 4th; *Mercury*, November 22d, December 13th; Atlanta *Constitutionalist*, November 12th; Knoxville *Register*, October 17th.

[34] Senator Phelan was particularly pessimistic.   The disgust with Van Dorn and his reverses had reduced the spirit in Mississippi "to a cold pile of damp ashes," and he believed that the army, heedless of the future, would dissolve at once if permitted to (O. R. ser. I, vol. XVII, Pt. II, 788).   Making due allowance for the Senator's pessimism and easy eloquence, the condition of affairs was undoubtedly serious.

bravely enduring." [35] Major W. T. Walthall requested the aid of troops to enforce conscription in North Alabama, where a conscription officer had been killed, a jail delivered of its deserters, and other forms of violence reported.[36] Out in the remote counties of Texas—Cook, Wise, Danton, Grayson, etc.,—the members of a newly organized anti-conscription and pro-Union association were being quietly hunted down and hanged.[37]

Such disturbances and resistance to conscription naturally engaged the serious attention of public leaders. There was a variety of opinion as how best to manage the disloyal communities. Some recommended suspension of conscription for a while, or indefinitely, since it appeared to them to be a failure. They claimed that fewer men were being conscripted than were required to hunt them, and many men who were neutral were being driven into the ranks of the enemy. Better let them stay at home, it was thought, and produce supplies for those who were willing to go to the army and for their families. With the elimination of competition from Kentucky and the Northwestern states they would have fine markets in the Confederacy and would, consequently, produce large quantities of food supplies. Others like General Cobb and General Floyd urged a modified form of conscription. Cobb referred to conscription as the "slow-coach process," and Floyd said the means then employed were "injudicious and wholly ineffectual" in Western Virginia. Cobb would make volunteering the major method and support it with conscription, while

[35] O. R. ser. IV, vol. II, 254.
[36] *Ibid.*, 207-258.
[37] The *Mercury*, November 22d.

Floyd would put conscription entirely in the hands of civil authority.[38]

Those who were responsible for the administration of the law were less inclined to experiment. Indeed, the President and the Secretary of War believed that there had been enough experimentation already to prove that suspension did not conciliate the disloyal, but rather encouraged them to believe that the Government was weak and powerless to punish. The Secretary was of the opinion that an "issue must be made with these people whether they will submit to the laws or not." The pressure of the enemy was too great, the President said, to let up in the enforcement of the law, and "to exempt the unwilling would be to offer a premium to disaffection." Conscription would force the disloyal into the ranks of the enemy where they would be less dangerous to the Confederacy, and would place the lukewarm patriots among loyal and tried veterans where their spirit would probably be toned up.[39] He was encouraged in his determination to enforce the law by many influential men throughout the Confederacy.[40] For example Senator Phelan wrote him that if the conscription acts were not enforced "as they should be, with iron and unrelenting firmness, our cause is lost."

Great pressure was brought to bear on the President from different sections to suspend conscription, but he steadfastly refused to do it, save in a few counties of

[38] O. R. ser. I, vol. XXI, 1022; vol. LIII, 273, 277.

[39] *Ibid.,* vol. XVI, Pt. II, 955; ser. IV, vol. II, 140.

[40] Among others, Governors Harris, Shorter, and Pickens and Congressman Wm. G. Swan of Tennessee and Senator James Phelan of Mississippi expressed the opinion that any relaxation would be disastrous. O. R. ser. I, vol. XVII, Pt. II, 788; vol. LIII, 269; ser. IV, vol. II, 87, 99, 138, 254, 258.

Florida which had furnished so many men that they could not spare more. Even Texas, which had generously furnished more than its quota of men, and the needy women and children of the Tenth Congressional District (composed of 15 hill counties) of North Carolina were promised relief from conscription until the following spring only upon condition that they first recruit their regiments in the field.[41] The suffering and the distressed were told that their needs bore heavily on the hearts of the administrators at Richmond and that everything possible would be done for their relief, while they were persuaded to see that the only feasible way of defending their localities and sections permanently was to defeat the enemy on the main battlefield.

Conscription continued to be retarded in some of the States by the persistent opposition of men of high position, especially in Georgia. Governor Brown after much protest submitted to the first conscription act, but when the second one was passed he became defiant. He refused to allow the new act to be enforced in Georgia until the legislature convened and deliberated upon it.[42] The legislature under the influence of the State supreme court's unanimous decision in favor of conscription and of influential Administration friends, like Senator Hill,

[41] O. R. ser. I, vol. LIII, 838; ser. IV, vol. II, 247.

[42] O. R. ser. IV, vol. II, 128. Brown's opposition caused anxiety throughout the Confederacy. Most of the Georgia papers ridiculed his position. The Milledgeville *Recorder* offered as an antidote to the Brown-Stephens propaganda the fact that the great States' rights man, former Governor Troup, favored Federal conscription in 1814. The *Enquirer* asked the people to recall where Governor Brown and the Vice-President stood before the war when the States were really endangered by the encroachment of Federal authority. It hoped that the unanimous decision of the Georgia supreme court in favor of conscription might lay to rest all of Governor Brown's misgivings. The *Enquirer*, October 31st and November 21st.

committed the State to conscription in spite of the opposition of Governor Brown and the Stephenses.[43]    It passed, however, a resolution of protest against the principle of Confederate conscription and authorized the Governor to raise two regiments of militia from men not actually in the Confederate service.[44]

The incompleteness of the conscription organization was itself a drag on conscription. All of the agencies prescribed by law had not been brought into action, and apparently in a few of the States even the camps of instruction had not been established.[45]    Many of the enrolling officers were said to be unfit for service, and when territory was regained from the enemy sometimes months elapsed before conscription was revived.[46]

Conscription could not of course fully succeed under the conditions that obtained. Reports from several States indicated that it was functioning very imperfectly.[47]    However, several of the governors claimed

[43] It is a significant fact that Honorable H. V. Johnson, candidate before the legislature to succeed Senator John W. Lewis, was not elected on the first ballot because of a rumor that he was opposed to conscription. Before the second ballot his friend, Mr. Briscoe (Representative of Baldwin County), read a letter received post haste from Johnson which was acceptable to the legislature. Johnson stated that he had believed the conscription act to be unconstitutional, but since the supreme court had upheld it he had counselled acquiescence in it and "a most earnest and undivided support of the Government and every measure thereof in the support of the war." He was elected on the second ballot. The *Enquirer,* November 25, 1862.

[44] O. R. ser. IV, vol. II, 128.

[45] *Ibid.,* 155, 171, 176, 286.

[46] O. R. ser. I, vol. XVII, Pt. II, 788; ser. IV, vol. II, 142, 215, 294.

[47] It was declared a failure in East Tennessee, Alabama, and Mississippi, as we have seen. Governor Brown predicted its failure in Georgia, and Governor Vance thought it would be "exceedingly difficult" for him, with all his popularity, to enforce the new act in North Carolina. However, Brown respected it enough to oppose it and Vance was soon report-

that their States were practically stripped of men, and
we know that Florida and Texas had furnished men to
the entire satisfaction of the Administration.[48]   The
claims of the governors that their States were about
exhausted of men must not be taken too literally, being
based, as they were, partly on superficial evidence and
on the rumors and suspicions extant in each State that
it was furnishing more than its due portion of men; and
partly, too, perhaps, on the fact that the governors regarded their States "exhausted" when the man supply
was drained down to about what they regarded as necessary for the defense of their States.   Nevertheless men's
names were somehow or other being placed on the army
rosters.[49]   The consolidated abstract of incomplete returns in the Adjutant and Inspector General's office,
December 21st, showed that 449,439 names were carried
on the army rosters,[50] and this number was only about
45,000 less than the Secretary of War had estimated
that the calls up to that time would furnish.   One won-
ders if the Secretary's estimate was too conservative, or
if those who were suffering or were very solicitous for

ing to the legislature that his militia officers were gathering up most of
those liable to service.  O. R. ser. IV, vol. II, 113, 147, 186.

[48] O. R. ser. I, vol. XIV, 703; LIII, 273, 834, 838; ser. IV, vol. II, 215,
649, 839.  The Vicksburg *Whig* said that "Texas was drained of her
troops till she was as helpless as a child," to which the Houston *Telegraph* replied, "Texas has undoubtedly been drained of her troops to a
greater extent than any other State . . . but, still, we hope we shall be
able to show our brothers of the *Whig* that our State is not helpless."
Quoted in the *Independent,* December 20, 1862.

[49] The fragmentary reports that came in showed that at least some men
were being conscripted.  Rhodes says the Southern army was consider-
ably increased in the fall of 1862.  O. R. ser. IV, vol. II, 10, 172, 176;
Rhodes, *History of the United States,* vol. III, 618.

[50] O. R. ser. IV, vol. II, 278.  Senator Yancey was of the opinion that
there were about 500,000 men in the service in December.  *Southern
Recorder,* February 3, 1863.

the Confederate cause overemphasized skulking and other forms of delinquency.[51]

While it is impossible to state even approximately the number of men actually conscripted, or induced because of conscription to volunteer, it is very clear from official and unofficial reports that thousands of conscripts had not been put in the army and that thousands of men who had gone to the front had deserted or were absent without leave. There were enough of these men to give victory to any of the Confederate armies, and during the closing days of the year a serious effort was made to secure them. The conscription system was revised; governors were requested to aid in arresting conscripts and deserters;[52] the President turned South on a speaking

---

[51] It does not seem probable that the consolidated abstract exaggerated the number of men, for it did not include a few of the commands. However, General Marcus J. Wright, agent for the War Department for the collection of war records, claims that there were more men in the Southern army in June, 1862, than at any other time, and the number at that time was about 340,250 (*South in the Building of the Nation,* vol. IV, 503). The disparity between the General's estimate and the abstract is probably not great after all, if he included only those present, for the abstract carried only 304,015 as the aggregate present. Livermore estimated that there were about 250,500 present for duty January 31, 1863. *Story of the Civil War,* vol. I, 94. The Knoxville *Register* (quoted in the *Republican,* January 6, 1863) estimated that there were 700,000 between 18 and 40 already in or preparing for the field.

[52] President's circular letter to the governors, November 26th, O. R. ser. IV, vol. II, 211. Apparently most of the governors responded favorably to the letter. They recommended to their legislatures that they should be allowed to use the whole State constabulary, if they did not already have power so to use it, for arresting conscripts and deserters and that persons harboring them should be punished. The recommendations of Vance, Pettus, and Shorter were especially strong (*Ibid.,* 180, 249, 254). Governor Pettus thought the legislature should disfranchise every man who refused to perform his military duties. Governor Shorter reminded the people that it was a "shame and an iniquity" that deserters and conscripts should successfully evade service, and called upon every community, however disagreeable the task, to force them into the ranks, for

to support a declaration of war was subject to two vetoes: the veto of the citizen who might not want to volunteer, and that of the State that might fail to appoint or might abrogate the appointment of militia officers. As a result of experience in the Revolution and Confederation period the States' power to furnish troops as they pleased was "discarded" in the new Constitution and Congress was given "complete power . . . to conduct war independently of the States." Since the constitution and laws made in pursuance of it were the supreme law of the land, it followed that any act of Congress in the exercise of its power and duty to protect a State against invasion was "constitutional and supreme, and all State action must yield to it, in accordance with the spirit and letter of the compact the States made with each other." The doctrine of the anti-conscriptionists that the States had a constitutional veto over laws enacted by Congress and the President he regarded a "new phase of State Rights"; [56] he could understand "a State having the right to veto a war which it disapproves by seceding from the government," but he could not understand the "rightful power to do so in any other way."

The argument was not that of a "fire-eater," as Yancey is unwarrantably supposed to have been on all occasions. It was calm, sane, clear, and even more convincing than the opinion of the Georgia supreme court, rendered a short while before. Yancey and Governor Shorter won the Alabama legislature to a full and sympathetic support of conscription. It went so far as even to turn the militia officers over to conscription.

The leading problems involved in conscription were

[56] As a matter of fact it was the recrudescence of the old idea of nullification which Yancey had before rejected,

tour that carried him before the Mississippi legislat
in December; and congressmen wrote letters to influent
men back home in defense of conscription, or return
home and expounded its principles to their legislatur
and pointed out to them the indispensability of the co
operation of the State authorities in recruiting and sup
plying the armies.[53] The addresses of Senators Benjamin
H. Hill and William L. Yancey to the legislatures of
Georgia and Alabama, respectively, were the outstanding
efforts of this kind.

The address of Senator Yancey is especially significant
because of its influence in Alabama and the lower South
generally.[54] It fell to the lot of this Cicero of secession,
whose eloquence in the Charleston convention had
snapped the last tie that bound the North and South,
to make the most able defense of centralized control
over military affairs at a time when the leading statesmen and jurists of the country were giving it serious
thought and discussion. The arguments, save a single
reference to the right of a State to secede, would have
been entirely acceptable to Chief Justice Marshall, and
it is doubtful if his facile pen could have added to the
strength of it.[55] With convincing clarity he pointed out
the fallacy of the contention that the power of Congress

"the evil is great and ruinous to our country's cause, and it is the par
of the patriot now to shrink from no task."

[53] Some of the leading newspapers warmly espoused this movemer
The *Mercury* (December 13th) urged that men and munitions be acquir
to defeat the projected Union attack on Vicksburg. The effect of s
would be "great on Europe, which has been invited by Napoleon to ir
pose for peace. The United States can never raise such a force a
and they are staking all on this campaign."

[54] Dubose, *The Life and Times of William Lowndes Yancey*, 671

[55] The address is quoted in full in the *Southern Recorder*, Febru
1863, and a synopsis is given in Dubose, 671.

projected in the fall of 1862. The status of conscription was highly unsatisfactory, but the measures adopted for improvement and the decisions of the high State courts in favor of conscription pointed to better conditions in the future. Chief among the remedial measures was the creation of the Bureau of Conscription with exclusive control over conscription east of the Mississippi River. The establishment of this Bureau represented a specialization of conscription and a recognition of the fact that recruitment was primarily a civil function.

It was time for drastic action. All of Kentucky, central and western Tennessee, a large part of Louisiana, and all of Arkansas, except the Red River Valley, had passed into the possession of the enemy, and Federal control of the whole Mississippi was imminent. By the aid of winter, the inferior numbers of Generals Lee, Bragg, Johnston, and their able lieutenants were holding back the Federals at vital points east of the Mississippi, while west of the river General Holmes' redoubtable lieutenants Kirby Smith and "Dick" Taylor, with a handful of men, guarded the large stores of cotton in the Red River Valley against General Curtis' invading army. A successful defense could not be maintained against the steadily increasing Federal forces unless the Confederate armies were greatly augmented before the opening of the spring campaigns; and the notion of an offensive by which to hurl Hooker out of Virginia and to roll the Federal armies of the West up the Mississippi Valley upon their bases of supply was futile unless the whole man power of the Confederacy could be mobilized. The failure of the first objective meant collapse, the success of the second meant European recognition and independence.

# CHAPTER VIII

## THE COURTS AND CONSCRIPTION

No narrative of conscription would be complete without a survey of the activities of the courts with regard to it. Incidentally such survey will also throw much light upon the subject of the legal character of the Confederate Government, for we Americans have formed the habit of allowing our courts to say what a law means, and to draw the line of demarcation between the authority of our National Government and that of our States in the twilight zone of political power. The conscription laws vested the Confederate authorities with a supreme leadership in the war, but this leadership, in some of its collateral aspects, contradicted the theory of a league of sovereign States, and many persons, inspired by turgid oratory and by a deluge of denunciatory editorials from leading papers, challenged it. Thus the courts were called upon, time and time again, to maintain the dignity and prerogatives of the States against the encroachments of the Confederate Government through the conscription system. But when the great powers of the Confederate Government were unsheathed by the courts, the new government looked so much like the old one that it was painful to the ultra-States' rights men. Their faith and respect for their judicial tribunals were seriously shaken, and some of them were no more ready to accept the interpretations of the courts than were the Abolitionists' Judge Taney's decision in the Dred Scott case.

The principle of State sovereignty apparently never established itself as firmly on the bench as it did in the councils of state and in the norms of political philosophy. Many of the Southern jurists, State as well as Confederate, were thoroughly grounded in the arguments of Chief Justice Marshall on behalf of the paramountcy of the Federal Government within the area of its jurisdiction. Moreover, they were as completely indoctrinated with the principle of *stare decisis* as were judges anywhere; hence we need not be surprised to find even State judges bolstering up the Confederate Government, which was fundamentally a replica of the Federal Government, with the irrefragable opinions and arguments of Marshall. The Confederate judges particularly found it easy to do this, for most of them had served as Federal judges. All of them cite as freely the decisions of the United States Supreme Court to support their arguments as if there had been no secession. The simple fact is, the courts of the Southern States were taken out of the Union, but they were by no means divorced from the principles of its system of jurisprudence. So far as the character of the decisions was concerned, it would be difficult as a rule for a reader of Southern judicial literature to discover that there had been a withdrawal from the Union.

With the above facts in mind the reader should be able to anticipate the arguments of the leading Southern jurists concerning conscription and its collateral issues. Even so, these arguments, emanating from a people who had revolted against an ever-expanding national government, will probably seem extraordinary.

The Federal court system was incorporated in the Confederate Constitution. Provision was made for a Supreme Court [1] with the same original and appellate jurisdiction as the Federal Supreme Court, and for "such inferior courts as the Congress may from time to time ordain and establish."

Congress passed an act, March 16, 1861, providing for the establishment of the district courts and for annual sessions of the Supreme Court, and setting forth in detail the relation of the Supreme Court to the State supreme courts. All cases before the latter involving an interpretation of the Constitution, treaties, or Confederate laws were subject to appeal to the former. The district courts were organized during the year,[2] but the act was amended, July 31st, so as to prevent the Supreme Court's meeting until it had been organized "under the provisions of the permanent Constitution." [3]  In this way the question of organizing the Supreme Court, ordained by the Constitution, was laid to rest for a year and a half. In January of 1863 Senator Hill revived it, observing that he thought it "high time the judicial department be thoroughly organized, for it [had] been a lingering concern long enough." Strenuous opposition to the appellate jurisdiction of the Supreme Court over the State supreme courts appeared at once. Senator Clay thought that such jurisdiction would lead surely to "the consoli-

[1] The Constitution as published in the 12th volume of the *Military History of the Confederate States,* 371, and in McPherson's *History of the Rebellion,* 99, contained the word "Superior" instead of the word "Supreme" in the old constitution. While this would be thoroughly consonant with the sensitive feeling of the States' rights men, General B. T. Johnson says the official copy of the Constitution, printed by Congress, retains the word "Supreme." *Southern Hist. Ass. Pubs.,* vol. 4, 88.

[2] *Southern Hist. Ass. Pubs.,* vol. 4, 83-84.

[3] *Ibid.,* 89.

dation of the Government"; and Senator Wigfall made a "long and venomous attack on John Marshall and the centralizing tendencies of the Supreme Court of the United States." The great learning and strong personality of Marshall, he said, had led the Court into the destruction of the Union.[4]

Apparently the subject was not broached again because it was felt that there was no public exigency requiring the establishment of the Supreme Court, and it would, for that reason, be inexpedient to force a schism in Congress with it when a concert of action was imperative.[5] It would be folly for Congress to wreck itself with debate concerning the correct relationship of the parts of a system which had not been established.[6]

The rejection of the Supreme Court as proposed by the Whigish element in Congress was but natural. The idea of a "common arbiter" set up by the Confederate Government to settle disputes between it and the States was thoroughly repugnant to States' rights men like Wigfall, Yancey, Toombs, Rhett, and Pollard.[7] Having seceded from the Union upon the doctrine of States' rights, it was hardly possible that they should surrender

Clay's proposed amendment to abolish the Supreme Court's appellate jurisdiction over the State courts was passed by a large vote in the Senate but the House Judiciary Committee smothered it until Congress adjourned, May 1st. *Southern Hist. Ass. Pubs.,* vol. 4, 84-87.

[5] It is said that a difference of opinion over this question led to the fight between Hill and Yancey, in which the latter was seriously hurt. *Southern Hist. Ass. Pubs.,* vol. 4, 94.

[6] This opinion is sustained by Colonel L. Q. Washington and Honorable J. A. Orr. *Southern Hist. Ass. Pubs.,* vol. 4, 95-101.

[7] It is said that President Davis was opposed to it. *Southern Hist. Ass. Pubs.,* vol. 4, 91. He may have opposed it at first as a matter of principle, but there can be little doubt that before the war was over he would have accepted it to override the "factious" opinions of Judge Pearson and a few others of his kind.

the principle within two or three years to the mercies of a court. The bold assumption of power by the Confederate Government and the frequent conflicts between it and State governments impressed them all the more with the dangers of a "common arbiter" created by the Confederate Government.[8] The misgivings about a supreme court, the great difference of opinion concerning what its true character should be, and the more or less general conviction that it was not a necessary functional agency during the war led Congress to table the consideration of it indefinitely.[9]

The district courts played an insignificant role. For the most part they were relatively inert. There are a few reports of cases litigated by some of them,[10] but others never held a session.[11] Honorable J. A. Orr of Mississippi, reflecting in 1899 over the activity of the district courts, told of the arrest and of the trial of Congressman Foote in a Virginia district court, "to show the Confederate judiciary performed its functions when called on."[12] The fact is they were not called upon often, and for several reasons: (1) The State courts were naturally more popular with those who had griev-

[8] An editorial in the *Examiner*, March 19, 1863, voiced clearly those fears.

[9] These facts are supported by Senator B. T. Johnson, Honorable John V. Wright, Honorable J. A. Orr, and Colonel L. Q. Washington in a symposium on why the Confederate States never had a supreme court, published in *Southern Hist. Ass. Pubs.*, vol. 4, 81-101. All of these men were in Congress or intimately associated with Congressmen when the supreme court question was up for discussion.

[10] Clarke County *Journal*, July 9, 1863; O. R. ser. I, vol. XXVI, Pt. II, 494.

[11] *Southern Hist. Ass. Pubs.*, vol. 4, 97; O. R. ser. IV, vol. III, 598.

[12] Foote was arrested while trying to go to Washington without a passport. When his identity was established he was offered a release, but he was so peeved he refused it and sought and gained his freedom before Judge John W. Brockenbrough. *Southern Hist. Ass. Pubs.*, vol. 4, 97.

ances against the Confederate Government; (2) the fact that the organization of the Cenfederate court system was never completed impaired the dignity of the district courts and neutralized the influence they might otherwise have had; (3) they had no appellate jurisdiction over the State courts; and (4) the Government usually prosecuted in the State courts, because it was thought that their opinions would be respected more than those of the Confederate courts.[13]

Thus it fell to the lot of the State courts to arbitrate most of the constitutional disputes between the Confederate and State governments. Ordinarily a central government would not feel secure to have disputes between itself and local government left to the arbitrament of local tribunals. This arrangement was acceptable in the Confederacy because of the opposition to a supreme court with appellate jurisdiction over the State courts; and it was believed, as noted above, by the supporters of the Administration that the State courts, in the nature of things, would command greater respect than the Supreme Court could, and therefore would be in a position to defend the prerogatives of the Confederate Government more effectively, if they would, than could the whole hierarchy of Confederate courts. In recognition of this fact the President ordered the Government test cases to be presented to the supreme court of the State concerned.

The passage of the first conscription act precipitated the question of the extent of the war powers of the Confederate Government. The constitutionality of the act

[13] Mr. Orr was of the opinion that the district courts did not function because "we were too busy with the war." "We had no use for Beat Courts, nor for County Courts, nor for State Courts, nor for Confederate Courts." *Southern Hist. Ass. Pubs.*, vol. 4, 97.

was vigorously attacked by some of the States' rights
politicians and journalists, and their dismay was not
dispelled by the elaborate opinion of Attorney-General
Watts in unqualified support of it. Those who objected
to being conscripted were encouraged by the opposition
of influential men to test the validity of the law in the
courts.

The State courts took the position that they had·con-
current jurisdiction over all questions cognizable in the
Confederate courts when it was not otherwise provided
by law; and, since the Supreme Court was not organized
and Congress made no provision for an appeal of cases
from them to the Confederate courts, their findings were
final, as a matter of course. Within a few months after
the conscription act was passed it was reviewed and upheld by the high courts of practically all of the States.[14]
A few of the lower courts declared it unconstitutional,
and dissenting opinions were entertained by some of the
judges of the higher courts.

Apparently the first test case before a State court
was that of Coupeland, which was reviewed by the Texas
supreme court in the early part of July, 1862. Judge
Magrath of the Confederate District Court of South
Carolina had upheld the constitutionality of the law a
few days before.[15] In the Texas case it was held that
the "power to raise and support armies is an express
constitutional grant to the Congress of the Confederate
States, and there is no limitation as to the mode or manner of exercising it. The conscript law does not violate

[14] Jeffers v. Fair, 33 Ga., 347; Jones v. Warren, 34 Ga., 28; Ex parte
Hill, in re Willis et al., 38 Ala., 429; Ex parte Coupeland, 26 Texas, 386;
Burroughs v. Peyton, 16 Va., 47; 11 Fla., 93, 100, 105; Simmons v. Miller,
40 Miss., 19; O. R. ser. IV, vol. II, 177; the Republican, March 15, 1864.
[15] Charleston Courier, June 30, 1862.

any of the abstract or guaranteed rights of citizens, nor
assume any control over them not delegated by the constitution.   The grant of power to make war carries with
it, unless expressly withheld, the right to demand compulsory military service from the citizen. . . . The general government is not dependent upon the will either
of the citizen or of the State, to carry into effect the
power to raise and support armies. . . . When Congress
calls for the military service of the citizen . . . the right
of the State government must cease or yield to the paramount demand of Congress."   The counsel for the de-
fendant before the Georgia court argued that all of the
able-bodied men of the State constitute its militia and
therefore the conscription act, which provided for calling
them out individually and not by organized units, officered
by State authority as prescribed by the constitution, was
invalid.   But the court overruled the objection on the
ground that Congress had acted on the broad grant of
power to raise armies, and not on the power to call
out the organized militia to suppress insurrections and
repel invasions.   The power to raise armies, it observed,
was granted in as broad terms as possible, leaving the
method to the discretion of Congress.   The conscription
law acted upon the people of the respective States as citizens and not as militiamen.[16]

[16] The Federal conscription law was upheld by a similar line of argument in cases before the Circuit Court of the Eastern District of Pennsylvania and the U. S. Circuit Court of Illinois. N. Y. *Tribune,* September
11, 1863; Illinois *State Journal,* June 17, 1864 (quoted in McPherson,
*History of the Rebellion,* 273).   The Supreme Court of Pennsylvania in
1863 declared the law invalid and attacked it with an argument that is
not paralleled by the decisions of any of the Southern courts. "The great
vice of the conscript law," it affirmed, "is, that it is founded on an
assumption that Congress may take away, not the State rights of the
citizen, but the security and foundation of his State rights. . . . The
Constitution of the United States committed the liberties of the citizen in

These decisions were generally acquiesced in, if not popular. It is said that the decision of the Georgia court in the case of Jeffers *v.* Fair was applauded so heartily that the Chief Justice had to call the court to order. However, there were some persons of influence who did not relish such decisions. Governor Brown suggested in a message to the legislature that the supreme court had given its decision "under heavy outside pressure and if not *ex parte,* under most peculiar circumstances." [17] This insinuation brought many of the friends of the court to their feet, and in the stormy moments that followed Linton Stephens, brother of the Vice-President, soared to the plane of Seward's "higher law doctrine," declared the court's decision to be void because of the circumstances under which it was made, and handed down a decision to the legislature against the conscript law; affirming, among other things, that "a State may shield her fighting men from any compulsory military service which she may deem injurious to her rights or destructive to her existence." [18]

Georgians did not generally warm up to Governor Brown's appeal. The *Confederacy* touched a popular

part to the Federal Government, but expressly reserved to the States, and the people of all States, all it did not delegate. It gave the General Government a standing army, but left to the States their militia. Its purposes in all this balancing of powers were wise and good," but the conscript law "upturns the whole system of government when it converts the State militia into 'National forces.'" Chief Justice Lowrie was defeated for reëlection a few months later and the court reversed its decision by a vote of 3 to 2. McPherson, 273-274.

[17] The case of Jeffers *v.* Fair.

[18] The story of this episode may be found in the *Confederacy*, November 13, 16, 19, 25, and 28, 1862. The Vice-President agreed with his brother as to this decision. He said he had not met in many a day such a rehash of the old Federal doctrine. If the court were correct the Southern States were in rebellion against the Federal Government. Johnston and Browne, *The Life of Alexander H. Stephens,* 429.

note when it asserted that the opinion of the court should terminate all argument. "When we know what the law is, let every man obey it and have no more agitation about it." Let "governor, officers, privates, and all cease all opposition." [19]

After the conscription act had been held and generally accepted to be constitutional, the question as to whether or not men of conscript age in the militia and reserve organizations were subject to it came up in one form or another many times. The fact that both the Confederate and State governments had authority under their respective constitutions to draft a militiaman into service gave rise to a question of precedency. As to this, the Alabama court observed: "When the lawful call of each government, Confederate and State, to perform military service, falls on the same person, the claim and call of the Confederate States must prevail over the claim and call of the State government, on the ground that the constitution of the Confederate States, and laws made in pursuance thereof, are the supreme laws of the land." [20] Similarly, the Mississippi court held, in the case of Simmons v. Miller, that the war power of Congress "must be exclusive" and that the States had no authority to hold their citizens, even though they should need them to repel invasion or suppress insurrection. "When the Constitution grants Congress and the States powers over the same object or person," it decreed fur-

---

[19] November 13, 1862. The Clarke County (Ala.) *Democrat,* December 27, 1862, observed: "The discussion in Georgia respecting the conscription law is disappearing. . . . The decision of the Supreme Court in its behalf has reconciled the people to it,—at least for the present."

[20] *Ex parte* Bolling, *in re* Watts, 39 Ala., 609. See the earlier decision of the court in the case of the State, *ex rel* Dawson *in re* Strawbridge and Mays, *Ibid.,* 367.

ther, "the powers are concurrent only to a certain extent. The power of the State is subordinate to that of the General Government, and the exercise of it by the latter precludes its exercise by the former. If the State has exercised the power before the General Government, it ceases to the State and the power of the General Government becomes paramount. . . . Where the nature of a power or the terms in which it is granted require that it should be exclusively exercised by Congress, the States are prohibited from it as fully as if forbidden expressly to act upon it." [21]

The conscription acts conferred much discretionary authority upon the War Department, in the exercise of which it formulated general policies and gave general instructions to the enrolling officers. Thus the Department and its subordinate officers were invested with quasi-judicial powers; that is, the enrolling officer had to judge the merits of each individual's case upon the basis of instructions from the Department, and the Department was often called upon to hear cases which were appealed from the enrolling officers. Quite generally those who were not satisfied with the rulings of the officers sought relief of the courts, alleging irregularity in the determination of their status. This raised two questions. First, did the War Department and its subordinates have the exclusive right to construe the conscription law and apply it to cases before them; were there no limits to their quasi-judicial powers? Second, if their rulings were

[21] 40 Miss., 19. This decision was grounded upon the decisions of the Federal courts concerning the concurrent powers of the United States Government and the State governments. The Government consented to the exemption of militia officers because of Governor Brown's vehement protests and because, at a later time, some of the other governors claimed them as State officers. O. R. ser. IV, vol. I, 1155; 60 N. C., 186.

subject to judicial review, were the State courts competent to review them?

The supreme court of North Carolina, *in re* Bryan, held that it was the province of the courts to interpret the law; that Congress had no power to make the Secretary of War a judge, or to authorize him to invest his subordinates with judicial power. "Congress can confer no judicial power on a department of the executive branch of the government," it affirmed. The "Secretary of War in carrying the acts of Congress into effect, puts a construction on them, but this construction must be subject to the decision of the judiciary, otherwise our form of government is subverted, the separation of the powers of government would no longer be true, and the executive would be left without a check." [22] Chief Justice Walker of the Alabama supreme court remarked that if this were the correct view the fugitive-slave law, in its bestowment of power upon the Commissioners, violated the Constitution.[23] The courts generally took the position of the North Carolina court. There was also a unanimity of opinion among the State supreme courts that State courts had concurrent jurisdiction with the Confederate courts in the matter. [24]

The Secretary of War challenged the authority of the State courts to release persons from the enrolling officers, and Chief Justice Pearson of the North Carolina supreme court set aside a day for hearing arguments pro and con on the subject, before the court proceeded with the examination of the many applications before it by writs of habeas corpus. President Davis appointed Attorney

[22] 60 N. C., 1.
[23] Dissenting opinion in *ex parte* Hill, 38 Ala., 458.
[24] *Ibid.*

General Strong and Honorable Thomas Bragg to represent the Government, and Messrs. Moore and Winston represented the court. "After this careful deliberation the Court was of the opinion that it has jurisdiction and is bound to exercise it, and to discharge the citizen wherever it appeared that he was unlawfully restrained of his liberty by an officer of the Confederate States." [25] The Government acquiesced, and the courts and judges of North Carolina shared concurrent jurisdiction with the courts and judges of the Confederate States in issuing writs of habeas corpus and in making inquiry into the cause of detentions by officers of the Confederate Government.

The Alabama supreme court held, *ex parte* Hill, that when the question was whether the officer had erroneously applied his authority or jurisdiction the State courts had authority to inquire into it, "unless the law, in its terms, inhibits such inquiry." [26] Chief Justice Walker wrote a very elaborate and able dissenting opinion in this case. He admitted that the interpretations of Confederate law by Confederate administrative officers were subject to judicial review but he denied vigorously the competency of the State courts to review them. "I maintain," he said, "that so much of that jurisdiction as is exercised in the application of judicial correctives to the irregularities and errors of the executive officers of that government, charged with the enforcement of the conscript law, is necessarily exclusive; and that such officers cannot be interfered with by a State court, although they may commit errors." Improper or invidious conduct by the conscript officers could "only be corrected by a

[25] *In re* Bryan, 60 N. C., 1.
[26] 38 Ala., 458.

Confederate court, through the instrumentality of the writ of habeas corpus. To hold otherwise would be to confess that the State has power to qualify the execution of Confederate law. It results that State tribunals cannot supervise and control the executive officers of the Confederate States in the exercise of their appointed functions by the writs of injunction, replevin, habeas corpus, or other processes, for there is a delegation in the Constitution of an unqualified right to execute the laws which Congress may enact." "Both Governments," he continued, "are paramount and supreme within the sphere of their respective powers, that they stand within those limits as equals." Hence the tribunals of neither could release persons in the charge of the executive officers of the other.

Manifestly, Judge Walker stood on solid ground. His opinion was based securely on the great decisions of Marshall, and set forth the only workable principle in a federal system of government.[27] But the majority opinion in the State courts concerning this subject was more compatible with the theory of secession. Even so, some of the judges apparently felt that they were on doubtful ground; they justified the jurisdiction of State tribunals over the conduct of conscript officers by the assumption that the Confederate courts were unable to mete out justice to the injured conscript, and by the fact that in the absence of a Confederate supreme court there could be no uniform rule of decision among the district judges. Concerning this, Attorney General Strong very well observed that a flaw in the Confederate court sys-

[27] It is illuminating to see such an irrefragable argument in support of the authority of the national Government coming from a Southern judge at this time. I have not discovered a case of this kind in which there was a unanimous opinion in support of State authority.

tem did not automatically enlarge the jurisdiction of the State courts.[28]

So far as the records show, the other State courts took the same position as that of the courts of North Carolina and Alabama;[29] and the Richmond authorities gave way. Thus the floodgates of judicial redress for grievances, great and small, were raised and a large variety of cases pertaining to conscription, exemption, and substitution flowed into the courts.[30]

Many technical questions were presented to the courts by the cunning of persons who were over-anxious to evade service. On the whole the State supreme courts, except that of North Carolina, supported liberally and ungrudgingly the Confederate conscription laws. The Government was usually given the advantage of the doubt, but there are a few cases in which the courts quite clearly set at naught the real spirit and purpose of the law. For example, the Georgia court in the case of Gates v. McManus [31] held that if a citizen applied for a detail on the ground that he was a manager of a plantation on which there was a large number of slaves and his petition was refused, he was not estopped from afterwards claiming exemption as a skilled mechanic habitually working for the public. Surely the law did not anticipate one's playing so many cards for exemption; every one was

[28] 60 N. C., 1.

[29] 38 Ala., 458; O. R. ser. I, vol. XXVI, Pt. II, 493.

[30] The decisions are recorded in the State court reports; the Official Records, as for example, ser. IV, vol. III, and ser. I, vol. XXVI, Pt. II, 493; and in the newspapers. The governors generally, as a matter of course, backed up the decisions of the supreme court of their States. Governor Vance wrote the Secretary of War, May 25, 1863, that since by the action of Congress no appeal could be taken from the supreme courts of the States to that of the Confederate States, "the decisions of the Supreme Court of North Carolina when formally rendered will be binding upon all parties." O. R. ser. I, vol. LI, Pt. II, 715.

[31] 33 Ga., 67.

presumed to have a major field of enterprise and it was as a laborer in this field that he was entitled to exemption, if at all. Again, the Alabama court maintained in the State, *ex rel* Dawson, *in re* Strawbridge *v.* Mays, that bonded overseers, who were exempted upon the condition that they should furnish a specified amount of foodstuffs to the Confederate Government, were liable to service in the militia.[32] One is inclined to agree with the dissenting opinion of Justice Stone in this case that the bonded agriculturists could not "be lawfully hindered in the performance of such service by the exercise of the right in the State to call out the militia." "Can it be," he argued, "that there rests at one and the same time, and on one and the same citizen, the duty to the Confederate Government of giving his personal attention and skill to the production of grain and provisions on his plantation, and to the State Government of serving in its militia away from his plantation?"[33] Since the bonded agriculturist was exempted by the Confederate Government upon condition, any claim that the State made upon his service that destroyed the obligation, forfeited its rights to such claim. The pressing need for troops for State defense probably influenced the court to take its doubtful position.

After the question of the constitutionality of the conscription law was determined by the courts, there were no other cases that opened up such serious constitutional discussions and interpretations as those pertaining to the abolition of substitution. There was a series of cases growing out of the second conscription act, which made substitutes between the ages of 35 and and 45

[32] 39 Ala., 367.
[33] The North Carolina court in the case of Wood *v.* Bradshaw followed Judge Stone's line of reasoning. 60 N. C., 419.

liable to service on their own account. Then another followed when substitution was abolished, January 5, 1864.

The first set of cases concerned the status of the principals whose substitutes had been taken from them by law. As was pointed out in a preceding chapter, the War Department took the position that such principals automatically became liable to service, since they no longer had proxies in the army.[34] The principles demurred that they had contracted with the Government to furnish substitutes upon the condition laid down by it; and that they and their substitutes had contracted with each other under the authority of a public law and with official sanction. For these reasons the Government could not make them liable to service before the expiration of the time for which their substitutes had been employed. Thus the courts were called upon to say whether a contract did exist in either case and, if so, whether the Government was legally competent to annul it or in any sense impair it. But some of them passed over these questions gently, observing *obiter* that substitution involved a contract with the Government, and liberated the principals on the ground that the Secretary of War had no constitutional authority to give the second conscription act, which did not affirmatively abrogate any right possessed by exempts under the first act, a retroactive application.[35] It was admitted that Congress might pass retrospective laws. Chief Justice Pearson observed, *in re* Bryan, that the situation was a *"casus omissus* for which Congress neglected to provide, and it

[34] See pp. 34 and 35 above.
[35] *In re* Bryan, 60 N. C., 1; *in re* Cohn, reported in the *Confederacy*, February 3, 1863, and in the Clarke County *Journal*, February 12, 1863; *in re* Ritter, 60 N. C., 76; *in re* Prince, 60 N. C., 195.

is too late for the War Department to attempt to remedy the mischief, by assuming to legislate under the name of regulations."

The courts seem generally to have maintained that the Secretary had power, under the discretionary authority conferred upon him by Congress, to conscript the principals whose substitutes had become liable to service.[36] This power of the Secretary of War was not impaired, even though a contract existed between the principals and the Government or between the principals and their substitutes, for in either case the regulation promulgated by the War Department, April 29, 1862, to the effect that when a substitute became liable his principal became liable again, was a part and parcel of the contract.[37]  As regards the contract feature, the supreme court of Georgia held in the case of Weems v. Farrell that in the process of substitution there was no contract between the principals and the Government, that substitution was a gratuitous privilege, and as such was subject to the will and discretion of Congress.

When Congress abolished substitution it produced a storm of indignation among the principals.  They rushed to the courts with the deposition that the law was unconstitutional because it violated two contracts; one between them and the Government, the other between them and their substitutes.  They met with little success.[38] Their claims were rejected even by the North Carolina supreme court, which in the case of Gatlin v. Walton reversed Chief Justice Pearson's opinion in the Bryan

---

[36] Mann v. Parke, 16 Va., 443.

[37] 33 Ga., 413.

[38] The courts generally were of the opinion that substitution was in nature *ex gratia,* and revocable as a matter of course.

case.[39]   It held that there was no contract between the
Government and the principals, but if there were, it
could be annulled "by virtue of the power inherent in
all governments whose organic law does not expressly
deny them that power." [40]   The Alabama court denied
that anything more than a legislative contract existed;
and averred that in every such contract there was "an
implied condition, that any succeeding legislature, acting
in good faith, and for the public safety, should have
power to repeal it."  "All exemptions," it observed further, "granted by Congress, must be taken under the
implied condition that, if the exigencies of the country
require, they may be revoked and set aside."  The "high
and solemn trust confided to the legislature, in the possession and exercise of the war power, it cannot surrender
or sell; it cannot abrogate or relinquish." [41]   In the cases
of Burroughs v. Peyton and Abrahams v. Peyton the
Virginia supreme court took the position that the other
State high courts did, and asserted the power of the Confederate Government with a baldness that must have
caused painful reflections to the disciples of State sovereignty.  It did not allow itself to be inveigled into a
discussion of the tangled skein of technical questions pertaining to substitution, but cut to the heart of things by
asserting that there was no contract between the Government and the principals, and if there were, there was
nothing to prevent the Confederate Government from
impairing it, since the constitution forbade only the States

[39] 60 N. C., 310.

[40] Chief Justice Pearson dissented vigorously.  The opinions filed in the
courts of Alabama, Georgia, and Virginia in support of the law only
tended to confirm him in his opinion.  The decisions in these states he
regarded as having been made *post litem motam*.  60 N. C., 310.

[41] *Ex parte* Tate.  39 Ala., 254.

to impair contracts.  Like the Alabama court in the Tate case and the Texas court in the case of Mayer,[42] it asserted that Congress had no power to enter into a contract with an individual whereby it could not demand military service of him thereafter.[43]

Thus, the State courts in a second great series of cases upheld the war powers of the Confederate Government, and projected the sound principle of constitutional law that Congress had no authority to enact a law which would obstruct it in the exercise of an obligation imposed upon it by the constitution.

There were inferior judges and a few superior judges in all of the States who maintained that the law was unconstitutional.  Most conspicuous among these was Chief Justice Pearson.  Since his court was not in session at the time of the passage of the law, he reviewed several cases at chambers and declared the law null and void.[44]

There were differences of opinion among the high State courts concerning some of the particulars in the application of the conscription acts.  In the absence of a central Confederate tribunal there was no way to harmonize these conflicting views, and the Government found itself face to face with the impossible task of accepting the rulings of each court and administering the law differently in the different States.  It adopted the only feasible expedient, namely, that of accepting the decision of a

[42] 39 Ala., 254; 27 Texas, 715.

[43] 16 Va., 470.  Other decisions along this line are reported in the *Republican,* February 9 and 15 and March 5, 1864.  For example, Judge O. A. Lochrane, of the Georgia superior court, Macon district, held in Fitzgerald *v.* Harris that if a contract existed it violated every principle of constitutional law.  Contracts and vested rights must bend to the exigencies of Government.  Judge W. B. Fleming of the eastern district of Georgia took a similar position in the case of Swindle *v.* Brooks.

[44] O. R. ser. IV, vol. III, 176; Raleigh *Confederate*, March 24, 1894.

court authoritative in the particular case but not as to the general principle involved.[45]   The Secretary of War, for example, wrote General Brandon, Commandant of Reserves in Mississippi, that the Department had "no power to dispense with the execution of this law [law pertaining to reserves], or to submit its actions under it to the final decision of any State tribunal."   "The decision of the State courts of Mississippi will be respected in any case within the jurisdiction of the court, and the opinion of the judge will be considerately examined in respect to the cases that are likely to arise, but the Department cannot pledge itself to adopt it as the basis of its action." [46]

The Government seems to have adopted as its working principle the consensus of opinion of the State superior courts, which was usually favorable to it.[47] The practice of honoring the decree of a civil court in a particular case but rejecting it as a general rule of action for the conscript officers, enabled the Government to free itself to some extent from the obstructions of the mischievous inferior courts.   The conscription officers were instructed to look to the Confederate Government for the interpretation of its laws and not to the State courts.[48]

The mischievous interposition of the courts in matters of conscription in the Confederacy presents a very striking contrast to the attitude of our courts in the World

[45] O. R. ser. IV, vol. II, 1056; vol. III, 891.   The War Department had "in a multitude of cases yielded to the exercise of authority by State judicial authorities in cases in which it was exceedingly clear the judgment was erroneous and the power to decide did not exist."   O. R. ser. IV, vol. III, 562.

[46] O. R. ser. IV, vol. III, 965.

[47] *Ibid.*, 201, 965.

[48] *Ibid.*, 176, 198, 891.

War.  Many of the inferior courts through the instrumentality of the writ of habeas corpus became marplots in the enforcement of the conscription laws.  The incursions of the enemy caused the higher courts in some of the States to become peripatetic, sessions were held infrequently,[49] records were lost, and appeals were irregular and difficult.  This gave the inferior courts, even the justice of the peace courts, whose incumbents often were ill-informed and sometimes unprincipled, an opportunity to function and many of them did it in an extraordinary way.  When there was no compelling power over them it mattered little if they did not have authority to issue a writ of habeas corpus.  Those who were generous in the use of it became widely known, and in those States where there were no limits as to the distance a judge might hurl the writ, the moral slackers were drawn to them from the uttermost parts.[50]  Saucy orders were sent out by these judicial dignitaries to the enrolling officers, and if they did not obey they had to answer for contempt.[51]  President Davis told of some ludicrous incidents of this kind.  In one instance a general on the eve of an important expedition, when every man was needed, was commanded by a judge more than 200 miles away "to bring, if in his custody, or send if in the custody of another, before him on habeas corpus, some deserters who had been arrested and returned to his command."  In another, a commandant of conscripts was ordered to

---

[49] The supreme court of Mississippi tried only nineteen cases during the war, and fifteen of these were tried in 1861. *Pol. Sci. Quar.,* vol. 16, 287.

[50] O. R. ser. I, vol. XXVI, Pt. II, 493; *Ibid.,* ser. IV, vol. III, 68.

[51] Judge Thomas ordered the enrolling officer of Oglethorpe County, Ga., put in jail because the officer disregarded a writ of habeas corpus issued by him. The *Confederacy,* December 21, 1862.

bring a certain conscript he had to a judge more than 100 miles away, although there was a judge resident near the camp who was competent to hear and dispose of the case. The commandant having a pressing need to stay at his camp, consulted an eminent attorney who, knowing the attitude of the distant judge, told him the conscript would undoubtedly be released, and informed him that he might avoid the journey if he would release the conscript and return the facts informally; that such a return would not be technically good but should suffice, inasmuch as it would accomplish the purpose of the writ. But not so; he was immediately summoned to appear before the judge to show cause why he should not be attached for his contemptuous conduct. Thus he had to leave his command and go before the judge, who was located some distance from the railroad, to purge himself of the serious crime of technical contempt.[52]  The President did not record what happened to the officer, but presumably a visit to Canossa and a humble confession of his sin was sufficient to liberate him.

Concerning the interposition of some of the judges, Assistant Secretary of War, Judge J. A. Campbell, wrote to Congressman Barksdale: "Some judges, apparently catching the distemper of the time to relieve from the burden of the military service that class of men who above all others are interested in carrying through a revolution commenced for the security of their rights and interests, have resorted to the most refined and astute discussions to dispense with these conditions. . . . In every State some local judges seem to have bestirred themselves to withdraw from the service all who by any subtlety could be released.  A widespread disaffection

[52] Message to Congress, February 3, 1864, O. R. ser. IV, vol. III, 68.

has been the consequence, both in and out of the Army. . . . "The Department has been forced to inquire into the extent of the jurisdiction of local judges to determine such questions." [53]

From the States came similar reports. Governor Smith of Virginia remonstrated that the remedy by habeas corpus, designed for extraordinary acts of official and individual tyranny, "is daily resorted to, to extricate the citizen from the holy duty of defending the country, . . . judges in chambers and in court feel constrained to apply the principles of the writ to those but little better than moral deserters." [54] Governor Shorter of Alabama wrote to General Johnston that most of the militiamen in Alabama who had become liable to service were seeking "pretexts in every manner to avoid duty, even to a resort to a *habeas corpus* before ignorant justices of the peace, who have no jurisdiction of their cases." [55] From General Greer, Commandant of Conscripts in the Trans-Mississippi Department, came the complaint that "the decisions of certain judicial officers of the State of Texas [had] seriously obstructed the execution of the laws of conscription," and "consequences disastrous to the Confederate cause" would probably result unless a suitable remedy were applied. "It seems to be the favorite scheme," he said, "of some of the Texas judges to override the Confederate laws and to discharge from service in the army any and all who apply to them for relief." He gave instances of the corruption of Judge W. P. Hill of the Confederate district court and of Judge B. W. Gray of one of the State

[53] O. R. ser. IV, vol. II, 656.
[54] *Ibid.*, vol. III, 909.
[55] O. R. ser. I, vol. XXVI, Pt. II, 139.

district courts; [56] but the judiciary as a whole, so far as he knew, was in favor of "law and right." A few other cases of corruption were reported.[57]

The Secretary of War wrote General E. K. Smith that his Department had experienced "much embarrassment from the eccentric decisions of inferior judges" east of the Mississippi and could "appreciate the difficulties that General Greer has had to encounter on that subject." A few months later he wrote to Governor Milton: "In some cases the judges have undertaken to examine a conscript in open court, and to pronounce in opposition to the Medical Board, that he labored under a physical incapacity for field service, and discharged him; in other cases have withdrawn a soldier from the Army to detail him to manage private business." [58]

[56] One S. D. Wood, who obtained exemption as an overseer by fraudulent methods, fully attested to by his neighbors, was apprehended and sent to the front. He then gave the son of Judge Hill 500 bushels of corn to sue out a writ of habeas corpus before his father, and upon the hearing he was discharged. One A. M. Walker, who had been a physician, abandoned his profession for the more remunerative business of speculation. He acknowledged to General Greer that he was caught and offered to pay through him into the Treasury $1,000 a month for a twelve months' furlough. Having failed with his scheme, he sued out a writ of habeas corpus before Judge Gray. The counsel for Walker misled the attorney for the Government and Walker was discharged upon an *ex parte* hearing. O. R. ser. I, vol. XXVI, Pt. II, 493. See page 126 of this source for the activities of the county courts in Texas.

[57] General Lee complained to the Secretary of War about the way slackers were being indulged by the courts. He reported three interesting cases. In one a soldier, who had been elected justice of the peace, was discharged by a judge; in another, a contractor on an insignificant mail route in Alabama was likewise exempted, though he lived and transacted business in Richmond and never saw his route; while in the third, a wealthy young man was discharged by a court to carry the mail on an unimportant route, whereupon he employed some one to carry it for him and stayed at home. O. R. ser. IV, vol. III, 660. Other cases are cited on page 660 of this source.

[58] O. R. ser. IV, vol. III, 562. See page 231 also.

Perhaps the courts in North Carolina gave more trouble than elsewhere, because of the example set by the cantankerous Chief Justice of the supreme court. Early in 1863 the Secretary of War complained to Governor Vance about the pernicious influence of Chief Justice Pearson's decisions, and expressed a hope that the Governor would make an effort to restrain the "too ready interposition of the judicial authority in these questions of military obligation." [59]   Governor Vance denied that the North Carolina judges had been too ready to interpose and countered with the petulant query: "Has the 'too ready interposition' of the judiciary of South Carolina and Georgia been rebuked for almost similar decisions rendered?" He declined to use his "influence in restraining or controlling that coördinate branch of the Government which intrudes upon nobody, usurps no authority, but is, on the contrary, in great danger of being overlapped and destroyed by the tendencies of the times." [60]

It has been noted already that Judge Pearson gave a great deal of trouble over substitution.[61]   At chambers he declared the act suspending it unconstitutional, and proceeded by writ to discharge principals from the custody of the enrolling officers. This and similar activity by inferior judges in many of the other States could not be tolerated. President Davis said that soon every case of enrollment would be followed by a writ, "and every enrolling officer will be kept in continual motion to and from the judge, until the embarrassment and delay will

[59] O. R. ser. I, vol. LI, Pt. II, 714. The Secretary thought that the conspicuous desertion of the North Carolina troops was due to the hope held out to them by some of the decisions of their supreme court. See also page 707.

[60] *Ibid.*, 715.

[61] Pages 46-48 above.

amount to the practical repeal of the law." He recommended to Congress the suspension of the privilege of
the writ of habeas corpus.[62]

The writ was suspended and Chief Justice Pearson
reluctantly yielded.[63] The supreme court convened in
June, and in the test case of Gatlin v. Walton it held
the act abolishing substitution to be constitutional, Judge
Pearson dissenting.[64] But the judge had not played his
last trump with the Government. Some time later, in
the case of Johnson v. Mallett, he held that the Governor's certificate on behalf of a State officer was not material, that all officers and agents provided for by the
constitution or laws of the State were exempted from
service without regard to any action of Congress.[65] This
was an adverse opinion because some of the laws of the
State provided for the employment of skilled mechanics
and artisans. It contradicted the purpose of the Government to exempt only such State officers as the governor
would certify to be indispensable to the administration
of the State Government.[66]

The War Department was greatly handicapped by the
fact that the laws which it had to enforce and its acts
under those laws were subject to review by the State
courts, which were really not the ultimate arbiters of
such questions under the constitution. It was unfortunate
that the conscription laws were in a large sense at the

[62] Message February 2, 1864, O. R. ser. IV, vol. III, 69, 231.

[63] The Government was still gravely concerned, however, for the Secretary of War wrote March 19th, "Judge Pearson is still, I fear, bent on
mischief," though he believed it would be hard for him "to stem alone
the changing current of public sentiment." O. R. ser. IV, vol. III, 238.

[64] 60 N. C., 310.

[65] O. R. ser. IV, vol. III, 755.

[66] The courts in the North also interfered with conscription. O. R. ser.
III, vol. V, 629.

mercy of the judges in the various States. If the Confederate court system had been fully organized, not only would there have been harmony and uniformity of construction of the Confederate laws, but the strong backing of them by the Confederate courts would have given them a force and dignity before the people that was impossible when they were being twisted, warped, applied with indifference or partiality, and in some instances flaunted by the State courts. The organization of the Confederate court system with a Supreme Court as a necessary capstone seemed inexpedient, but probably more was conceded to the ultra-States' rights men than was necessary. The Supreme Court and the State high courts would have been of the same mind concerning the constitutionality of the conscription laws, and with the support of the State courts in this important way the Supreme Court could have weathered the storm of opposition and instituted harmony and uniformity of interpretation in the courts. Once thoroughly established, it could have eliminated the pernicious influence of the inferior State courts.

The judges in the inferior courts and some of the judges in the high courts embarrassed the Government and seriously obstructed the enforcement of the conscription laws.[67] Their activities were so detrimental and exasperating that the Government was forced to resort to a suspension of the writ of habeas corpus. It was the opinion of the President at the time of the expira-

[67] The Government apparently held most of the State supreme courts in high regard. For example, Attorney-General Davis wrote the Secretary of War, November 30, 1864, that he had every confidence that the Virginia supreme court would adjudicate the case before it "with a due regard to the constitutional rights of the Confederate States." O. R. ser. IV, vol. III, 875.

tion of the last suspension that the effects of the suspension of the writ had been "most salutary," and that it accounted very materially for the "increased efficiency of the military preparations." "In my judgment," he said, "it would be perilous, if not calamitous, to discontinue the suspension while the armies of the enemy are pressing on our brave defenders with persistent effort for their destruction and for the subjection of our country." [68]    But his message fell on deaf ears; the writ was not suspended again, and doubtless there was much foundation for Colonel W. H. Taylor's despair, voiced a few weeks later: "With enrolling officers to exempt and detail and judges to discharge we are in a sad way." [69]

[68] O. R. ser. IV, vol. III, 429. The writ was suspended from February 15, 1864, to August 2, 1864, partly to secure a better enforcement of the conscription laws.

[69] Endorsement by Colonel Taylor of Captain H. C. Thorburn's complaint, September 9, 1864. *Ibid.*, 660.

# CHAPTER IX

## THE DUAL SYSTEM

THE need for a better enforcement of conscription east of the Mississippi led to the creation of a Bureau of Conscription in the Adjutant and Inspector General's office with complete control over conscription.[1] But it had scarcely had time to exert a systematic influence before the Inspector General tried to promote a general system of field recruitment. By a circular, January 8th, he urged the field commanders to detail officers and men at once to gather volunteers from those sections of the country in which their regiments had been raised. It was hoped that they might by kindness and persuasion induce conscripts to volunteer.[2] This sort of recruitment had been permitted from the outset, but apparently the field commanders had not generally attempted to reinforce their armies by means of it.[3]

General Bragg responded promptly to the circular.

---

[1] For some time the need of a bureau of conscription had been urged upon the President. Richmond *Dispatch,* quoted in the Clarke County *Journal,* January 15, 1863; O. R. ser. I, vol. XXIII, Pt. II, 921. Conscription in the Trans-Mississippi Department was left in the hands of the Commander of the Department, who was responsible only to the Secretary of War.

[2] O. R. ser. IV, vol. II, 305. Those who volunteered were promised all the benefits guaranteed by law to volunteers.

[3] *Ibid.,* vol. I, 1098; vol. II, 165. Enough officers had been detailed to evoke criticism from Commandant Jno. S. Preston of South Carolina. He said the country was already "flooded with ignorant subaltern officers" (p. 307).

He needed at least 20,000 more effective men before breaking camp at Tullahoma, and since the regular conscription agencies did not seem able to supply them he adopted a novel plan. He ordered Brigadier-General G. J. Pillow to organize "a volunteer and conscript recruiting bureau" for his army.[4]

With characteristic celerity Pillow organized his bureau with headquarters at Huntsville, Alabama, and dispatched his officers to various parts of Alabama, Mississippi, and Tennessee. The selection of Huntsville, which was, according to Senator C. C. Clay, the citadel of Union sentiment, for headquarters illustrates the audacity of the man. Requests were made for military aid and soon volunteers and conscripts, some of whom had exemption certificates in their pockets, began to trudge along toward Tullahoma. Thus there were two rival bureaus of conscription operating in the same area: one was poorly organized, timid, and heedful of its legal limitations; the other was precise, bold, and attentive to military necessity. The one was civil, the other was military.

Although the orders of the War Department were clear on the point that field recruiting would in no sense supersede the regularly established conscription system, within three weeks after General Pillow was ordered to organize his bureau complaints were made that his officers were violating law and utterly ignoring the commandants of conscripts. Prompted by the complaints

[4] O. R. ser. I, vol. XX, Pt. II, 498. General Pillow was one of the many Tennessee conservatives who opposed secession, but when the war began he raised an army of 35,000 and advanced out of his own means a large part of the money for equipping it. The energy and devotion thus displayed probably commended him to General Bragg. But, along with General Buckner, he was made to suffer for General Floyd's disaster at Donelson and was never in favor with the President and the War Department.

of Superintendent G. J. Rains, the War Department laid down the law (February 7th) to Generals Johnston and Bragg concerning the duties of General Pillow. His officers must respect certificates of exemption issued by regular enrolling officers and report punctually all conscripts gathered by them to the commandants of conscripts. They must not interfere with conscripts already in the custody of enrolling officers, and in no case could they grant exemption or details.[5]

Still there was not an orderly relationship between the two bureaus. They became competitive in spite of the designs of the War Department. General Bragg's bureau was very conscious of its identity, and its personnel was self-sure, energetic, impatient, and arrogant. It seemed utterly unable to accommodate itself to the fact that the Richmond Bureau had "exclusive control of the whole subject of conscription," and that it was to act in a supplementary way only.[6] General Pillow issued orders as "chief of the Volunteer and Conscript Bureau" and his officers styled themselves conscript officers.[7] These titles suggested a connection with conscription proper, and the high rank of General Pillow caused con-

---

[5] They must refer all doubtful cases as to exemption, or cases of appeal from their decisions to the regular enrolling officers, or to the commandants of conscripts (O. R. ser. IV, vol. II, 389). Pillow relied "upon superior energy and industry" for the success of his enterprise, and Commandant W. T. Walthall was confident of being able to conscribe with "equal efficiency and at less expense" than could General Pillow's force. Major Walthall was commandant of the camp of instruction at Talladega, Alabama. O. R. ser. IV, vol. II, 389, 435.

[6] O. R. ser. IV, vol. II, 433.

[7] W. G. Swanson, commandant of the camp of instruction at Notasulga, Alabama, reported that Colonel J. W. Echols of the 34th Alabama had established his headquarters in Montgomery and was styling himself "Chief of Volunteer and Conscript Bureau," and that he was "producing much confusion and dissatisfaction." O. R. ser. IV, vol. II, 440.

fusion when his orders conflicted with those of the officers of lower rank in command of the camps of instruction. For the sake of clarifying the situation, the War Department ordered General Bragg to see to it that his recruiting officers divested themselves of their titles.[8]

The ink was scarcely dry on the order of February 7th before General Pillow and his force were usurping authority again, and they had the endorsement of General Bragg. While this order made it clearly General Pillow's duty to supplement the regular conscription agencies, he made bold to give orders to some of the conscription officers, including the commandant of conscripts in Tennessee.[9] The tail was about to wag the body. Reports were not faithfully made to the commandants of conscripts, and officers with the mien of a sheik, it was claimed, passed upon the validity of exemptions, details, and discharges.[10] It mattered not at all that conscript officers and medical boards had the sole authority under law and orders to exempt and to discharge. The necessity for men and the numerous abuses and frauds upon the law were sufficient to provoke military men to desperate means;[11] but the Administration could not allow the legal system of conscription to be broken down by the extra-legal activities of General Pillow. He was reprimanded by the Secretary of War, in reply to which he reduced the charges made against him to the minimum and exonerated himself of these

[8] O. R. ser. IV, vol. II, 433. A month later, according to Superintendent Rains, they were still clinging to their titles. *Ibid.*, 431.

[9] *Ibid.*, 404, 433.

[10] *Ibid.*, 431, 432, 433, 435, 436, 438, 439, 440, 441, 456; ser. II, Vol. V, 857.

[11] See pages 212-214 below.

under the plea of necessity.[12]   What he had done was
done for "advancing the best interests of the service."
"In my overzeal," he said with fine sarcasm, "to be useful and to accomplish much in the pressing wants of
General Bragg's army, I presumed too much upon your
appreciation of my services and your approval of what
I thought was evidently right under the circumstances."
When it was clear to him that his bureau must play a
subordinate rôle in conscription he jumped to the extravagant conclusion that it could not conscript at all and
asked General Bragg to relieve him.   General Bragg
was yearning for a powerful army with which to win
victories that would silence his critics, and was not in
tune with the Richmond plan of strategy for his army,
so he found it easy to endorse Pillow's usurpations.   In
a fit of peevishness he accepted Pillow's resignation and
hurled the information at the War Department with
this to think about: "In six weeks he has done ten times
as much to strengthen his army as all the conscript officers. . . . As requested, he will be relieved and this
army will again decrease." [13]   The War Department ordered him relieved and his bureau closed.   Undoubtedly
the conscription officers breathed a sigh of relief.

There was a variety of opinion as to the accomplishments of General Pillow's bureau.   He and the officers
of the army of Tennessee felt that it had accomplished
a great deal, and that instead of being abolished it
should have been given absolute jurisdiction over conscription throughout the Confederacy.   Pillow claimed

[12] O. R. ser. IV, vol. II, 404, 456.
[13] *Ibid.*, 444.   The Clarke County *Journal* (January 29, 1863) said that
many persons were volunteering because they could go to the army without passing through the camps of instruction.

that his bureau put more than 12,000 men in General Bragg's army during the first month of its service.[14] After it was abolished he read to the Administration a lesson on conscription, drawn from his research and experiences. The Richmond Bureau he asserted was a failure, and inevitably so, because it was based upon the supposition that enrollment and orders would bring men into the army. Experience had proved that there must be force back of conscription, ready to be applied whenever necessary. If the Government would give him exclusive control over conscription and support him he was certain that he could put 100,000 men in the service in a short time.[15]

The Administration and the higher conscription officers, generally, did not place a high estimate on the services of General Pillow. Superintendent Rains thought that, while his extreme measures might seem to have some justification "from their apparent immediate good effects in recruiting the Army more rapidly," just as much might have been attained by "calmness, system, and an apparent as well as a real respect for law, without unsettling whole communities and engendering a spirit of hatred and resistance to the very name of conscription."[16] Conscription officers reported that the high-handed methods of Pillow's officers were causing much dissatisfaction and disturbance, and the character of their appeals to conscripts discredited conscription.[17]

[14] O. R. ser. IV, vol. II, 403. The *Weekly Sun*, March 24, 1863, said that General Pillow's system was very efficient in "placing truants in the services of their country."

[15] *Ibid.*, 450.

[16] *Ibid.*, vol. II, 431.

[17] They encouraged men to volunteer by telling them if they did not they would sooner or later be conscripted and disgraced. This sort of argument tended to strengthen the conviction that conscription carried a

They claimed also that the men who were forced into service by these arbitrary methods deserted at every opportunity because they felt that they had been unjustly taken. Commandant Preston said, concerning Pillow's system: "In every instance this has unduly disturbed the production of the country . . . has violated legal rights . . . has failed to send men into the field . . . and has been unjust to the general service." [18]  The Bureau circular, issued immediately after General Pillow's removal, reveals the Administration's estimate of his service. Conscription officers were advised that "the execution of the conscript act [was] a matter of responsibility and delicacy and the rights conferred by the acts of exemption important in a personal and public view, and that summary proceedings, in every way subversive of the true interests of recruiting as well as offensive to law and humanity." They were warned that they could not serve their country "by hasty action, practically nullifying the right of appeal" from their decisions. Men must not be "assigned or dragged to the Army till their cases have had a fair hearing." [19]

The year 1863 opened inauspiciously for the Confederates. Their forces were outnumbered two to one,[20] and there was a feeling of uneasiness in all of the camps.

taint with it, and, of course, reacted unfavorably on the conscription service.

[18] O. R. ser. III, vol. V, 698. Preston's judgment must not be fully trusted. His criticisms were not consistent, and inasmuch as he had predicted its complete failure he was prepared to see it. O. R. ser. IV, vol. II, 307.

[19] O. R. ser. IV, vol. II, 463. The essential facts of this interesting episode in conscription can be found in the second volume, fourth series, of the *Official Records*, 305-463.

[20] Livermore, vol. I, 90, 94.

With such odds against them it really made little difference if Secretary Seddon were correct in his view that the Army was "fully equal, if not superior, in all the elements of strength" to what it had been at any time before.[21]   The imperturbable Lee begged the Secretary of War to use every means in his power to fill up the ranks.[22]   General Johnston laid before the Adjutant and Inspector General the dire needs of the Department of the West;[23] and, as we have seen, General Bragg became so alarmed over his insecurity before General Rosecrans that he created a special bureau of conscription for his army.   The scarcity of men was due in considerable measure to desertions and improper leaves of absence.[24]

The Administration bent its efforts toward filling up the regiments already in the field.   Secretary Seddon believed that if this could be done the army would be "fully adequate to all future needs and exigencies," and he thought conscription could be relied upon to do the task.[25]   Strange as it may seem, when generals were beg-

[21] O. R. ser. IV, vol. II, 279.

[22] O. R. ser. I, vol. XXI, 1086; ser. III, vol. V, 695.   He thought the governors should be urged to put the plain facts before the people and to aid the enrolling officers in every possible way.   The people should be told that if they would have "the honor of [their] families [free] from pollution, [their] social system from destruction, or [themselves from] degradation worse than death" they must make every effort to fill up the ranks.   Such pressure should be brought to bear that men would be forced into the ranks "from very shame" to stay out.

[23] Ibid., vol. XX, Pt. II, 495.

[24] The great number of officers and men absent with leave surprised General Bragg.   Since the preceding October the granting of such leaves had been reserved to him, but more than 2,200 had been granted by other officers.   Out of a total enrollment of 82,783 he had present on February 19th, only 49,002.

[25] O. R. ser. IV, vol. II, 280.   The Republican (January 20th) said that demagogues must be set aside and "the unpatriotic and cowardly whipped into the ranks."   The Examiner warned that if 75,000 to 100,000 young

ging for men, leading newspapers were doing their utmost to stimulate conscription, and patriotic women were threatening men with hate and scorn if they did not go, the Secretary and the President recommended to Congress the extension of the exemption system.[26]   Congress was on the brink of a new election and was not prepared to take a detached view of the question.   It considered seriously a rigid contraction of exemptions, and did so modify the "twenty nigger" clause as to make many planters liable to conscription.[27]

The two bureaus added a considerable number of men from Alabama, Mississippi, and Tennessee to General Bragg's army during the winter months.   It is impossible to say how many men the Richmond Bureau was able to gather from the other States, but such evidence as we have indicates that it functioned feebly.[28]   February 9th, General Beauregard wrote Congressman C. J. Villére that only a few conscripts had joined the "worn-out standards."   His hostility to President Davis led him to lay the whole blame of this, as of everything, at his feet.   The Government, he said, was a "dead weight" to the people instead of an aid.[29]   Two days later General Lee wrote Seddon that conscripts were coming in

men were not added to the forces of the Southwest within two months the country would come to grief.   January 20th and 22d.

[26] O. R. ser. IV, vol. II, 287, 348; the *Confederacy*, January 3, 1863; the *Mercury*, February 6 and March 14, 1863.

[27] See pages 73-74 above; O. R. ser. IV, vol. II, 553.

[28] Jones complained in his *Diary* January 21st: "Conscription drags its slow length along.   It is not yet adding many to the army."   Vol. I, 243. Three weeks later he complained that Congress had not restricted exemptions and conscription was still dragging.   Under the conditions it would be necessary to call out those between 40 and 45 (257).   General D. H. Hill reported from North Carolina: "The business of conscription is miserably managed" (286).

[29] O. R. ser. IV, vol. II, 391.

very slowly. Only 421 had reported and 287 deserters had returned, while his losses from death and desertion amounted to 1,878.[30]

According to the official records more than 50,000 men had been enrolled by the end of April.[31] In a special message, April 10th, President Davis told Congress that the contrast between conditions of the past and at that time was such as "to inspire full confidence in the triumph of our arms. At no previous period of the war have our forces been so numerous, so well organized, and so thoroughly disciplined, armed, and equipped as at present."[32] An enrollment of 500,000 at the end of April looked large, to be sure, on the Confederate side of the ledger, but it loses some of its impressiveness when it is noted that there were only slightly above 300,000 men present for duty. Probably the number actually present for duty was smaller at this time than at the latter part of January.[33] The rosters of the armies in the Department of the West were larger than ever,[34] but according to the records General Pemberton,

[30] O. R. ser. III, vol. V, 695. The *Courier* (April 2d) said that very few persons had been added by "the vigilance and activity of the enrolling officers." It seems from General Lee's letter that there were no details made from the army of Northern Virginia for recruiting purposes, but details were sent out to pick up deserters and absentees.

[31] O. R. ser. IV, vol. II, 380, 530. Livermore's estimates are more conservative (vol. I, 104). His estimate at the end of January, for example, places the total at 2,839 less than the official total for December 31st, while according to the official record 23,565 were enrolled during January.

[32] *Ibid.*, 475. A few weeks earlier he told his Raleigh audience that he found the Army of the West in good condition. The *Republican*, January 6th.

[33] Consult the tabular statements, O. R. ser. IV, vol. II, 380 and 530.

[34] Some of the departments of the interior were materially increased, as were some of the State defense troops, by special concessions. O. R. ser. I, vol. XV, 939; vol. LII, Pt. II, 405; ser. IV, vol. II, 400, 419. I have found evidence that the forces west of the Mississippi were augmented.

with his roster enlarged by 12,078 at the end of March, had 7,771 less effectives than on January 31st. There were not many thousands added to the army of Northern Virginia during the spring.[35] Having dispatched a few thousand troops to the south, General Lee was forced to fight the battle of Chancellorsville with less men than he had in the battle of Fredericksburg the preceding December.[36]

The report of June 30th showed conditions to be about as they were in April. The total enrollment may have been slightly over 500,000,[37] but the number present for duty was the same as that carried by the April report. If these estimates are at all accurate, it is obvious that the armies were recruited some in May and June, for several thousand men had been lost at Chancellorsville and in the skirmishes in Tennessee and Mississippi.

The Richmond Bureau had had the whole field of conscription to itself since March, and while it furnished small increments of effectives, they were in all probability composed partly of returned deserters. There was a general feeling that the exemption system was in large measure responsible for the ineffectiveness of conscription. Rumors of corruption in the exemption system were widespread,[38] and the Assistant Secretary of War, J. A. Campbell, who was directing conscription through his son-in-law, Colonel George W. Lay, was accused of

[35] At the middle of April, according to Jones, Virginia was furnishing conscripts at the rate of only 700 per month. (*Diary,* 1, 292.)

[36] The total enrollment of the army of Northern Virginia was about 16,000 less on May 31st than on January 31st, according to the records of the War Department. O. R. ser. IV, vol. II, 380, 615.

[37] The report (O. R. ser. IV, vol. II, 615) was incomplete, but by supplementing it with Livermore and other sources I have arrived at the above conclusion.

[38] Pages 78-80 above.

being entirely too liberal with exemptions.[39]   Jones complained that Judge Campbell's "judicial profundity" was keeping many men out of the service.   He lamented the fact that Campbell could ignore the opinions and orders of Secretary Seddon.[40]   His aspiration to become a major of conscription in Richmond probably helped him to be a severe critic of conscription.[41]

The baleful practice of skulking and deserting grew apace and seriously undermined the strength of the armies.   At the opening of the spring campaign there were about 90,000 absentees from Lee's, Bragg's, and Pemberton's armies, and by the end of June the number of absentees from all of the commands totaled about 136,000.[42]   Many of these deserters and conscripts banded themselves together in out-of-the-way places to resist arrest, and freely sniped conscript and other officers who came their way.   From Virginia, North Carolina, Tennessee, Georgia, Alabama, Mississippi, and Texas came reports that the conscript law could not be enforced and deserters could not be picked up without the use of armed forces.[43]   By appeals to their chivalry and to their fears patriotic women tried to call them to their duty.

[39] The *Examiner*, June 6th, questioned Judge Campbell's motives, calling attention to the fact that he was late coming over to the Confederate cause.   The idea of Campbell's excessive liberality runs through *Jones' Diary*.

[40] *Diary*, vol. I, 234, 258, 260, 275, 378.

[41] *Ibid.*, 262, 263.

[42] See sources referred to already.   Many of those absent were technical deserters, that is, they did not leave their commands outright but failed to return at the expiration of their leaves of absence.

[43] O. R. ser. I, vol. XV, 925-939; vol. XXV, Pt. II, 814; vol. III, Pt. II, 711-715; ser. IV, vol. II, 301, 360, 419, 460, 563, 604, 607, 618, 638, 680; Jacksonville *Republican*, January 8th; *Weekly Sun*, February 3d; *Mercury*, March 14th; Clarke County *Journal*, April 14th.

"It is impossible," a certain group of them said, "for us to respect a coward, and every true woman who has husband, father, brother, or lover . . . had rather see him prostrate before her with death's signet on his noble brow that has never been branded by cowardice or dishonor, than have him forfeit his good name and disgrace his manhood, by refusing to do his duty to his country." [44] Governor Vance, who prided himself upon the magic of his words over the masses of his fellow-North Carolinians, hurled fiery darts of eloquence at the derelicts of the mountains which were calculated to make them shudder to behold themselves slinking about, and to drive those who were harboring them to close their doors against them. With powerful rhetoric he threatened them with civil prosecution, and warned them of the awful retributory justice that would be meted out to them when the war was over and the patriots came home. Then they would wish for the mountains to fall upon them. But a whole dictionary of verbal castigation and of threats would not have budged them.[45]

The numerical superiority of the enemy made a rigid concentration of the Confederate forces necessary. It had become clear that it was strategically unwise to sacrifice strength at the vital spots by trying to prevent invasions in every locality. Secretary Seddon informed the governors early in June that troops would be called from the local defense, and urged them to organize troops out of the industrial and professional reserves to be used

[44] The *Confederacy*, January 3, 1863.
[45] Conditions in North Carolina became the subject-matter of serious correspondence between General Lee, Secretary Seddon, and Governor Vance. O. R. ser. I, vol. XXV, 707, 709, 715, 746, 814; ser. IV, vol. II, 180-191.

in local emergencies.[46]   But the policy did not furnish enough men to save Vicksburg.

Fourth of July came and the South was steeped in gloom.   Vicksburg had fallen and the invincible Lee had been stopped at Gettysburg!   A successful invasion of the North, with its many salutary results, no longer seemed possible, and the fall of Vicksburg cut off the great food resources of the West and the supplies of small arms through Mexico.   The "Anaconda" plan of attack was now accomplished; the main part of the Confederacy was completely blockaded.   Lee's army recoiled upon Richmond to save it and the Tredegar Iron Works— the Krupp Works of the Confederacy; Pemberton's army was annihilated; and Johnston was in retreat before Grant to some interior position.   The plan of concentration was deterred by the threat of the Federal navy to occupy the leading seaports and to hold them as a basis for advances into the interior.   Grant would probably soon move to help Rosecrans crush Bragg, and if Chattanooga fell the mountain region would be opened; traffic between the upper and lower South over the Virginia and Tennessee railroad would be interrupted; the shuttle-like movement of troops between Richmond and the Mississippi behind the line of defense would be prevented; and the foundations of an advance upon Richmond from the South would be laid.

President Davis' troubles were coming upon him "not single spies, but in battalions."   The problem of readjustment and of toning up the spirit of the people after the heartbreaking reversals at Vicksburg and Gettysburg would have been stupendous under the most favorable circumstances.   It fell to the lot of President Davis

[46] O. R. ser. IV, vol. II, 580.

to undertake it under the most unfavorable circumstances. His health had been wretched for months, and his enemies, numbered by the thousands, were attacking him without mercy. The conscription, impressment, and tax-in-kind laws had turned a large mass of people against him who needed only to be led to espouse a course of active opposition to his administration. The movement in Congress, supported by some of the influential newspapers, to save the cause by enlarging the President's powers touched off the guns of the opposition. The *Mercury* forgot its prayer for proper conduct, concocted at a moment when it felt more kindly toward the President, and assailed him with all its might.[47] It had a powerful ally in the *Examiner*. Richard Smith's *Sentinel*, the new Government organ, and the *Enquirer* now reinvigorated by the "Irishman," John Mitchell, defended the President with enthusiasm. By the middle of July they were advocating the extreme expedient of conferring dictatorial powers upon him. This only deepened the widespread feeling that the President had secret designs against the liberties of the people. The thought of such was more than the editors of the *Mercury* and *Examiner* could bear. They were opposed to the dictatorship of any one, and especially to that of President

[47] Mr. Rhett adopted this prayer from an old writer "with alterations and editions suitable to the present conditions of the Confederate States of America." It serves the purpose, at least, of showing what he thought were the dangerous sins of the times. It ran: "Almighty God and Merciful Father, guard us in each State of the Confederacy from sedition, conspiracy, rebellion, and insurrection; and our Army and infant Navy from disaffection and insubordination, from mutiny and desertion, from cowardice and panic, from intemperance and blasphemy, and from the want of generalship which either fails to obtain an advantage or to improve it when obtained. . . . Take not from us the sharpness and the point of the two-edged sword; but enable us to win one victory after another over every spiritual and natural foe," etc. *Mercury,* March 27, 1863.

Davis whom they charged with having banished from him the heart and brains of the Confederacy.[48]    The Richmond press duel over the new plan of salvation for the Confederacy was reproduced in some of the other cities; and the opposition crystallized and began to elect Congressmen to check the despotic tendencies at Richmond.[49]    Toombs had a sympathetic hearing when he unnecessarily remarked that he "would rather see the whole country the cemetery of freedom than the habitation of slaves." [50]

[48] *Examiner,* July 30th.
[49] See O. R. ser. IV, vol. II, 489; Stephenson, *The Day of the Confederacy,* 92-98.
[50] Stephenson, 90.

# CHAPTER X

## THE DUAL SYSTEM (Continued)

SWIFT measures were adopted to oppose the advance of the enemy in Tennessee and Virginia. First, President Davis called out the reserves between 40 and 45. Second, he called upon the governors to raise State troops for State defense, so that the regulars might be transferred to the main battle-fields. Third, Colonel John S. Preston, who had attracted considerable attention as commandant of conscripts in South Carolina, was put in charge of the Bureau of Conscription. Colonel Preston was expected to put life and order in the conscript system. The former superintendents, according to Secretary Seddon, had been too much interested in field affairs to give conscription their full energies. He appointed Preston because it had become "most important to secure the promptest and most efficient execution of the law of conscription throughout the Confederacy." [1] Fourth, General Johnston, upon his urgent request, which was sanctioned by the governors of the States concerned, was given complete jurisdiction over conscription in his department (Department No. 2).[2] He set up a bureau of conscription, put General Pillow

[1] O. R. ser. IV, vol. II, 635, 636.
[2] O. R. ser. I, vol. XXIII, Pt. II, 912; ser. IV, vol. II, 868, 911. The request was made and sanctioned, it was said, because the conscript law was not being enforced in this department.

in charge of it, and turned over the whole business of conscription to him.

The dual system of conscription east of the Mississippi, thus revived, obtained until the middle of December. Under this system the Richmond Bureau retained control of the seaboard States,[3] except Florida, which, along with Tennessee, Alabama, and Mississippi, was given over to General Johnston's military bureau. A clean-cut contest between conscription by civil processes and by the military resulted. Each was on trial; the more efficient would probably prevail for the remainder of the war. Superintendent Preston recognized the competitive relationship of the two bureaus and hastened to offer an alibi.[4] Conscription headquarters at Richmond and at Marietta took on a business-like appearance. The governors and army officers in Department No. 2 were friendly to the Marietta Bureau, but the Administration leaned to the Richmond Bureau, which was "bound to be more regular and measured, respecting the legal rights of exemption and disability." Preston was sure of Judge Campbell's sympathy, because of the judge's prepossessions for civil authority and because his son-in-law, who had for a long time been practically in charge of conscription, held an important position under Preston. And Judge Campbell was the dominating personality of the War Department.

Because of the separation of the territorial jurisdiction of the two bureaus, there was much less danger of

[3] It also retained control over east Louisiana, but there were few conscripts to be had there.

[4] He said there were fewer conscripts in his States in proportion to the population than in those under Pillow's jurisdiction; in fact, he maintained, there was but little material for him to work on. O. R. ser. IV, vol. II, 694.

conflict between Preston and Pillow than formerly between Pillow and Rains.[5]  There was a feeling in administrative circles, however, that as between the two bureaus permanency and paramountcy lay with the Richmond Bureau.  It was still the *Bureau of Conscription*.
Preston had no authority over Pillow until October, and
then only that of reviewing appeals from Pillow's decisions when they were referred to him by the War Department; but he kept an inspector of conscription in the field
who reported to him the conditions of conscription in
Pillow's department.[6]

There was much for the bureaus to do.  Conscription
was at a low ebb and the crime of desertion, if, as Judge
Campbell remarked, so general a habit could be considered a crime, was rampant.  General Lee complained
of the inefficiency of conscription;[7] Governors Harris,
Brown, and Shorter thought the cause was lost unless
the system could be enlarged;[8] and the officers of the
Army of Tennessee implored the President to recruit the
armies with fresh levies at once, either by calling upon
the States for enlarged quotas, or by assembling Con-

[5] Pillow was anxious for this arrangement since it would avoid conflicts and "misrepresentations made to the War Department in *ex parte*
statements."  O. R. ser. IV, vol. II, 637.

[6] O. R. ser. IV, vol. II, 717, 761, 799.

[7] O. R. ser. I, vol. XXVI, Pt. III, 1041.  The *Examiner* said that the
chief evil of the time was the escape of "innumerable individuals from
the service under false pretenses and by the criminal indulgence of those
who are appointed to enforce the law."  There was no use to extend the
law until the Government was able to get and keep those whom the law
had given it.  The *Republican* said there were as many men out of the
army as in it.  It called upon the Confederate Government and the
States to put the men in the field and keep them there.  Any man who
stood between the citizen and the service—Governor or peasant—was a
traitor and should be treated as one.  Quoted in the *Enquirer*, July 11,
1863.

[8] O. R. ser. IV, vol. II, 750, 753, 754.

gress to modify the exemption system so as to make available the needed men.[9] The *Enquirer* advanced the opinion that the States must come to the rescue of the Government. Additional conscription machinery, machinery in more intimate touch with the people and supported by potential force, was required and the States alone could furnish it. As things stood only the willing and the patriotic were collected.[10] It was difficult to conscript men and keep them in the service when they had lost confidence in their Government,[11] and when they were so spiritless that the hero-worshippers of Richmond could let the great hero of Chancellorsville ride past them without cheering him.[12]

General Pillow took up his duties promptly. He proceeded to conscript through the old agencies of conscription and to organize a supplementary force.[13] His complete organization consisted of the old camps of instruction and a large number of rendezvous and outposts. The former was the "conscript branch" of his bureau, the latter the "supernumerary branch." [14] The General thought he had an organization equal to the work to be done. "It is a complete net-work of organization," he wrote General Cooper, "which is spread like a map all over those portions of the States in our possession, and

[9] O. R. ser. IV, vol. II, 670.

[10] The editor believed that a concert of action among the people, the States, and the governments would soon put 600,000 men in the field. August 12, 1863.

[11] Jones said some persons believed that Lincoln and Davis were prolonging the war because they feared peace would prove their undoing (*Diary*, II, 15).

[12] *Jones' Diary*, II, 32. The burden of returning deserters was attached to the conscription service early in 1863. O. R. ser. IV, vol. II, 750.

[13] He did not complete his organization in Mississippi until about September 1st. O. R. ser. IV, vol. II, 748, 805.

[14] *Ibid.*, 821.

with an active corps of officers with supporting forces of cavalry will soon sweep the country clean of deserters and conscripts, and must, to the exhaustion of the population, rapidly build up our armies." [15]

But conscription and returning deserters was not altogether a matter of machinery. Within a few days after Pillow took up his duties he discovered that the prospect in his department was "gloomy enough." Deserters and "tory conscripts" in north Alabama—to the number of 8,000 to 10,000, he said—had banded together, killed several of his officers, and defeated several small bodies of cavalry sent against them; and in central and southern Alabama nearly all of the conscripts were already in the army. In those portions of Tennessee and Mississippi yet within the Confederate lines it was almost impossible to get the men out of the thickets, swamps, and mountains. He requested ten companies of cavalry to enforce the law in north Alabama, and the privilege of extending his jurisdiction over Georgia. Without Georgia, which he asserted was full of men liable to duty, it would be impossible for him to add much strength to the armies of Tennessee and Mississippi.[16] A few days later he applied for authority to extend his organization to northern Georgia and those portions of West Virginia and North Carolina that lay west of the Blue Ridge.[17]

[15] O. R. ser. IV, vol. II, 805.

[16] Ibid., 680, 751. One gets the impression that Pillow's anxiety to make an impressive showing, as a means to extending his jurisdiction, prompted him to make a heavy bid for Georgia. In two other communications he incidentally admitted, for example, that there were a large number of conscripts in his department (Ibid., 676, 760). It was Inspector August's opinion that there were 15,000 conscripts in Mississippi (Ibid., 763).

[17] O. R. ser. IV, vol. II, 805.

The longer Pillow was in the conscription business the more ambitious he became. If he were not to be allowed to win laurels as a commander in the field, he might do the next best thing to it; he might get charge of conscription throughout the Confederacy and save it by putting its able-bodied men in the field, and thus succeed where other men had failed. The idea was captivating, and the failure of the War Department to reply to his request for Georgia did not restrain him. He not only renewed his petition for Georgia but suggested the advisability of extending his system over the whole Confederacy.[18] The system of conscription set up by law was a failure because it lacked force; no man could take the organization of the Richmond Bureau and put the conscript population in the army. His system had proved its merit to the satisfaction of the generals and governors in his department, and if applied to all the States would fill the armies and keep them full.[19]

Secretary Seddon and Judge Campbell did not entertain General Pillow's high esteem for his system. They admitted the temporary success of it but anticipated disastrous results from its blunt and extra legal methods. Already, they said, Pillow and his officers were compared "to the press gang sweeping through the country with little deference to law or the regulations designed to temper its unavoidable rigor, without detracting from its

[18] He said two weeks before that he did not want the service, (O. R. ser. IV, vol. II, 751) but the War Department understood that he did (*Ibid.,* ser. I, vol. XXIII, Pt. II, 922). Pillow knew, of course, that he was being pushed for the position of Chief of Conscription by the generals in his department.

[19] O. R. ser. IV, vol. II, 741. General L. Polk, of General Bragg's army, had at an earlier date urged this upon the War Department. He thought "something more concentrated, direct, and stringent" was required (ser. I, vol. XXIII, Pt. II, 921).

legal force." This indicated a revival of the "remonstrances, indignant and bitter," which came up to the Department during Pillow's former incumbency.[20] He was told that his bureau was merely a temporary device, but he was not unhorsed. For several weeks he continued to lay before the War Department jeremiads on the weakness of the old system and panegyrics on the efficiency of his own.[21] He failed to make the desired impression. By telegraphic orders he was deprived of the power to pass definitively upon applications for exemption. These orders wounded his pride; it was not befitting to one of his rank to masquerade, merely, as a superintendent of conscription. So he asked to be transferred to the field. General Johnston urged the War Department to restore his power, but instead he was ordered (December 16th) to report to General Hardee, and the Richmond Bureau resumed jurisdiction over Department 2. Thus ended purely military conscription and the rôle of General Pillow as a conscript officer. General Cooper and Judge Campbell concurred in the opinion that two bureaus on the same subject were not only superfluous but conducive to confusion; and the Bureau of Conscription retained undisputed control till near the end of the war.

General Pillow was expected to put into the army at once the conscripts in Alabama and Mississippi whom the conscription authorities had failed to procure, and to return to the army a large number of deserters. This was an extremely difficult task. But Pillow had orders to

[20] O. R. ser. IV, vol. II, 748, 806.

[21] He went so far as to send one of his officers to Richmond to explain the merits of his system, and requested a personal interview with General Cooper in case he should remain unconvinced. O. R. ser. IV, vol. II, 749, 805, 851.

get them, and like a good military man, he pounced upon them in a direct and vigorous manner. Picking up men and arms wherever he could find them,—the generals could not spare him many able-bodied men, and guns were so scarce that household firearms must be used— he succeeded in organizing a force of 2,000 men who made it very difficult for those of military age to stay at home. Most of those who had expected exemption or detail were disappointed, and the law-defying conscripts and deserters generally found it necessary to go to camp or to retreat into the enemy's lines. According to Pillow's reports he probably put 25,000 to 30,000 men in the field within three and a half months.[22] He claimed at the time of his retirement that the conscript population was about exhausted.[23]

It is not possible to say how many effectives Pillow put in the field. It was impossible to keep every man in the field who was driven in at the muzzle of a gun. In fact, desertions were frequent;[24] Pillow said that he sent some men to the front as many as four times. He advised that the only way to keep them there was to send them away from home by putting them in the army of northern Virginia. The Secretary of War allowed this to some extent, but he was unwilling to make a Botany

[22] No reports for November and December have been found. Early in October he claimed that he was averaging 500 men per day, but November 17th he wrote General Cooper that the number would probably begin soon to "fall off", owing to the exhaustion of the population. O. R. ser. IV, vol. II, 859, 963.

[23] *Ibid.*, 1019. Within 60 days he said there would be practically nothing left for his bureau to do.

[24] The Bureau of Conscription claimed that the number of deserters and stragglers in Alabama and Mississippi exceeded that in Virginia, the Carolinas, and Georgia (*Ibid.*, 965). This was not an impartial claim, but conditions were acute in Pillow's department after the fall of Vicksburg and the reversals in Tennessee.

Bay colony of General Lee's Army.[25]  It is sufficient to notice that enough effective men were added to justify Pillow's system in the minds of the governors and of the officers of Johnston's and Bragg's staffs.  The War Department, too, admitted Pillow's zeal, vigor, and efficiency, but it feared a popular reaction against his exercise of unlimited powers.[26]

Colonel Preston took charge of the Bureau of Conscription August 1st.  Concerning his appointment Jones observed: "The law will now be honestly executed— if he be not too indolent, sick, etc." [27]  Like General Pillow his first problem was that of organization.  The organization he said was not complete in any State and the service was "confused and languid, and the administration of the conscript laws necessarily unsatisfactory."[28]

He called attention to the low status of conscription and proposed a plan of reform.  Recruiting for special organizations, military conscription in some of the States, and unrestricted volunteering had the conscript system "down to the condition of some of our cavalry corps, with scarce strength left to brush away the vermin which now attack it in the form of details for railroads, telegraph offices, express offices, etc."

The plan of improvement consisted of four propositions: (1) all recruiting and volunteering of men between 18 and 45 should be done through the Bureau of Conscription; (2) the number of enrolling officers should be greatly enlarged by the use of disabled soldiers,

[25] O. R. ser. IV, vol. II, 869.
[26] O. R. ser. III, vol. II, 806, 911.
[27] Diary, vol. I, 386.
[28] O. R. ser. III, vol. V, 697; ser. IV, vol. II, 723.  General Pillow gave a similar picture of the conditions of conscription in Department No. 2 when he took charge (p. 850).

or "invalid" conscripts, who could furnish their own horses to act as cavalry; (3) the State governments should be requested to furnish aid to the enrolling officers; and (4) commanders of armies, posts, and garrisons should be required to furnish aid to the enrolling officers when called upon. Adopt this plan, he urged, and "I will promise that in six months the military force under the law will be in the field." If it had been adopted at the outset, the conscript law, in spite of its "glaring defects," would have been "as smooth in its execution and as sure of its results as the tax law, or the election law, or any other customary law of the country." [29] He warned against the continuation of military conscription, for military officers were ill-suited to meet the "most cherished prejudices of the people." They would soon drive the people and the States into rebellion. It will be recalled that Pillow was at the same time claiming that he could glut the army with men if given the whole field and plenty of armed troops to support him.

Neither Preston nor Pillow could see much that was good in the other's system, but it should be said to their credit that their criticisms were confined to systems and never touched personalities. It is significant that they were agreed, with a single exception, upon fundamentals. Each believed that there was a need for more and better men in the conscription service, and each urged the indispensability of backing up the conscription agencies in their conscription work and in their activities as an external police for the armies. In other words, each recognized the fact that men could no longer be put in the

---

[29] O. R. ser. IV, vol. II, 723. He enclosed with his communication a letter received from Major W. T. Walthall, commandant of conscripts for Alabama, which supported his own opinions.

army and kept there by mere orders.[30]   Each, too, advocated a unified and centralized system in which all the sources of conscription would become confluent.   But they were by no means agreed as to which system should be the one and only system.   Their chief difference lay in the fact that Pillow would use the supernumerary military force for all conscription duties, while Preston would use it to enforce the decisions of the enrolling officers. Each would have had more respect for the other's system if he himself had been in charge of it.

In rebuttal to General Pillow's contentions and requests, Colonel Preston reiterated and expounded upon his original recommendations.  His system, he contended, was not only more consistent with the law than Pillow's but would be more efficient if given the additional forces and powers requested by Pillow.  The Bureau of Conscription possessed a superiority in adjusting the rights of citizens and maintaining the internal police and production of the country.  "If General Pillow's plan is adopted," he expostulated, "to the full extent proposed, my opinion is that before the 1st of January more than one State will by law prohibit its execution within their limits, and that in many localities such armed resistance will be made to it as will require more men for its execution than are the objects of its search."[31]   The War Department accepted Preston's views.  Several weeks before Pillow was removed the Secretary called the Presi-

[30] Assistant Secretary Campbell said that the machinery proposed by Pillow and his friends was substantially the same as that of the Bureau of Conscription.  He understood their proposals to amount to a recommendation to put efficient officers in the place of disabled soldiers and to place Pillow at the head of the Bureau.  He was highly in favor of using select officers if the commanders of armies could spare them.  O. R. ser. I, vol. XXIII, Pt. II, 922.  See page 750 for a similar opinion by Preston.

[31] O. R. ser. IV, vol. II, 749, 867.

dent's attention to the potentialities of the Bureau, "with slight modifications" and with an adequate supporting force of armed men.[32]

By early September Superintendent Preston's organization was about complete.[33] Several practical measures were adopted to promote its efficiency. First, commandants of conscripts were ordered to see that their officers functioned with increased vigilance and activity, and that they secured all possible aid from the State governments. Their officers must be "active, intelligent, and efficient." Second, they were ordered to assemble their Congressional district enrolling officers once a month to canvass the conditions of conscription and to report fully to the Bureau the results of their deliberations, with regard to schemes for improvement as well as to prevailing weaknesses. Third, a system of inspection was instituted. Inspection officers were sent out with authority to remove incompetent officers and to set aside improper decisions, or to do anything else found necessary to promote efficiency. The obstructionist activities of the governors of South Carolina and Georgia led Preston himself to go out on a tour of inspection in October.[34]

Preston had barely begun his work before he discovered two serious impediments. First, he found that the volunteer system had, because of the activities of army recruiting officers, degenerated into a method of avoiding service. Men in large numbers—"indeed large major-

---

[32] O. R. ser. IV, vol. II, 999. There was at this time a consensus of opinion among administrative, conscript, and military officers that the conscript law could not be executed and deserters could not be returned without the use of armed forces.

[33] Ibid., 798.

[34] See O. R. ser. IV, vol. II, 703, 717, 736, 768, 781, 867, 1022.

ities in some localities"—held back from volunteering until they could dodge the enrolling officers no longer; then they accepted "offers of recruiting officers who tender them rewards and extended furloughs for the chance of getting the names on their rolls, thus delaying the volunteer beyond the conscript." He had seen "furloughs of ninety days given by recruiting officers to men who held certificates six months old that they belonged to certain companies, and who had never been in the field." In other instances men escaped after enrollment and joined companies from which it was difficult to reclaim them.[35] The next, and the more serious, impediment was the extensive aggregation of conscripts and deserters in inaccessible places.

The reports that came to Preston's office in August convinced him that the task of arresting deserters and renegade conscripts would be a difficult one. Armed bands of conscripts and deserters were reported from all the States within his jurisdiction. From Virginia, relatively free up to this time from desertion and skulking, came the report that in a dozen or more of the upper counties even the best citizens were becoming demoralized and disloyalty was widespread. Deserters had become defiant. When asked by enrolling officers for their authority to be away from their commands they would merely "pat their guns and say, 'This is my furlough,'" and the officers turned away as "peaceably as possible."[36] From the hitherto loyal South Carolina came the unwelcomed news that there was "a most lamentable and fearful condition of affairs in the mountains

[35] O. R. ser. IV, vol. II, 694. Orders were soon issued to the army recruiting officers to stop the abuses (*Ibid.*, 731).
[36] *Ibid.*, 721.

of Greenville, Pickens, and Spartanburg [counties]."
Commandant C. D. Melton wrote that there were few
families in this section which had "not a husband, a son,
a brother, or kinsman, a deserter in the mountains," and
it was no longer a reproach to be known as a deserter.
Conscripts and deserters had organized and taken up
headquarters in the mountain fortresses, or in cottages
converted into blockhouses, from which they sallied forth
in force to harvest the crops, or to do the less irksome
labor of plundering their yet loyal neighbors.  It was
dangerous for an officer of the law to approach them or
for a neighbor to tell tales about them.[37]  In North Carolina, according to Inspector George W. Lay, conditions
had gone from bad to worse.  Not merely the Western
part now, but the central portion as well, was reported
to be on the verge of desperate action.  Under the leadership of W. W. Holden, editor of the *Standard,* and
"Tory" of the first water, it seemed that these sections
might soon espouse *en masse* the cause of peace.[38]  Conscripts and deserters were organized and holding themselves in readiness for defense by regular drills, and in
one place 500 of them were intrenched in a camp.  In
another place, in Cherokee County, they had assumed
a sort of military occupation of a town.  Enrolling officers were shot on sight and the country round about was
subject to pillage and all sorts of violence.[39]  Requests
were made for troops from the army to relieve the

[37] O. R. ser. IV, vol. II, 771, 769, 773, 774, 784.  Union meetings in the
Anderson district were reported.  O. R. ser. I, vol. XXXV, Pt. I, 536.

[38] Davis became alarmed and wrote Governor Vance to know if it
would be advisable to take steps against the "reckless" Holden.  Vance
replied that it would be "impolitic in the very highest degree" to bother
Holden, and that the patriotism of the people could be relied upon to
check him.  O. R. ser. I, vol. LI, Pt. II, 739, 740.

[39] O. R. ser. IV, vol. II, 783.

orderly and helpless citizens of this scourge.[40]   The
Governors of North Carolina and South Carolina took
joint action against the affiliated bands along the boun-
dary line between their States,[41] and President Davis
recommended that a general officer should be stationed
there with a brigade.[42]

After weighing all of the evidence Judge Campbell
was of the opinion that "the condition of things in the
mountain districts of North Carolina, South Carolina,
Georgia, and Alabama [menaced] the existence of the
Confederacy as fatally as either of the armies of the
United States." [43]   According to the records conditions
were quite as serious in the States embraced in Department No. 2, and the States of the Trans-Mississippi Department also were having their troubles with derelicts.[44]
In truth, the practice of desertion and evading the conscription law, which began in the summer of 1862, had
become extensive throughout the Confederacy owing,
among other things, to the almost unbearable conditions
of the service and to the despondency following the defeats of the summer of 1863.[45]   The President's proclamation of Amnesty, August 1st, to all deserters who
would return to their commands at once, and his appeal
to the women to drive them back, did not get the results

[40] O. R. ser. I, vol. XXIX, Pt. II, 676; ser. IV, vol. II, 733.
[41] O. R. ser. IV, vol. II, 741, 765. See page 795 for Governor Vance's
proclamation of September 7th warning those who were opposing the
military laws that they would be punished as traitors.
[42] Diary, II, 46.
[43] Ibid., 786.
[44] O. R. ser. I, vol. XXII, Pt. II, 949; vol. XXVI, Pt. II, 119, 194.
[45] In addition to the citations made already, see ser. I, vol. XXVI, 549,
550; ser. IV, vol. II, 675 et passim. Jones' Diary, vol. II, 86; and the
Mercury, Sun, and the Virginia papers for the summer and fall of 1863.
The Enquirer, August 12th, said that half of the men on the army rolls
were absent from their commands.

hoped for. The *Independent,* August 15th, commenting on the President's proclamation, touched upon an ironical truth when it observed: "Let all the appeals be made which may possibly do any good; but if you want soldiers don't forget the appeal of the law." Pollard characteristically remarked that proclamations and patriotic appeals to deserters were "paltry quacking." [46]

No data has been found by which to measure the success of Preston's efforts. In anticipation of a Congressional inquiry in December he had instituted as early as September "a most admirable system" for securing minute information about conscription and urged the commandants of conscripts to be prompt and circumspect in their reports,[47] but only a few reports seem to have come to the office. Indeed, it is certain that no reliable reports had been made by the last day of grace, November 1st. From the "scanty material" in the office it was roughly estimated, November 7th, that three-fifths of the material (75,000 men) under the law in Virginia, the Carolinas, and Georgia, had been put into the army since the spring of 1862, and that there were about 25,000 yet to be conscripted.[48] Undoubtedly Preston drove a considerable number of men into the army. Jones squared himself with his *Diary* by substituting for a former ridicule of Preston's efforts the following observation: "Our armies are augmenting from conscription." [49] It is hardly to be supposed that Cooper, Seddon, Campbell, and the

[46] *Third Year of the War,* 183.

[47] O. R. ser. IV, vol. II, 830, 946, 1022.

[48] *Ibid.,* 939.

[49] He did not hope for large results, however, until honest men were in charge of all the agencies of conscription and the exemption and detail systems were amended and purified (vol. II, 85).

President could have placed their stamp of approval on Preston and his organization if no tangible results had been accomplished in more than three months. It stands, of course, to the discredit of Preston's organization that he could not get through it prompt and accurate reports, but this resulted in part from the frequent changing of conscript officers and the uncertainty of communcation. Even General Pillow found it impossible to get prompt and accurate reports through his military machine.

It is impossible to say how many men were added to the armies in 1863. Secretary Seddon estimated that 80,000 to 100,000 were added. Of these he thought three-fourths volunteered to avoid conscription. He did not include in his estimate a large number of conscripts who had volunteered into the local State organizations.[50] Whatever the actual increments may have been, they were not large enough to keep the number of effectives present up to the standard at the beginning of the year. The abolition of a large number of details, the use of men, not available for field service, in the non-combatant enterprises, the revision of the medical boards, the adoption of an inspection system, etc., failed to produce the needed results. Sickness, casualties of battle, captures, desertions, and discharges had brought the total roster, December 31st, down to 464,646, and the aggregate present for duty down to 233,586.[51] The President was generous in his interpretation of the records when he told Congress it was believed that the army was "in all

[50] For statements concerning the size of Lee's and Bragg's armies from time to time during the fall see O. R. ser. I, vol. XXIII, Pt. II, 920, 941, 945, 957, 962; vol. XXIX, Pt. II, 659, 709, 811, 898.

[51] O. R. ser. IV, vol. II, 1073. This report did not include the State defense troops which probably numbered 50,000.

respects in better condition than at any previous period of the war." [52]

Conscription in 1863 performed very imperfectly its two-fold duty of putting men of conscript age in the army and keeping them there.[53]   It was ineffective because of: (1) the defects of the conscription laws; (2) the failure of the spirit of the people; (3) the incompetency of the conscription machinery; (4) the confusion growing out of the dual system of conscription and the voluntary recruiting system; (5) the volunteering of conscripts in the local defense organizations; and (6) the lack of armed forces to support the conscript officers.[54]   The opinion prevailed generally among civil and military leaders that there were enough men between the ages of 18 and 45 to supply the needs of the army.   Secretary Seddon and Adjutant General Cooper believed that there were at least as many within these age limits as the country could equip and sustain.[55]   The great need of the country was to remove the obstacles in the way of enrolling them.

While those in direct charge of conscription strove to systematize and energize its machinery, the President endeavored to tone up the spirit of the people.   He gave out optimistic interviews, wrote encouraging letters, and made an extensive tour of the country which was calculated, among other things, to arouse hope and inspire action.   It was said that he succeeded in relaxing his austerity and talked heart to heart to the people, but

[52] O. R. ser. IV, vol. II, 1040.

[53] According to Pollard, Secretary Seddon said that the effective force of the army was "not more than half, never two-thirds of the soldiers in the ranks." *Third Year of the War,* 189.

[54] Conflicts between State and Confederate authority and the continued opposition of influential men were also contributing factors.

[55] O. R. ser. IV, vol. II, 696, 996.

the effect was only momentary. Sweeping victories were needed to stimulate the spirits of the people. The victory of Chickamauga, for example, was electrical in effect, but the subsequent defeat at Chattanooga restored the long faces of doubt and fear.

Toward the close of the year chief attention was focused upon the weakness and abuses of the conscript law. Generals in the field, governors, legislators, and public leaders generally, demanded the abolition of substitution and the termination of abuses connected with exemptions and details. In response to these demands searching investigations were instituted, corrections made, and the policy of substituting disabled soldiers for the able-bodied clerks in the Quartermaster and Commissary departments was pushed. But it was the opinion of the Richmond authorities that the law would have to be radically changed before abuses could be successfully eliminated and the able-bodied men of conscript age released for field duty. They formulated a program which they believed would recruit the army and at the same time maintain essential production. They proposed, first, to create a definite labor reserve by conscripting able-bodied whites over 45 years for purposes of labor, and by using free negroes and slaves around Government works and in the armies as cooks, teamsters, etc.[56] The Government could not compete with the industries for high-priced labor, hence it must by law establish a prior right to labor, or continue the practice of detailing men between 18 and 45 to do its work.[57] Second, substitu-

[56] The President thought that able-bodied whites above 45 might be used for light military duty also.

[57] There were probably 100,000 whites above 45 years able to labor, and 50,000 free blacks. (The census of 1860 gave the total number of free negroes at 135,630.) But, of course, many of the able-bodied men above

tion should be abolished and a system of Executive details should be substituted for the exemption system. Third, the conscription organization should be perfected and the conscript officers should be supported by local military forces organized for the purpose. The conscription system thus revised might be given the additional duties of checking upon the use of details, and of keeping the War Department informed of available labor, free or slave. Fourth, there must be legislation to retain all those whose terms of enlistment would expire in the ensuing spring and summer.[58] This was a radical program, and it provided for a large expansion of Executive power. It was not likely to be adopted *in toto* by a Congress possessed of much anti-Administration sentiment and fresh from a people who were discouraged, and distrustful of their President.

As the last sun of 1863 went down the odds were fearfully against the Confederates. The Assistant Adjutant General penned a grim truth when he wrote Secretary Seddon: "The crisis is a fearful one, and men must be found to constitute our armies, else all is lost." [59]   The dual system of conscription had failed to keep the strength of the army up to the previous year's standard. The need was imperative for more men and supplies than before, but they must be drawn, if at all, from a greatly reduced area. The Trans-Mississippi region had been ripped off and the Confederate defense pushed back to a zigzag line extending from Dalton, Georgia, to Mobile. So complete had been the subjugation of Tennessee, Louisiana, and Arkansas that President Lincoln formulated a

45 could not be taken from the farms and employed twelve months in the year at Government works.

[58] O. R. ser. IV, vol. II, 946, 990, 1024.

[59] *Ibid.*, 947.

plan for their political reconstruction and for encouraging the peace men in the other States. Nor were the political reverses of the Administration less decisive. Anti-Davis parties had sprung up and carried some of the States with a slate of relatively obscure candidates, while in other States some of the old members of Congress were frankly in the anti-Davis column.[60] Ominous signs of conflict with the State authorities appeared, and confusion, distrust, and apathy prevailed. A large group despaired of success, while others were too busy making money to lend a helping hand for victory, just as many a Northerner was more interested in the great commercial and industrial advance of his section than in the advance upon Richmond. A greatly reduced army, a greatly contracted area from which to draw men and supplies, divided civil and military counsels, a skeptical and mummering people, a countryside full of deserters and skulkers,[61] preparation in the States for local defense regardless of Richmond plans, and two powerful and well generaled Union armies—the one north of the Rapidan, the other at Chattanooga—ready at the dawn of spring to drive toward a common meeting ground, this was the panorama of menace before those who looked for a hopeful sign as the sun rose upon a new year.

[60] O. R. ser. IV, vol. II, 726; vol. III, 1187; Stephenson, *The Day of the Confederacy*, 94-98.

[61] General B. H. Hill said that more than half the men and officers of General Bragg's army were absent from duty, and that the battle of Chattanooga was lost because of it. Jacksonville *Republican*, December 19th. The *Republican* said that Lee's army was weakened almost as much from the same cause, and that if he lost a battle it would be because officers and privates were "railroad passengers, hotel guests, and lady gallants instead of being soldiers." See also the *Sun*, December 5th and 22d (quoting the Richmond press).

# CHAPTER XI

THE inherent character of the Confederate political system made unity of purpose and coördination of effort during the war impossible. Friction between the Confederate Government, with full constitutional power to raise armies and to wage war, and the States, severally capacitated by the possession of sovereign power not only to judge the acts of the Confederate Government but to redress themselves against any apprehended encroachment, was inevitable. Some leaders were unable to see the logic of surrendering State sovereignty to the Confederate Government as a means of establishing it against the Federal Government. The character and extent of the conflicts would be determined, of course, by the temperament and attitude of mind of those sponsoring the governments, and of influential citizens everywhere. To the extent that men failed to see and to reconcile themselves to the inexorable demands of war, just so far would they be unable to make the compromise of political prepossessions, official prerogatives, personal pride, and State autonomy that was necessary to avoid working at cross purposes.

The first year of the war demonstrated the imprac-

[1] The South is divided into three sections for the purpose of this investigation: the lower South, including Alabama, Florida, Mississippi, Louisiana, Texas, and Arkansas; Georgia and North Carolina; and the upper South, South Carolina and Virginia.

ticability of raising and equipping armies through the instrumentality of the States, each as sovereign as the other, and therefore acting in its own way. It also demonstrated the supersensitiveness of some of the governors concerning the rights of the States, and their high regard for their own prerogatives. They insisted on furnishing troops on their own conditions; protested against "independent acceptances" of troops; and remonstrated vigorously when there was any prospect of encroachment upon their power to officer the State troops.[2]

The conflict with State authorities during the first year of the war was a mere tempest in a teapot compared with the storm of opposition produced in some of the States by the conscription act. This act seemed to many of the States'-rightists an unbearable aggression upon the sovereign powers of the States. It seemed all the more monstrous because they had been made apprehensive of some such wanton manifestation of despotism; the stage had been set by the flaming diatribes of such papers as the *Examiner* and *Mercury* for the appearance of a despot, who loved secrecy, mystery, and power, and whose "imperious conceit seemed to swallow up every other idea in his mind." The degree of their opposition was determined by the extent to which they were ridden by political predilections, by personal temperament, and by personal feeling toward President Davis. Already he had been dubbed "our Moses" by some, a "despot" and "an incubus to the cause," by others.

[2] President Davis' assurance to Congress, March 28, 1862, that a harmonious and cordial relationship existed with the governors was more generous and tactful than true. An examination of the Official Records, ser. IV, vol. I, and ser. I, vols. LI and LII, Part II, will convince one that there had been considerable friction between the War Department and the governors.

Strange as it may seem, E. A. Pollard, States'-rightist *par excellence* and Typhon of Southern journalism, and R. B. Rhett, the powerful apostle of State sovereignty and secession, supported the conscription policy, and each thought enough of it to claim credit for having originated it. Each one believing he was responsible for the idea had a keen interest in its success, and became a merciless critic of all shortcomings in the administration of it. They looked with impatience and disdain upon Governor Brown's stubborn and tawdry opposition. Their papers spoke for the large mass of people who regarded conscription constitutional, or who were practical enough to see the danger of agitating against it when universal coöperation was imperative.

Considerations of expediency did not deter Governor Brown from ventilating his political obsessions, and his scrupulous regard for State sovereignty and for the powers of his office. His implacable spirit would not allow him to keep quiet while his State was being stripped of its "constitutional military powers" and he was being reduced to the status of a puppet, "suspended upon the stage to amuse the women and children and a few non-combatant diseased men left by the operation of the conscript act." Through the spring and summer he boldly engaged the President in a long-drawn and rancorous pen duel, which finally resolved itself into a mere sparring over the meaning of words. This extraordinary correspondence made its way into the dailies and into pamphlet form, and the pamphlets were hawked, Pollard said disdainfully, in every city in the Confederacy.[3]

[3] Governor Brown's former experience as judge of the Blue Ridge circuit probably gave him confidence in his opinion as to the constitutionality of the conscription act.

The act, Governor Brown said, was "a bold and dangerous usurpation by Congress of the reserved rights of the States and a rapid stride toward military despotism." Granting that conscription was necessary, but he was positive it was not, since Georgia had always furnished promptly all and more men than the President had asked for, he was not at all sure that States' rights and States' sovereignty "must yield for a time to the higher law of necessity." He expressed a willingness, "as an individual," to assist the President "in the discharge of the laborious and responsible duties assigned" him, but he could not "consent to commit the State to a policy" which was in his "judgment subversive of her sovereignty and at war with all the principles for the support of which Georgia entered into the revolution." He refused to have anything to do with the enforcement of the law and threatened to use the armed forces of the State to protect its civil and military officers.[4]

The Governor laid aside his pen in the summer because, as he wrote Vice-President Stephens, no other governor had raised any objections to conscription and he feared that he "might be considered by good and true men in and out of Congress too refractory for the times."[5] He allowed the conscription of all persons except his military and civil officers, "rather than that Georgia's fidelity to the cause should be questioned" or the enemy should be comforted by the development of internal strife in the Confederacy.[6] Thus through considerations of expediency he yielded a grudging toleration to the conscription act and retreated before the jeers and

[4] O. R. ser. IV, vol. I, 1082, 1116, 1133, 1156.

[5] *Toombs, Stephens, Cobb Correspondence*, Amer. Hist. Ass. Report, 1911, vol. II, 605.

[6] O. R. ser. IV, vol. II, 128.

taunts of the hostile press in his State. But this strong-willed martinet of State sovereignty never surrendered in mind or soul. He wrote the Secretary of War in August of 1863 that his views of conscription had undergone no change, and he never wavered from his purpose not to lend it the aid of his industry and personal influence.[7] This powerful challenge to the legality of conscription laid the basis for serious conflicts in Georgia.

The other governors either accepted the constitutionality of conscription or acquiesced in it without debate, in the interest of the public cause. It was the opinion of Governor Letcher of Virginia that the conscription act was unconstitutional, but, on account of the unusual circumstances at the time of the passage of the act, he forebore to debate it. "Harmony, unity, and conciliation are indispensable now," he said, and he urged the people to respond cheerfully to the law. Governor Milton of Florida said the constitutionality of the act was a judicial question; and in his message to the legislature in December he pleaded with patriotic fervor the necessity of coöperating with the Confederate Government.[8] Governor Clark of North Carolina desired "to carry out the conscription act fairly and to the fullest extent of the wants of the country." Governor Lubbock of Texas believed the act was constitutional and offered the help of the State officers in enforcing it; while Governor Pettus of Mississippi asked the Secretary of War for "all the information necessary to put the [law] in full operation as soon as possible," and pledged to the President every man in the State.[9]

[7] O. R. ser. IV, vol. II, 753.
[8] The *Confederacy*, December 6, 1862.
[9] The *Republican*, March 14, 1863. O. R. ser. IV, vol. I, 1091, 1093.

Since the original conscription act did not contain an exemption clause, the governors became deeply concerned about the security of their governments. Governor Brown, always reconnoitering for evidence of encroachments from Richmond, was quick to call the President's attention to the fact that a literal enforcement of the law would disorganize, if not annihilate, the State governments. He claimed the exemption of all State civil officers from himself down to tax collectors and receivers; and his staff officers and the field officers of the militia. These, he said, he would protect, if necessary, with all the "remaining military force of the State." [10] The Governor was wasting ammunition, for while he was writing his letter Congress passed an exemption act for the protection of the State governments.[11] This act, apparently, was acceptable to all of the governors, except Brown; he was displeased with it because it did not specifically provide for the exemption of his militia officers, and because it did not recognize other classes of persons whom he thought should be exempted.

Apparently all of the governors, except Brown, showed a willingness to aid the processes of conscription, but there was a misunderstanding concerning the way Congress intended that the governors should coöperate. The conscription act was silent on this point and the governors assumed that they would be allowed to superintend the activities of their officers in the conscription service. Some of them promptly undertook to enroll all conscripts with a view to turning over a complete list

[10] O. R. ser. IV, vol. I, 1083.

[11] The Administration recognized the fact from the beginning that by implied limitation the war powers of the Government could not be so exercised as to destroy the State governments by conscripting the officers necessary to their existence.

to the Confederate authorities. For example, Governor Pickens of South Carolina, set his enrolling officers to work and promised to have a complete list of conscripts by June 15th.[12] Governor Shorter of Alabama elaborated a plan by which he proposed to dispatch the business of conscription and laid it before the War Office June 24th, only to be sidetracked with the thanks of the Secretary for his proffered assistance, the assurance that it would be gladly accepted wherever the law permitted, and a pledge to bespeak to Major Swanson "the assistance of the Governor", when the Major should have formulated and reported his plans.[13] Shorter said with evident piquancy a few months later, when requested to use the State officers to enforce the law in Randolph County where the Confederate officers had stirred up a hornet's nest of opposition, that since conscription had been "discharged and directed solely by the Confederate officers" he questioned the "policy of calling in State officers" to enforce the law at that late hour and under such adverse circumstances.[14] Governor Clark and Major Mallett had a disagreement concerning the use of State officers.[15]

The high hopes of some of the governors that they would be permitted to direct conscription within their States were exploded before conscription was many months old. Disappointed though they were, they yielded generally with good grace and allowed such militia officers as they had for enrolling purposes to be used by the Confederate authorities. In August, 1862, the Secretary of War recommended that the law requiring the use of the State enrolling officers should be repealed

[12] O. R. ser. IV, vol. I, 1140, 1141, 1144, 1153; vol. II, 74.
[13] *Ibid.*, I., 1170.
[14] *Ibid.*, II, 87.
[15] *Ibid.*, 68.

because the, military system in many of the States had fallen into fragments and there were either no enrolling officers or none that could be depended upon.[16]

Though perhaps not understood at the time, this little skirmish between the governors and the Administration was premonitory of many greater conflicts that inhered in the Confederate political system.  Conscription, aided by the mysterious secretiveness of the Administration and the officious conduct of officers, threw many bones of contention into the field of disputed jurisdiction.  The enervating effects of the long-drawn struggle, the scarcity and high cost of the necessities of life, the impressment system, the tightening of the reins of authority to check the forces of disintegration, and the harrying forays of the enemy were so many plagues that vexed the souls of the people, and accentuated and enlivened the natural points of friction between the military system of the Confederacy and the State governments.  It became an easy matter for a designing executive or a disgruntled political leader to focus the currents of discontent upon conscription, which was depicted as the chief power-reaping agency operated by the "janizaries" of the "Monarch" at Richmond.

The conflicts in the lower South were not nearly so frequent and not generally so intense as those in Georgia and North Carolina.  Governor Milton of Florida set a fine example for all.  It was his policy, and his fine spirit was reflected in the Legislature, not to compromise the "honor and dignity of the State in her obligations to her sister States for the maintenance of the war" by opposing the Confederate authorities.  Even at the critical period of the war, when other governors round about were

[16] O. R. ser. IV, vol. II, 44.

adopting desperate means, he counseled a faithful support of the Confederate Government as the only means of preserving the sacred rights of the people. "It is best therefore," he wrote Governor Brown, "where it can be honorably done, to avoid all conflicts and competition between the State and Confederate authorities for political power" during the war, and went on to assure him that after the war "the rights of the States and the constitutional powers of the Confederate Government [would] be adjusted by an intelligent, brave, and free people." [17]  The wisdom of this advice did not sink very deeply into the mind of Georgia's belligerent governor, but it was very effective ballast for Floridians during the perilous hours of the war, and accounts in no small degree for Florida's enviable war record.

There were other reasons for the pacific attitude of the governors in this section in the early years of the war: (1) there was relative political sterility; (2) the great pioneer of State sovereignty pursued a sane course, and the fact that the President came from this section probably inclined leaders to be charitable; (3) early in the war this region became sort of "no man's land," the contending armies surged back and forth in it and there was little opportunity for the development of a vigorous political life; [18] and (4) the propinquity of war perils caused the leaders to be more anxious about coöperating with the Confederate authorities in beating back the enemy than about the maintenance of every detail of State sovereignty by working, if need be, at cross pur-

[17] O. R. ser. IV, vol. III, 304.

[18] As Professor Stephenson has said, after "the loss of New Orleans, one thing with another operated to confine the area of full political life to Virginia and her three neighbors to the South." *The Day of the Confederacy*, 74.

poses with those authorities. At least this was the case as long as there was any hope of material aid from Richmond.

But things had changed by the end of 1863. Public leaders had become grim, irritable, and critical under the awful strain of war; they were being forced by the sheer momentum of events into a policy of resistance to Confederate authority. The fortunes of war had given their States a position of semi-isolation; these States were "neither in nor out of the Confederacy," as Professor Stephenson happily puts it.[19] In the lower South the States east of the Mississippi were completely separated from those west of it, and the Confederate authorities had made up their minds to fight it out along the Virginia line. That part of the lower South that lay east of the Mississippi was to occupy the position of basis of supply to the major field of operation. But there was an importunate demand for every available man in this unhappy region to resist the frequent incursions of the enemy, and to protect society from the predatory mobs that had begun to emerge from their dens in the swamps and mountain fastnesses. The instinct of self-preservation became stronger than the fidelity to the Richmond plan of strategy, and the hitherto pacific governors began to compete with the President for the man power of their States. This drew the President into an administrative duel with the State authorities in this section over conscription,—a duel with which he was already painfully familiar in Georgia and North Carolina.

The first conflict of note between State and Confederate authority in the lower South grew out of the sus-

[19] Stephenson, 114.

pension of the writ of habeas corpus.[20] The habeas corpus act had expired by 1863 but some of the military officers continued to treat civil authorities as if it were still in force. It took several orders from the War Department to quash the practice, because of the acute need for men and the officers' contempt for the mischievous attitude of the local courts. Some sharp conflicts between arbitrary enrolling officers and local civil officers evolved. For example, the *Southern Advertiser* records the case of one Rhodes in Alabama who was enrolled, although he had by the exercise of his wits induced a local court to exempt him. The court ordered the Colonel in command of the local rendezvous arrested for his impudence, but to no good purpose, for the soldiers protected their Colonel against the sheriff. The judge who had issued the warrant of arrest became belligerent over this new outrage, but was seized by the soldiers for his temerity. Some afterthought led the Colonel to release him and appeal the case to the supreme court.[21] Probate Judge Curtis of Winston County, Alabama, was arrested by a squad of cavalry and murdered while being taken to jail at Jasper; and Probate Judge Fitzpatrick was arrested by an enrolling officer.[22] Governor Shorter

[20] It is worth noting that there was no conflict over the enrollment of militia officers in this section until well toward the end of the war. Some of these States did not allow their militia officers to claim exemption, even after Governor Brown had bombarded the War Department with a few menacing notes and extracted from it the policy of exempting militia officers. In December of 1862 the Alabama legislature made all of the militia officers liable to conscription; and Governor Milton said, in an open letter August 12th, that nearly all of the militia officers of Florida had volunteered as privates and he saw no good reason why the others should not. He warned those who had not volunteered to do so before they were "liable to be made a conscript." O. R. ser. IV, vol. II, 49, 212.

[21] Cited in Stephenson, 117-18.

[22] O. R. ser. I, vol. LII, 614; The *Sun,* November 4, 1863.

remonstrated against such military tyranny and the Government apologized and ordered the conscription officers to respect the decrees of civil authority.[23]

The effort in the early part of 1863 to revive the habeas corpus act as a means of enforcing conscription, and other war measures, produced a war dance among the more impetuous of the States'-rights men. There was nothing new in the proposal to resurrect the act of suspension, but things had happened that gave it a new significance. The war burdens had rubbed the patience of many persons to the quick, and the various desperate war expedients adopted gave much strength to the arguments of the hostile press that a despot with an overweening ambition was being elevated at Richmond by the patience and pariotism of the people. There was much alarm throughout the South. If the writ were to be suspended again, as it was to be in 1864, for the purpose of facilitating conscription, it would put the States of the lower South at a great disadvantage in the contest for their man power.

The inability of the Government to protect the States against local invasions led the President to call upon the States in the summer of 1863 to organize local defense troops to serve for six months. It was expected that these troops would be raised out of the fragments left by conscription,[24] but conscripts from the outset passed quietly into the ranks of the local defense. Leaders in the lower South were coming to the Brown and Vance

[23] General G. J. Pillow, who was in charge of conscription in Alabama, Mississippi, and Tennessee, was moved at last to order his enrolling officers "to give implicit obedience to the inferior courts"; if their decisions seemed improper the officers were instructed to appeal to the higher courts.

[24] O. R. ser. IV, vol. II, 581,

viewpoint, namely, that their first problem and duty, owing to the impotency of the Richmond authorities to furnish their States adequate protection, was to prepare for self-protection. Some of the legislatures passed acts claiming all able-bodied men not actually in Confederate service, and the governors proceeded promptly to execute the acts.[25] All this was done without opposition from Richmond, and before the end of the year many skulking conscripts had gone into the home service, especially in the "bomb-proof" units,—the companies stationed away from the theater of real action. The cavalry units were especially popular, some of which sprang up spontaneously and operated without authority from any source.

These emergency troops proved to be a thorn in the flesh of the Government in 1864. The period for which they were mustered into Confederate service expired January 31st, but the governors retained them as State troops. They contained, besides derelict conscripts, many men and boys who were made liable to service by the new conscription act, and others of the latter classes rushed into them before the promulgation of the act. It will be recalled [26] that this act provided for junior and senior reserves, thereby setting up a permanent system of local defense troops under Confederate authority. Thus there were two kinds of State defense troops: the State troops, containing derelict conscripts and a large number of reservists; [27] and the Confederate reserves, composed of boys of 17 and men of 45 to 50 years. If

[25] O. R. ser. I, vol. XXXIV, Pt. II, 1095; ser. IV, vol. II, 926; III, 8, 172, 322, 463.

[26] Page 308 below.

[27] The reservists were readily accepted in the State troops on the assumption that it was immaterial who enrolled and organized them so long as they were available to the Confederate commanders.

the Confederate system prevailed the governors would have to surrender those in the State organizations who were subject to the conscription act. When the "generals of reserves," appointed to the States, proceeded to enroll the reservists in the State troops and the conscript officers to extract the derelict conscripts strenuous opposition was encountered.

The governors thought that the State troops were "troops of war" and as such could not be taken from the States by conscription. The War Department took the view that the troops were simply militia, since they were not in active, permanent service.[28] The governors were not satisfied with this interpretation, but if they must give up the troops, they demanded the right of presenting them as organized. Some of them requested that since the reservists would be retained in the State for local defense they should at least be allowed to hold some of the companies as organized militia, with the understanding that they would always be sent to any locality upon the request of the general in charge. The Secretary of War courteously declined the request on the ground that he did not have legal authority to grant it, at the same time expressing an unfeigned desire "to cordially coöperate with the Governors of the States in the great struggle." The governors did not yield all of the disputed ground. Superintendent Preston complained in June that "these claims by local authorities for troops, . . . are having the effect of entirely defeating the law, in relation to the reserve forces." If the governors persisted in their course, he said, the contemplated effect of the act of February 17th would be neutralized.[29] The

[28] O. R. ser. IV, vol. III, 173, 256.
[29] *Ibid.*, 464.

actual character of the controversy can best be understood by following the course of it in the respective States.

The enrolling officers in Alabama greatly irritated Governor Watts by conscripting his militia organizations, officers along with privates. The legislature shared the Governor's wrath. It imposed a fine of $1000 to $6000 and imprisonment for six months to two years upon conscript officers who forced exempts into service; and reversed its former position with regard to militia officers by declaring them no longer subject to Confederate conscription.[30]

Governor Watts would not entertain for a moment the plan of the Government to disband the troops and conscript the young men into the reserve forces according to the law. He wrote the President that he would "regard such action as a great calamity." Moreover, he regarded the State troops as "troops of war," and therefore he had the legal right to direct the disposition of them. He thought that faith should be kept with the young men by allowing them to be received as organized.[31] A few weeks later he warned Secretary Seddon that the enrolling officers were "harassing these men and requiring them to be enrolled and sent to camp." "I have resisted by remonstrance," he said, "the action of the enrolling officers, and I may feel myself justified in going farther unless some stop is put to the matter by you." [32]

[30] Acts December 12th and 13th, Fleming, *Civil War and Reconstruction in Alabama*, 98.

[31] O. R. ser. IV, vol. III, 323.

[32] *Ibid.*, 463. He thought it was "egregious folly" to take these men from the counties where they had been organized, except when their services were actually needed. They should be allowed to stay at their

Seddon ignored this warning and four days later the Governor hurled the following ultimatum at him: "Unless you order the commandant of conscripts to stop interfering with such companies there will be a conflict between the Confederate General and State authorities." [33] This drew a capitulation from Richmond, or a swift reply that one had been made a few days earlier. The Secretary informed the Governor that a letter had been addressed to him sometime before, notifying him that it was the President's opinion that "in this case as stated it would seem proper to receive the companies as organized either in the reserve or active force." [34] Thus Governor Watts preserved the units that had been organized under his authority and kept them in their respective counties, producing food supplies when they were not called out by the Confederate authorities to drive the enemy from their borders. Perhaps the Governor's obstinacy with regard to his troops was due to the fact that their real character was a technical constitutional question, and he felt, owing to his legal training and experience, that he was about as well prepared to interpret the constitution as were the President and his Cabinet.

In Mississippi there was similar confusion and conflict. Many State troops had been organized at the request of the Confederate commanders, and men of any age were allowed to volunteer in them. Various "floating companies" of cavalry, existing without State or Confederate authority, were reported. General Pil-

work, drilling enough to keep them in training and ready to respond to a moment's call.

[33] O. R. ser. IV, vol. III, 466.

[34] *Ibid.*, 323, 472.

low wrote Secretary Seddon in August, 1863, that he was embarrassed by numerous organizations of cavalry, operating under orders from the Governor and composed mainly of men liable to conscript duty. He said they enrolled in these units to avoid conscription and were sustained by their officers in their opposition to entering the Confederate service. Governor Pettus proposed to keep these organizations intact as mobile State troops, as did Governor Watts, to be sent at any moment to meet emergencies when requisitioned by the Confederate authorities. General Pillow recommended that the Governor's proposal be accepted, since it would be difficult to disband the troops and sift out the conscripts, and much discontent would be produced. His recommendation was not approved, however, and he proceeded to conscript those who were liable, at the same time warning the Governor of the danger of conflict if he persisted in his course. The Governor replied in a pacific manner, assuring the General that no conscripts would be enrolled and indulging the hope that the conscript officers would reciprocate the courtesy by ceasing to detail the exempts to specific duties so as to place them beyond the State military laws.

The conflict became more intense during the incumbency of the new Governor, Charles Clark. Officers under color of authority from him raised new corps and permitted conscripts to volunteer in them. In January, 1864, General Chalmers served notice on him that no more conscripts would be permitted to enlist under the State banners, at the same time expressing the hope that no "misunderstanding or bad feeling" might grow out of this position which the law compelled him to take. Governor Clark requested an opinion from the Secretary of War concerning the effect of the Conscription Act of February 17, 1864, on the State organizations, but he refused to accept it when he discovered that the Secretary regarded them as militia, pure and simple. He had "no doubt of [his] right to them as troops of War of the States," and he informed General Brandon that he would "secure volunteers for six months without regard to age, if mustered into service previous to enrollment or conscription." [35]    General Brandon reported that the Governor's position "virtually arrested the volunteer enrollment of the reserves and the conscription of men of the military age. All are rushing into the State organization greatly to the detriment of the service." The Secretary of War instructed him to proceed to the execution of the law, but to do it in such a way as to be least offensive. He disliked to have a conflict with the State authorities but he said he was bound to enforce the conscription acts, which were no less binding on State authorities than upon those of the Confederacy.

The Governor and the General came to daggers' points. To avoid the worst the former proposed to submit the question to the State supreme court. The War Department finally agreed to accept the decision of the court in the case proposed, but would not pledge itself to accept it as a basis of future action. The case was decided against the Governor early in 1865 and he forthwith offered to turn over the troops as organized to the Government. [36] The episode ended by the Depart-

[35] O. R. ser. IV, vol. III, 710. The Governor was probably encouraged by General Taylor's statement to him that it made no difference who mustered the forces so long as they were placed under the command of the general of the department (740).

[36] This was a clever move. It meant that since the reservists among the troops would be retained for local defense, those between eighteen

ment's yielding to the Governor's request that the troops be mustered for Confederate pay, after which they were temporarily organized into companies and held for the emergency of the moment.

Governor Clark had his way till the war was so nearly over that it made little difference how the troops were disposed of. The controversy added, of course, much to the confusion and turmoil of the time, and according to contemporary evidence greatly impaired the strength of Mississippi in the critical period of the war. It is notable that General Brandon gave Governor Clark credit for having been "actuated by patriotic motives and an overweening solicitude for the defense of the State . . . and not from a factious spirit of opposition." This was doubtless true; one would hardly expect a maimed Confederate general to oppose the Government through a spirit of recalcitrancy. The same thing might have been said about Governor Watts, perhaps, since he had served as soldier and Confederate Attorney-General. It is not likely that these men, who had had an opportunity to see the needs and problems of those who were directing the destinies of the war, were impelled in their opposition by any purpose other than the redemption of their States from their sad plights.[37]

The isolated and remote Texas also had a controversy with the Confederate Government over conscription.[38]

and forty-five who were a part of the organizations would be kept for State defense also.

[37] For the whole story, see O. R. ser. IV, vol. II, 742, 759, 761, 925; III, 8, 172, 710, 740, 821, 824, 902-4, 1162; ser. I, vol. XXXII, Pt. II, 601; XXXIX, Pt. III, 893.

[38] Governor Rector of Arkansas assumed a belligerent attitude in the spring of 1862, going so far as to ignore the conscription act and to threaten to withdraw Arkansas from the Confederacy (p. 171 above). The records are very incomplete as to Arkansas.

After the fall of Vicksburg, Texas was completely separated from the States east of the Mississippi and was forced to rely on the resources of the trans-Mississippi Department, so called, for self-preservation. But by 1864 her sister States in this department had been virtually eliminated, and large areas of them were going through the preliminary stage of reconstruction. With enemy bases on all sides from which quick slashing expeditions could be sent out, and without a ray of hope for help from the theater of war beyond the Mississippi, there was a painful feeling of insecurity. Like Alabama and Mississippi, her companions in sorrow, Texas organized troops for self-defense, and like them was reluctant, too, to give up her troops to be ordered here and there by Confederate commanders to meet the military requirements of the department as a whole.

The dangers that confronted Texas at the end of 1863 led the legislature and the new Governor, Pendleton Murrah, to veer off from former Governor Lubbock's admirable policy of coöperation. It had been sort of a slogan with Governor Lubbock that each State must give a "cordial and determined support to the Government." [39]  An act of the legislature made it incumbent upon Governor Murrah to put in the State troops all able-bodied men who were not actually in the Confederate service or were not exempted by State law. The result was that large numbers of derelict conscripts were incorporated. General J. B. Magruder said that thousands of conscripts were enrolled and detailed by the Governor to such useless duties as hauling cotton, etc.[40]

[39] In March of 1863 he delivered a powerful message to the legislature on the need of State coöperation "in all things tending to a proper and vigorous execution of the war." The *Republican*, March 14, 1863.

[40] O. R. ser. I, vol. XXXIV, Pt. III, 726.

General Magruder, whose task it was to organize the reserves under the conscription act of February, 1864, corresponded with Governor Murrah for several weeks concerning the disposition of the conscripts and reservists in the State troops. Like most of the governors, Murrah tried to preserve the State organizations intact, and when he saw this was impossible attempted to turn them over to the Confederacy as organized. Magruder refused to accept them except as provided by law and orders, and warned the Governor of the "dangerous and yawning chasm created by the efforts to impede the execution of the conscript law." To the State Adjutant General he wrote: "If the Governor's chasm cannot be bridged I will leap it," and if he insisted upon the "extreme State-rights construction of the laws of Congress, as inopportune as it is wrong, he must take the consequences." The firm stand of Generals Smith and Magruder forced Governor Murrah to capitulate. To General Magruder he wrote: "As you have declined receiving the State troops as State troops, I shall be forced, in view of the dangers surrounding the State and country, to coöperate with you in organizing them under the recent law of Congress." Manifestly, he acted under duress and with a heavy heart; but likely, as General Magruder said, his reluctance was due to the drastic laws enacted by the Legislature. Thanks to military methods, the controversy lasted only a few weeks.[41]

Such evidence as is available indicates that there was more or less conflict with the Louisiana authorities, and that it developed along the usual lines. Governors

[41] Magruder gave him credit for having been prompted by "the loftiest patriotism." See O. R. ser. I, vol. XLI, Pt. IV, 1006; LIII, 926; XXXIV, Pt. III, 726, 735, 739, 747, 786.

Moore and Allen complained of the neglect of the State, and the latter tried to keep in the "Home Guard" boys and men who were made liable to service as reservists by the act of February 17, 1864. Early in the preceding year the legislature passed a militia act which conflicted with the Confederate law. These difficulties seem to have been promptly disposed of by General Smith, with the aid of the President's conciliatory letters.[42]

The dispatch with which the Texas embroglio was smothered contrasted sharply with the months of bandying opinions, interpretations, and menacing innuendoes between the Governors of Mississippi and Alabama and the War Department. Perhaps Governor Watts' audacity was inspired in part by the fact that he had learned while a member of the President's official family that there was some regard there for civil authority and for State rights scruples.

The exemption of State officers was another bone of contention between the Government and the State authorities in the Gulf States. The indispensability of exempting State officers essential to the successful operation of the State governments was recognized at the outset, but there was no definite policy determined upon. The first exemption act provided that all civil officers of the States, not required to serve in the militia, should be exempt from service in the Confederate armies. This act was amended May 1, 1863, so as to include other State officers whom the governor would claim to have exempted for the proper administration of the laws, provided that such exemptions should cease at the end of the next regular session of the legislature unless it exempted them by law. Finally, the act of February 17, 1864,

[42] O. R. ser. I, vol. LIII, 819, 843, 982, 985, 986.

provided for the exemption of all State officers whom the governors would certify to be necessary for the proper administration of their governments.[43]

It was pointed out in a preceding chapter [44] that practically all of the governors abused the trust confided to them. They certified many petty officers whose functions were not indispensable; indeed, they were little more than relics of the elaborate administrative mechanism of former State governments. Some of the Governors went so far as to claim that persons in the service who were elected to office should be discharged, and there are some cases recorded where the courts ordered the release of such persons. Congress conceded the point so far as members of Congress and of the legislatures, judges of the supreme courts, district attorneys, clerks of the courts of record, sheriffs, ordinaries, judges of probate, one tax collector, and a parish recorder, were concerned.[45] The governors then claimed that other local officers, who were elected subsequent to the passage of the act of February 17, 1864, and before they had been notified to report for duty, were entitled to exemption. The Government, however, maintained that all persons made liable by the act were enrolled by it.

These dissentient opinions formed the basis of conflict. The governors' solicitude for the petty officers of the State, many of whom were slackers, and their failure to furnish a list of all certified officers as a security against fraud, disgusted the enrolling officers and some of them developed the habit of not implicitly following their instructions regarding local State officers.

[43] See O. R. ser. IV, vol. II, 161, 553; III, 179, for these acts.
[44] Pages 122-123 above.
[45] Act of April 2, 1863, O. R. ser. IV, vol. II, 914.

From Texas came the complaint that minor offices were being sought by "able-bodied men liable to conscription for the sole purpose of screening them from duty." [46]  Governor Clark of Mississippi certified freely, and when any of the petty officers were conscribed he protested vigorously.  To the Secretary of War he wired: "Justices of peace and other civil officers declared by my proclamation exempt have been forced into service.  I respectfully demand your order . . . for their discharge."  The Secretary replied that officers certified by him would be exempted, but suggested that the Governor would probably have less trouble if he would give a special certificate in each case instead of certifying officers by a blanket proclamation.[47]  There is no record of the Governor's entertaining the suggestion.  The conscript officers continued to enroll the petty officers and he recommended action to the legislature.  The legislature protested but finally agreed to claim only those civil officers "named in the constitution," and "necessary to the preservation of the American form of government." [48]

The sharpest conflict over the conscription of petty civil officers was in Alabama.  Governor Watts got on the war-path.  He wrote General Withers, commander of reserves, that some of his officers were enrolling State officers who were not only certified by him but also by Colonel Lockhart, commandant of conscripts.  This sort of thing could not continue, he asserted, "without a conflict between the Confederate and State authorities.  I shall be compelled to protect my State officers with all

[46] O. R. ser. I, vol. XXVI, Pt. II, 494.
[47] O. R. ser. IV, vol. III, 446, 450.
[48] *Pol. Sci. Qr.,* 16:228.

the forces of the State at my command." General Withers expressed a desire "to perpetuate the most frank and cordial coöperation" with the Governor, and suggested that if he had the list of certified officers which was promised it would help to avoid future trouble. He advised the Governor that he should address himself to the Confederate Government concerning mooted questions of authority.

Governor Watts apparently acted on the General's suggestion, only he was in no mood to debate. He sent the Secretary of War a hot ultimatum. "Unless you interfere," he warned, "there will be a conflict between the Confederate and State authorities. Officers of the State cannot be conscribed without the consent of the State. I learn that your enrolling officers have instructions to enroll officers of the State who have been elected since the 17th of February, 1864. I deny such right and will resist it with all the forces of the State. The police officers of Selma have been enrolled by force. These officers are indispensable to the administration of the State government." The Secretary wired promptly: "Officers of the State of Alabama, certified by you to be necessary to State administration, are exempt. Officers of police of Selma are, I suppose, not considered State officers. Cannot the courts decide? I only wish to enforce the laws, and deprecate conflict with the authorities of the State." The agitation continued and the question was boiled down to the naked proposition of whether the claim of the State for civil service was paramount to the claim of the Confederate government for military service. The Secretary of War said this was unmistakably a judicial question and, as such, was not a proper subject for protracted debate between the executives of the Confederate and State governments. He thought that any difference of opinion between the Government and Governor Watts concerning it "scarcely entitled him to take up arms, or to menace with resistance by force the administration of the Department."

Governor Watts' position was a curious one for a constitutional lawyer. Probably he thought that an attorney who had succeeded in splitting legal knots for the President was able to do the same for the Governor; and that he had no reason to defer to the legal opinion of a War Secretary, and little to learn of the fundamentals of the Confederate constitution from the opinion of a State judge.[49]

Governor Milton exhibited his usual moderation. He said that, although it might be his duty to issue commissions to the "many persons" then in the Confederate service who had been elected to inferior offices, he would not do so unless the attorney general ruled that it was his legal duty. He did not deem them necessary to the administration of the State government.[50]

Conflicts in all of the Gulf States, except Florida, between the Confederate and State governments in 1863 and 1864, over the conscription of State officers and the maintenance of State troops, greatly embarrassed the Government and thwarted some of its plans. It produced, besides, rancorous feelings and facilitated the general dissipation and crash of military strength that characterized this infelicitous section in the closing scenes of the war. Governor Milton's encomium of the President and his Cabinet was as a strange soliloquy in

[49] The records of this controversy can be found in O. R. ser. IV, vol. III, 817, 818, 820, 821, 849.
[50] O. R. ser. IV, vol. II, 880.

a wilderness of doubt and misgiving. He was happy to report to the legislature that "the President of the Confederate States and the distinguished gentlemen, the heads of the different departments who compose his Cabinet have consistently acknowledged the right of the States whenever their attention has been invited to interference with them. Nevertheless, in a few instances insurmountable obstacles have prevented a compliance with applications, the justice and propriety of which were not disputed." [51]  This was a unique bit of gubernatorial charity in the lower South at that time.[52]

[51] O. R. ser. IV, vol. II, 973.

[52] Governor Lubbock of Texas said early in 1863, before the critical period was reached, that he had been able to work in harmony with the Government. The *Republican*, March 14, 1863.

# CHAPTER XII

## CONFEDERATE VERSUS STATE AUTHORITY IN GEORGIA AND NORTH CAROLINA

In Georgia and North Carolina conflicts were most frequent and lively.[1] Governors Brown and Vance pushed forward in defense of State rights when other governors hesitated because of the danger of internal discord. Arguments and persuasions of the President for coöperation in the interest of the common good, and for the vindication of the Confederate system of government, that were sufficient to unhorse other governors usually made little or no impression on these strongheaded executives.

We have already encountered Governor Brown as an enemy of conscription and a lecturer to the President upon States' rights in the summer of 1862. The passage of the second conscription act provoked him to measure pens with the President again, and he was more certain of his ground than ever because of a recent decision of Judge Harris, of the superior court of Georgia, against conscription. The prospect of Georgia's being stripped of her man power at a moment when it seemed that the Emancipation Proclamation might produce servile insurrections alarmed him. He served notice on the President

---

[1] These States are considered together because of the similar and unusual conditions that obtained in them.

that his duty impelled him to oppose the enrollment of conscripts under the second conscription act until the State legislature convened. "No act of the Government of the United States," he said, "prior to the secession of Georgia struck a blow at constitutional liberty so fell as has been stricken by the conscription act. The people of this State had ample cause, however, to justify their separation from the old Government." The brilliant successes of the Confederate armies he said had invalidated the plea of necessity advanced in the preceding spring; hence, the President should call upon the States for troops, and he might "have them as volunteers much more rapidly" than his officers could "drag conscripts like slaves in chains to camps of instruction." He warned the President that Georgians, whose fathers opposed Federal encroachments under Jackson, Troup, and Gilmer, would "refuse to yield their sovereignty to usurpation and would require the Government, which is the common agent of all the States, to move within the sphere assigned it by the Constitution." [2]

The President ignored this threatening letter. A month later, however, he addressed a circular letter to the governors, appealing to them to coöperate with the War Department in the discharge of its duties and assuring them of his "unfaltering reliance on their patriotism and devotion" to the cause. Colonel William M. Browne was dispatched to deliver in person this letter to Governor Brown, and to represent to him the grave necessity of filling the decimated ranks of the Georgia regiments. He was to express to the Governor the President's hope "that the decision of the supreme court of Georgia," which had just been rendered, might "be

[2] O. R. ser. IV, vol. II, 128.

regarded as conclusive of the constitutional question presented," and to assure him that the President would be highly pleased to have his unstinted aid at that critical moment.[3]

This conference did not affect the Governor's frame of mind. He submitted his proposition for obstructing the conscription laws to the legislature, and made a strong bid for its endorsement. If the legislature did not accept his recommendation he would have to advise "the people of Camden and the ladies of St. Mary's that while the State collects taxes, and requires them to bear other public burdens, she withdraws her protection from, and leaves them to the mercy of negro invaders, who may insult and plunder them at pleasure."[4]  A lively debate ensued. Linton Stephens, the Governor's right bower, under the stimulus of a strong backing and a strong cause, rose, and pulling out all of the stops of his organ of oratory struck up with shrill, fustian notes the then beautiful tune of State sovereignty. He observed that if all of the fighting men of Georgia could be taken without her consent, or against her will, by an external power she could have no residium of sovereignty. "To speak of such is mockery; it is insult added to injury and robbery." He would have Colonel Floyd and his 40,000 militiamen ordered to Savannah under Georgia's "retained right" of keeping troops in time of war for her own protection. He would have them stand upon the seaboard as a "monument to Georgia's sovereignty." "The essence of conscription is the right to take away the fighting men of the States against the wills of both the citizens and the States." It is "the right to coerce sovereign States . . .

[3] O. R. ser. IV, vol. II, 141, 211, 216.
[4] The *Confederacy*, November 16, 1862.

which Mr. Lincoln is now claiming over us and which we are resisting with our blood." [5]

Aided by the decision of the supreme court, the powerful journals of the State, and by the addresses of Senator Hill and the newly elected Senator, H. V. Johnson, in defense of conscription,[6] the anti-Brown forces voted down the Governor's nullification proposition.[7] The legislature, however, passed a resolution of protest against the principle of Confederate conscription, in accordance with Senator Johnson's suggestion that it should be done to the end that the principle might not be quoted as a precedent in future days.[8]

This controversy in the Georgia legislature marked the parting of the ways as between its leaders. The one faction led by Brown, the Stephens', and Toombs, was immoderately anti-Davis and was opposed to conscription and its kindred policies; the other, led by the Hills, the Lamars, the Cobbs, and Johnson was friendly to Davis and accepted the extreme measures of the Administration for winning the war.[9] It was a battle of giants;

[5] Reported in the *Confederacy,* November 7, 1862.

[6] Senator Johnson defended it only on grounds of necessity.

[7] Toombs had predicted that the "spineless" Know Nothings, whom he had in a moment of unguarded generosity permitted to enter the legislature again, would support the Administration. "They are a terribly whipped set of scoundrels," he said, "and are afraid even to do right lest they may be thought to be what they really are—traitors to public liberty." *Amer. Hist. Ass. Rep.,* 1911, vol. 2, 608. This probably was easy for Toombs to say. since the Know Nothings of the legislature did not support him for the Senate.

[8] The *Confederacy,* November 7, 1862. The *Sun* observed (March 31, 1863) that "a string of resolutions very similar to those of the celebrated Hartford Convention were introduced and discussed from the beginning to the close of the session."

[9] Senator Johnson supported conscription only on grounds of expediency, and Howell Cobb doubted the wisdom of continuing it after the summer of 1862.

an inter-governmental and an intra-State political conflict which many a Georgian made use of to keep off of the tented fields.

Senator Johnson carried with him to Richmond the Brown notion of the insecurity of the States. He proposed an amendment to the constitution allowing any State to secede peaceably when its grievances were not satisfactorily redressed. That the principle of peaceable secession at will was incorporated in the spirit of the Confederate system was "lamentably true," the *Republican* observed. It said that Johnson's proposition was like chanting a funeral dirge at the birth of an infant. "If we are not prepared to concede something of State sovereignty, the right to pull down and destroy at the pleasure or caprice of the parties to the compact, we may as well abandon all idea of a permanent government at once." [10]

Governor Brown's captious correspondence with the President as to the constitutionality of conscription and his nullification proposition made his rôle unique among the governors. With characteristic bluntness he stated his policy at the outset, and he clung to it with unequivocating tenacity throughout the war. It was briefly this: because of the exigencies of the times he would throw no obstructions in the way of enforcement of conscription "further than might become absolutely necessary to preserve intact the State government in all its departments, civil and military." [11] Plainly, the Governor had resolved himself into an umpire to judge between the pervading activities of a system that was repulsive to him and the self-sustaining activities of an institution and

[10] February 10, 1863.
[11] O. R. ser. IV, vol. I, 1085, 1129.

system for which he had the deepest solicitude. Conflict resulted inevitably.

The Georgia umpire was not long finding something to do. The War Department was inclined to conscript militia officers in the same way as privates in the militia. Governor Brown objected, and assumed that the Department had yielded when the Secretary informed him that no State officer was liable to conscription.[12] He was gratified over this promise, for he said, by way of warning, that "it would have been impossible for [him] to have consented to the enrollment of the State officers of the militia, and if insisted upon conflict must have been the inevitable result." [13]

The incident, however, was not closed. The enrolling officers enrolled some of the militia officers, and the Governor unbottled his wrath. He sent Secretary Randolph two telegrams in swift succession, assuring him that he would not allow his militia officers to leave their commands. He requested a telegraphic order releasing the officers and directing Major Dunwody to cease enrolling them or, he said, "I shall order the arrest of each officer who arrests a State officer." [14] The Secretary wired back that Major Dunwody had been instructed not to enroll militia officers recognized by the State authorities as in commission, and offered a word of sound advice; namely, "If you attempt to get men to fill up the Georgia regiments now, in the face of the enemy, you will cause great mischief. I think we might as well drive out our common enemy before we make war on each other." The

[12] O. R. ser. IV, vol. I, 1085, 1129.

[13] *Ibid.*, 1126, 1129.

[14] Judge Thomas, who was no doubt encouraged by Governor Brown's attitude, a few months later ordered the enrolling officer of Oglethorpe County put in jail because he disregarded a writ issued by the court.

Governor agreed that a conflict would be most unfortunate and pointed to a way to avoid it. The Confederate Government should "respect the constitutional rights of the State so far as not to force her to the alternative of permitting any department of her constitutional government to be disbanded and destroyed, or to defend the existence and integrity of her government by force." [15] He suggested that in the future much friction could be avoided if the enrolling officers, when they encountered opposition, would cease executing their orders upon notice from him until the question at issue could be referred to the Department. If given this consideration he pledged that he would not raise a false issue with the officers. The Secretary of War accepted his proposition.[16] So the Governor won his point, but he did it at the expense of a severe drubbing by the press of the State.[17]

[15] O. R. ser. IV, vol. I, 1154, 1155, 1169. The Secretary's anxiety over Governor Brown's attitude is evinced by his telegram to Major Dunwody, June 21st. He ordered Dunwody to send the Governor a copy of his instructions as regards the militia officers and to notify him of the fact by wire.

[16] *Ibid.,* vol. II, 22, 219, 263, 633.

[17] The Southern *Confederacy* observed: "His protection of militia officers and not privates is absurd and unjust. . . . Officers are retained to train the militia with no militia to train. Resistance in this way is folly and anything short of an entire and complete resistance to its operation upon every one within the limits of the State, is ridiculous, absurd, and had better for the credit of the State be abandoned." The victory as to militia officers "is fruitless, empty and vain" (June 20th, 21st). The *Sun,* August 2, 1862, said the militia was "a name without meaning, a shadow without substance—in short, an antiquated humbug." "No one seems to know what has been done about the militia, and all seem to rival each other in not caring to know. We beg pardon; we now remember that there had like to have been a terrible 'bust up' between our estimable Governor and the Confederate authorities on this very subject." At a later time (June 20, 1863) it charged that Brown's course had encouraged straggling in north Georgia. The Governor had been able to retain his "pets" by "Bullying threats . . . flashing over the wires to Richmond, announcing what the great Empire of Georgia intended to

Having succeeded in retaining his militia officers, Governor Brown struck boldly to establish the right of the Georgia troops in the field to select their officers and his own to commission them. One of his objections to the conscription acts was that they took from the State regiments in the field the right of electing their officers; a right, he said, guaranteed them by the Confederate constitution and the laws of Georgia. He did not contest this point thoroughly, however, until the spring of 1863, when Colonel Slaughter of the Fifty-first Georgia was killed and the commanding officer appointed his successor. The War Department approved the appointment and Governor Brown protested vehemently.[18] He was surprised and mortified at the position of the Government, and accused it of committing "a most unjustifiable breach of its plighted faith" with the men of this regiment. He also accused it of acting illegally, for "the act of Congress, so far as it confers the right of appointment in this case upon the President, is a nullity, on account of its conflict with the Constitution, and it follows as a necessary consequence that any regulation of your

do in case a few militia officers" were not immediately released. "The people . . . do not endorse the mad attempts of a few ambitious demagogues to get up a conflict between the State of Georgia and the Confederate Government." The *Republican* (May 12, 1862) accused him of making war on the Confederacy and of cutting "high fantastic figures"; and the Macon *Telegraph* said he was like a man who when aroused by a fire bell at night and found his neighbors fighting the flames stopped them and demanded documentary evidence that they were acting under regular orders from the fire department.

[18] This regiment was received into the Confederate service before the passage of the first conscription act, and the mooted question was whether it was received as part of the organized militia of the State or not. Brown regarded it as part of the militia and hence the State had a right to officer it; but the Secretary of War claimed that it was merely a part of the Confederate troops and therefore not in any sense subject to State jurisdiction.

Department carrying into execution that which is void is also unauthoritative." He seems to have hazarded a hope that the Secretary might set aside this act of Congress if led to believe it unconstitutional. This would be a dangerous wedge to drive between the Executive and Legislative departments of the Government, but if it were not driven, he warned, "it will be my duty to communicate the facts to the General Assembly of this State when again convened, and to ask them to take such action in the premises as will secure justice to their injured fellow-citizens and constituents and protect their plain constitutional rights."

Secretary Seddon stood firmly. He denied the Governor's charges of bad faith, and as to precedents in deference to State authority, cited by the Governor, he said they probably resulted from a "transient or casual toleration of an existing opinion without a full consideration of the import of the legislation of the Congress of the Confederate States." He did not feel that he had any authority to dispense with the conditions of the conscription laws, "however agreeable it might be to conform to the wishes of those who have maintained this opinion." Governor Brown regretted the immovability of the Secretary but concluded that it was useless to bandy opinions longer since, as he said, "I perceive your decision is made up, doubtless, after conference with the President, and it is determined that you shall enforce your construction." Because of the President's superior strength he was "obliged for the present, reluctantly, to acquiesce" in what he considered "a great wrong to thousands of gallant Georgia troops and a palpable infringement of the rights and the sovereignty of the State." As he beat his forced retreat he fired the sordid shot that "the denial of these rights of the States can only increase the power and patronage of the President, but cannot, . . . result in practical benefit to the public service." [19]

Further trouble with Governor Brown, over the appointment of officers to the so-called Home Guards, was encountered in the fall of 1863. He claimed the right to officer these local troops and General Howell Cobb, who had been appointed to organize them, advised the Department to yield to him so that harmony might be preserved. The Secretary declined to do it, but averred that the President would naturally give weight and careful consideration to any recommendations which Governor Brown might be pleased to make.[20] Indeed the President had already expressed a desire to have the Governor make nominations and pledged a deferential consideration of them. But these concessions did not appease him; he was after the substance of principle and power. He threatened to put the question before the legislature at its next meeting, meanwhile to make all appointments when election returns were sent to him.[21] The former threat he made good, but the legislature was not as bellicose as he. It shared his opinion as to the appointment of the officers, but it went no further than to request Georgia's representatives in Congress "to use their zealous efforts to procure, at the earliest practicable day," such a change in the Confederate laws as was necessary to secure the troops in their right. The Governor favored the President with a copy of these resolutions and his endorsement of them.[22]

---

[19] For the facts of this controversy, see O. R. ser. IV, vol. II, 129, 610, 620, 671, 737, 1063.

[20] O. R. ser. IV, vol. II, 854; see also ser. I, vol. LII, Pt. II, 523.

[21] *Ibid.,* 878.

[22] *Ibid.,* 1062.

The anti-Brown forces made a serious effort to defeat him in the election of 1863. The Milledgeville *Recorder* touched upon the facts stressed by the opposition when it pointed out that to vote for him would be to endorse his opposition to conscription; his "slanderous message" to the legislature concerning the supreme court's decision in support of conscription; his "foolhardy correspondence" with the President; and his "unjust protection of militia officers." [23] But he proved to be invincible. He won the election decisively over his two opponents, Honorable Joshua Hill, and Honorable T. M. Furlow.[24] His splendid victory gave him encouragement to forge ahead with his defense of State rights.

The conflict with Governor Brown over the exemption of State officers became particularly acute in 1864. In view of the Governor's attitude toward conscription it is not surprising that he was very generous to the State in claiming officers. Acting upon the courtesy extended to the governors by the act of May 1, 1863, he set claim to all officers of the State, "civil and military, appointed under her laws." The adjutant and inspector general of Georgia explained that, "In making this claim thus broadly His Excellency advances it in no spirit of opposition . . . but as the best method of avoiding unnecessary discussions and of securing without acrimony the just rights of the State and of the Confederate Government." [25] This apology shows the Governor's pur-

[23] Quoted in the *Republican,* June 23, 1863.

[24] Hill was an influential Union man and Furlow was a secessionist of the straitest set. Brown's biographer, Herbert Fielder, claims that Furlow was brought out with a view to throwing the election to the legislature in which it was believed Brown could be defeated. *Life and Times of Jos. E. Brown,* 109.

[25] Letter to Colonel Charles J. Harris, on conscription duty in Georgia. O. R. ser. IV, vol. II, 569.

pose in claiming all State officers, however insignificant their position. Out of scrupulous regard for the needs of the civil service of the States, Congress allowed the governors to claim all officers who were really necessary for the administration of the government of the States. Governor Brown through a supersensitive regard for State sovereignty, claimed and certified, not for the real administrative needs of his State, but for the preservation of its sovereignty in theory as well as in fact.

The act of May 1, 1863, made the list of officers which the governors might claim subject to the action of their respective legislatures at the next regular session. The Georgia legislature, acting under the spell of Governor Brown's representations, ratified his broad claims at its regular meeting in December. He was now satisfied; the three organic mouthpieces of the sovereign State of Georgia had spoken and claimed all of its officers, and necessarily they must ever afteward be immune to Confederate conscription.[26] With a feeling of solid security, he re-claimed all of the State officers and prepared an exhaustive list of them, observing that if he had omitted any officer whom it was his duty to protect he would include him later. On his certified list appeared county surveyors; coroners; all municipal officials; financial agents appointed by the Governor to aid in the execution of the laws pertaining to the exportation of cotton and importation of supplies for the State troops in the service, and to the importation of cotton cards and articles for repair of the State railroad; all officers and necessary employees of the State road; officers and cadets of the

[26] Brown dug up a decision of the Georgia supreme court in which it declared that if the Government should enroll the States' officers, "without whose agency their machinery must stop," it would transcend its powers. O. R. ser. IV, vol. III, 382.

G. M. I.; and officers and employees of the cotton card factory at Milledgeville.[27]

Governor Brown's conduct led to a long and acrimonious correspondence in the spring of 1864 between himself and General Cobb who had been made commandant of the reserve forces of the State. Cobb viewed the subject from the standpoint of the spirit of the law and of the relative need for the services of the men involved, as between the Government and the State; while the Governor viewed it solely from the angle of protecting the integrity and prestige of the State. Cobb ridiculed him for protecting more than 2,000 justices of the peace and upwards of 1,000 constables, when one justice of the peace to the district and one-fourth of the constables would suffice. He knew he said, of districts where there had not been a justice of the peace for years, which were then being supplied by able-bodied conscripts to obtain exemption.[28] As for the militia officers, he did not see how the 3,000 or more of them could be necessary for the proper administration of the State.[29] He presumed that

[27] O. R. ser. IV, vol. III, 345.

[28] "Neither Congress nor our supreme court, nor anybody else," he told the Governor, "but your Excellency, ever conceived the idea that justices of the peace who never held a court, constables who never served a warrant, and militia officers who have no men to command were necessary for the proper administration of the State Government."

[29] Governor Brown said that Cobb had greatly overestimated the number of militia officers. Cobb reduced the number to 2,726. Governor Bonham of South Carolina estimated the number at 5,000 to 7,000. (O. R. ser. I, vol. XXXV, Pt. II, 519.) One J. V. Mather of Guyton, Ga., wrote to President Davis that nine-tenths of the militia officers were between 18 and 45. "The idea," he said, "of keeping up such a militia is simply absurd," and he believed that the masses in Georgia looked to the President to stop "this outrageous wrong." The commandant of conscripts in Georgia did not doubt the truth of the statement, for he knew there was a wholesale exemption of militia and civil officers of the ages 18 to 50. O. R. ser. IV, vol. III, 259, 260.

a law that could be enforced in other States, without impairing their rights or violating their sovereignty, "might be enforced in Georgia with equal impunity and responded to with equal cheerfulness."

Governor Brown replied that he had no choice in the matter; the legislature had claimed all of the civil and military officers of the State and its authority as to their status was absolute, so far as he was concerned.[30]   He regretted that able-bodied young men were being elected to office, but when they were elected and the returns were duly made to him he could not refuse to commission them.

Brown and Cobb could not get together on this subject.   Brown claimed that Congress did not have constitutional power to conscribe State officers, as the Georgia supreme court had held, and therefore could not confer upon him the power to turn the officers over to conscription "in the teeth of an act of the legislature declaring that they shall be exempt."   The State had not claimed the exemption of its officers under the acts of Congress, nor did it accept it as a "matter of grace or favor from Congress."   It claimed and accepted their exemption as a "reserved right under the constitution."   Cobb championed the viewpoint of the Government: namely, the subject had not been referred to the legislatures because they had any jurisdiction, but simply to check upon the certifications of the governors.   Three months after the legislature of Georgia had acted upon it, Congress, still of the conviction that it had plenary authority, committed

[30] Cobb claimed that the legislature had no legal or moral right to tax Governor Brown's "conscience with a certificate which the laws of the country had submitted to [his] own decision."   He was positive that the legislature did not intend that every insignificant officer should be exempted.

the subject unqualifiedly to the discretion and patriotism of the governors.

This extraordinary correspondence between a general in the field and the governor of a State degenerated into one of personal criminations and recriminations, and caused much agitation in the State. It was inevitably reflected into the State's politics which Governor Brown, clever politician that he was, saw and took advantage of. With amusing self-purgation, he accused General Cobb, now prince of the "Conflict-croakers," of raising an obstreperous howl for political purposes every time he could "by a stretch of the imagination" discover a conflict, even "in the misty distance." It was Cobb's "political stock in trade" he said.[31]

Governor Brown's obstructionist tactics [32] and his vituperative correspondence with General Cobb overcame Secretary Seddon's patience. He was convinced that the spirit and temper of the Governor precluded "all hope of a change in his policy and rendered further attempts at conciliation, harmony, and coöperation useless." I am weary," he wrote to Colonel W. M. Browne, "of vain attempts to obtain his good will or assistance in the work of conscription, and am moreover inclined to believe that a course of firmness and decided action in dealing with him will be both wiser and more effective." He instructed the Colonel to proceed with the execution of "the law strictly, without respect to any claims or pretensions" made by Governor Brown which did not come within the fair intent of the law. His claims for the exemption of militia officers within the conscript age, or

---

[31] This correspondence is contained in the *Official Records,* ser. IV, vol. III, 345, 347, 381, 417, 432.

[32] See O. R. ser. IV, vol. III, 259, 344, 416.

for any more local officials, and his details for industrial purposes were not to be respected. If he interposed his authority Colonel Browne was to insist upon the enforcement of the law, and let him know that the issue would be "distinctly made and met before the people of his State." He thought that a few judicious examples made of the delinquent reserves "would probably strike wholesome terror" and induce others to respond to duty.[33]

The suspension of the writ of habeas corpus in 1864, as a means of enforcing conscription, aroused another controversy, and the hiatus between the Government and the Georgia authorities was broadened. It deepened Governor Brown's suspicion and distrust of the Government and led to his astoundingly acrimonious reproach of the President,[34] his refusal to comply with the President's requisition for his militia, and his threat to use the militia to oppose the "usurpation of power" by the Richmond authorities. Governor Brown was not the only or most significant person in Georgia who was aroused by the suspension of the writ.[35] The Vice-President now took up boldly the cudgels of opposition and cachinnated eloquently about this palpable "blow at the very 'vitals of liberty'." He, too, could see the ghost of despotism stalking abroad. His colleague, the President, he had never regarded "as a great man or statesman on a large scale." While he had regarded him as "weak and vascillating, timid, petulant, peevish, obstinate," he had given him credit for being a man of good intentions. But he had begun to suspect him of "aiming at absolute power." His abandonment of his former States' rights principles;

[33] O. R. ser. IV, vol. III, 530.
[34] See O. R. ser. I, vol. LII, Pt. II, 736, 778, 803.
[35] *Ibid.,* vol. LII, Pt. II, 648.

his reticence concerning the usurpations of generals in the field; and the earnest advocacy of a dictatorship by editors of journals that were generally understood to speak *ex cathedra* upon all topics in which the President had a vital concern, Stephens thought were consistent with the hypothesis that the President was entertaining notions of autocratic power, and they aroused his "suspicion and watchful jealousy." [36]

Governor Brown had had the encouragement and aid of the Vice-President and his brother from the outset.[37] The Savannah *Republican* asserted that Brown was put forward as the tool and exponent of "far shrewder men," with whom rule or ruin was the great maxim of life. "Uncle Billy" Holden of North Carolina undoubtedly "spoke by the card" when he said there was a party in Georgia who stood at Governor Brown's back.

Stephens was the rallying point of the recusants in this episode of conflict. He was the power behind the Governor's chair, advising, as he said, his impassioned message to the legislature on the new conscription act and the suspension of the habeas corpus "from stem to stern." [38]  It is claimed by one who admired Stephens that he lodged at the Executive Mansion, frequented the lobbies of the two houses, and watched the proceedings with an anxiety not second to Governor Brown's.[39]  He

[36] See O. R. ser. IV, vol. III, 278, for this very interesting delineation of President Davis by the Vice-President.

[37] Johnston and Browne, 409, 415, 429, 445; the *Republican,* March 15 and 28, 1864.

[38] The *Republican* understood that this "extraordinary message" was not the "sole concoction" of the Governor (March 15th).

[39] "Senex," a prominent correspondent of the *Republican,* affirmed the above facts. He lamented the fact that so able a man as Stephens should have been associated with such an affair, and hoped that his good judgment might yet save him (*Republican,* March 28th).

directed his brother, Linton, in the formulation of the denunciatory resolutions adopted by the legislature,[40] and at the crucial moment addressed a large assemblage of legislators and citizens on conscription and the suspension of the writ of habeas corpus.[41]

Excitement ran high in Georgia, and the leading features of the controversy were canvassed by the press throughout the country.[42] The pro- and anti-administration forces clashed sharply through the press, and in the lobby rooms and legislative halls at Milledgeville. Even the military officers left their commands and lobbied freely for the Administration,—an interesting legislative drama, it was, of inter-governmental, politico-military conflict; of trim uniforms and dappled civilian garbs, hobnobbing here and elbowing there, for the victory of a cause endeared by patriotic and partisan feelings.[43] The

[40] These resolutions condemned the habeas corpus act as "unreasonable and unconstitutional" and called upon Georgia's representatives in Congress to have it repealed. O. R. ser. IV, vol. III, 234; the *Republican*, March 18th.

[41] *Ibid.*, March 21st.

[42] The press of the country was generally against Governor Brown and he was lambasted without mercy by the press of Georgia. The *Republican* and the Columbia *South Carolinian* asserted that the only Georgia paper that supported him was Stephens' organ, the *Chronicle and Sentinel*. The *South Carolinian*, noted for its States' rights proclivities, said a Hartford Convention odium would attach to the Governor and his compatriots. The *Republican*, March 15th.

[43] "Senex" informed the readers of the *Republican* (March 26th) of extraordinary political chicanery on the part of Governor Brown. He said the Governor lobbied senators and representatives publicly and privately, and sat in the lobby of both houses when discussions and voting were going on. Nor was this the worst of it. He sold cotton cards to members of the legislature at $10 per pair, "Senex" said, when they were sold to nobody else, and were worth $40 to $60 in the market. He exchanged State for Confederate notes (to the extent of $200 to each member of the legislature) dollar for dollar when the former were worth twice as much as the latter. All these favors were bestowed on Friday, the day before the vote was taken on his measures. "Senex"

Government and its military lobbyists were defeated, but the officers returned to camp and secured the adoption of resolutions condemnatory of Governor Brown and the legislature.  The Governor and his allies were accused of being willing to sacrifice everything to "self-aggrandizement and personal ambition" and of "prostituting the dignity of high office to the accomplishment of unholy ends." [44]

Governor Brown thought well of his and Stephen's addresses and the legislature's resolutions; and with Stephen's approbation he committed the grave indiscretion of circulating them among the Georgia troops in the field.[45]  He did not stop at this.  In order that he might give the anti-Administration movement in Georgia the broadest and most sympathetic foundation, he sent copies of his address and of Linton Stephens' resolutions to the clerk of the court in every county within Confederate lines; and hoped to place A. H. Stephens' address

thought he drew 36 members to him by making them his aids. Two of these had resigned before the vote was taken, but the other 34 voted his way.

[44] Brown accused them of expecting promotion by condemning him and lauding the President with fulsome praise.  O. R. ser. IV, vol. III, 373.

[45] The Governor thought Stephens had spoken the last word concerning the constitutionality of the suspension act.  He wanted it extensively circulated, so he wrote Stephens, April 5th: "Privately, the Messrs. Wartzfielder of this city say they will pay for 1,000 copies to be circulated in the army, and I have to-day written to Steele at Atlanta to know if he struck off enough that I can get them.  The Messrs. W. do not wish their names known but they are ardently with us and have plenty of money to pay for the copies and not feel it."  He said that he had sent copies of his message and of Linton's resolutions to the captain of each company in the Georgia regiments and hoped that A. H.'s address might "take the same range."  He pledged $50 along with other contributors for the publication of this address, which he proposed to put into the hands of every lieutenant in the Georgia units.  *Toombs, Stephens, Cobb Correspondence,* 639, 640, 641.

in the hands of every sheriff.[46]   The over-anxious conduct
of the Governor and the Vice-President laid them open
to suspicion, and the "consolidation" leaders accused them
of treason.[47]

Although the anti-Administration forces were able to
secure a legislative indictment of the habeas corpus act,
for whatever that might mean, there were other con-
troversies with the Government which had not been settled.   For example, the War Department had recently
determined that many of the Governor's claims for the
exemption of officers, including his militia officers, should
not be honored; and the most acute conflict of all, namely,
that growing out of his effort to raise and maintain a
militia for the purpose of opposing Sherman, was just
going through its incipient stages.   Brown and his forces
left no stones unturned in the controversy of ever increasing intensity with Richmond.   He looked to Linton
Stephens and Toombs to out-general the Administration
or "Consolidation" party, which he thought would make
an effort to capture the legislature before its next meeting.   A vacancy had occurred in one of the judicial cir-
cuits of the State, so he sought diligently for a competent man who he was sure had no "consolidation"
proclivities.   And he did not neglect the press, though
he thought the papers were getting tired of the fight.
If those that were at all friendly could be spurred to
action they would be a powerful asset, as they had been.[48]

[46] *Toombs, Stephens, Cobb Correspondence,* 640, 641.

[47] Brown said that Cobb had called him a Tory and a traitor, and had
expressed the belief that he should be hanged and would be soon; and
while he had never been to a hanging he would go some distance to see
this one.   Brown thought the wrathful Cobb was serving well his master,
the President.   *Ibid.,* 640.

[48] He became much concerned because the *Constitutionalist,* which formerly supported him, had passed into the ownership of the "Consolida-

The last and most serious of Governor Brown's conflicts with the Confederate authorities developed into disastrous proportions in the fall of 1864. It was a conflict concerning State troops. The loss of Atlanta was the signal for the outburst. Governor Brown was in a bad mood. Numerous conflicts growing out of conscription and other war expedients had produced in him impatience and a deep-seated feeling of jealousy and distrust. On the other hand, the Administration after three years of sincere effort to secure his co-operation had come to the conclusion that he was hopelessly intractable, and resolved to enforce the laws of Congress in spite of him. The Governor had never been able to take the General Staff point of view, and it was useless to expect him to do so now. So far as he was concerned the war had primarily been a Georgia problem, and when Sherman captured Atlanta and encamped his forces on Georgia soil it became his sacred duty to mobilize the man power of the State to protect it against further invasion. The plan of the Chief of Staff, the President, to have one unified and harmonized military force to move at his behest, hither and thither according to the rules of strategy, against the invaders was of no consequence to him.

When Sherman began his advance toward Georgia Governor Brown set about to raise a militia force. He took men without much regard to their status, and thus came into conflict with the conscription authorities. Enrolling officers complained that he was forcing Confed-

tionists." When Henry Cleveland, the editor, informed him that Administration men had bought up a majority of the stock, he proposed to A. H. Stephens that they should raise enough money to put the "paper on right lines." It "would be a misfortune," he said, "for the paper to be lost to the cause of liberty." *Toombs, Stephens, Cobb Correspondence,* 643, 644.

erate details into the service, and in various ways obstructing the enforcement of the conscript law.[49]    The Secretary of War served notice on him that the detailed men were in Confederate service and could not be enforced to militia duty.    Brown defied him.    He said that since his request for reinforcements had not been granted he had called for the reserve militia and would "require those in civil pursuits with Confederate details as well as others to report and do their part," and would "compel obedience to the order."[50]    He ordered the militia of the first division, whom he furloughed September 10th, to bring back with them, "under arrest if necessary, . . . all persons who remained at home attending to their ordinary business under Confederate exemption or details."[51]

The President now made an adroit move to transfer the conscripts from the militia to the army in such a way as to avoid, if possible, serious trouble with Governor Brown.    He made a requisition on Georgia for her 10,000 militiamen, but Governor Brown upset all calculations by a flat refusal to comply with it.    There was no precedent for such refusal in Confederate history and no solid constitutional grounds for it, but that mattered little to the Governor, for he was striking, as he said, to protect his State against "external assaults and internal usurpations."    He felt that the Government had grossly neglected Georgia, and he would not at that critical moment turn over its last soldiers to be disposed of according to the "whims and caprice" of an authority in which he had not a modicum of trust.    But there were other

[49] O. R. ser. I, vol. LII, Pt. II, 710, 711.
[50] *Ibid.,* 712.
[51] *Ibid.,* 736.

reasons. He saw in the requisition a discrimination against Georgia (no other State was requisitioned at that time) and a design of the President to appropriate to himself the appointment of the officers by disbanding the militia and reorganizing the troops. Past experience, he charged, had shown that the President would "surmount all obstacles to secure to himself the appointment of the officers who are to command troops under his control." To comply with the requisition then would terminate a former controversy in favor of the Administration. What was of more vital consequence, if this last reserve power of the State were turned over to the President, the State would be powerless to protect itself "against the encroachments of centralized power." It would mean a virtual surrender of all contested points.

Governor Brown accompanied his refusal to comply with the requisition with a severe indictment of the President's purposes, his conduct of the war, and his "imperial" designs against the States and the people. He demanded that if the President persisted in his policy of indifference to the sufferings of Georgia "he permit all the sons of Georgia to return to their own State . . . to strike for their wives and their children, their homes, and their altars and the 'green graves' of their kindred and sires."

This was too serious to be passed over lightly by the Confederate authorities. The Secretary of War broke away from the policy of coaxing, of dignified and courteous expostulation, and with pointed language ably defended the record of the Administration and exposed the Governor's record of opposition to conscription and other war measures. As to his demand for the return of the State's troops, the Secretary preferred "to consider them as inconsiderate utterances rather than the foreshadowing of a guilty purpose to array [his] State in armed antagonism against the Confederacy." He took the Governor to a severe trimming, comparing his conduct to that of the New England governors in the War of 1812.

To his indictments the Governor made the smart reply that he had been unable to understand the expressions frequently used by the authorities at Richmond, such as "refractory Governors" and "loyal States." Such "imperial utterances" coming out of Washington would not be strange, "but such expressions are so utterly at variance with the principles upon which we entered into this contest in 1861 that it sounds harshly to our ears to have the officers of a Government, which is the agent or creature of the States, discussing the loyalty and disloyalty of the sovereign States to their central agent—the loyalty of the creator to the creature—which lives and moves and has its being only at the will of the States; and to hear their praise of the governors of sovereign States for their subserviency, or their denunciation of those not subservient as 'refractory.' " He denied that he contemplated arraying the people of his State against the Confederacy, but he would use the State's forces, if necessary, to resist abuses by the central Government.[52]

From the fall of 1864 till the surrender at Appomattox, Governor Brown was in virtual rebellion against

[52] This extended and caustic correspondence is recorded in the *Official Records*, ser. I, vol. LII, Pt. II, 736, 754, 760, 764, 778, 796, 803. Although they never agreed upon some of the facts of record, the correspondence is highly instructive. It was the product of years of misunderstandings, of working at cross-purposes, and of the awful strain of the war.

Confederate authority.[53]  Thus far had his States' rights dogmas, conflicts with conscript officers, some of whom he said seemed "to take pride in annoying the authorities of the State . . . upon a variety of technical pretexts," and the fortunes of war driven him.

North Carolina embarked upon a policy of opposition to conscription in the fall of 1862, when conscription was extended and Z. B. Vance was elevated to the Governor's chair by a large majority over his pro-Administration opponent.  His inauguration signalized the opening of an administration duel between Raleigh and Richmond. Elected overwhelmingly upon a platform of opposition, it was his business to oppose, and he did it in a way that made a distinct impression upon the Administration.  He discarded the creed of opposition to State sovereignty, by means of which he had projected himself from obscurity into a position of leadership, and with the zeal of a new convert threw himself into the cause of States' rights as against the power-reaping tendencies of the Confederate Government.  His masterly leadership of the masses of untutored, provincialistic, and suspicious peasant farmers of North Carolina made him the most dangerous man with whom Davis had to deal.[54]  His nimble wit and Lincoln-like intuition were more than a match for the methodical and unimaginative statecraft of the President.

Immediately after his inauguration Vance began the preliminaries of a manifold struggle against Confederate

[53] As late as March 13, 1865, he was still defying the Government as regards Confederate details in the militia.  He refused to allow the agricultural details then in the militia to be conscribed.  O. R. ser. IV, vol. III, 1138.

[54] Dodd, *Jefferson Davis*, 337.

authority. With unerring instinct, the first note of opposition he touched was the keynote of leadership among
an unsophisticated constituency; namely, "patronize home
talent." When his following showed any signs of stray-
ing off he could always enchant it back into line by the
blare of this note. He requested the President to employ
only North Carolinians as conscript officers in the State.
Like a good magician, he held this out as a sedative to
the sensitiveness of his people, and to the Confederate
authorities as a means of a thorough execution of the conscript law. He called upon the President to impress him
with the wisdom of the request, but failed. He then
laid this subject and that of officering the State troops
with North Carolinians before the legislature for it
"to take such steps as [would] preserve the rights and
honor of the State." "It is mortifying," he told the
legislature, "to find entire brigades of North Carolina
soldiers in the field commanded by strangers, and in many
cases our own brave and war-worn colonels are made to
give place to colonels from distant States, who are pro-
moted to the command of North Carolina troops over
their heads to vacant brigadierships." [55] He took occasion, also, to put the State on record as opposed to the
suspension of the writ of habeas corpus, by condemning
the recent act of Congress conferring upon the President
the power to suspend the writ. This power, he said,
he would not intrust to any living man. He saw "but
little good, but a vast tide of inflowing evil, from these
inordinate stretches of military power which are fast
disgracing us equally with our Northern enemies."

Other complaints and signs of opposition appeared

[55] O. R. ser. IV, vol. II, 189.

before 1863, which must have convinced the President
and his official family that they had a formidable recusant,
at least in the making, in the Executive chair of North
Carolina.[56]

Governor Vance started out with an apparently serious
purpose to aid conscription, since it was the adopted
policy of recruiting the armies.[57]   He had not gone far,
however, before he found cause for reprimanding the
Administration.[58]   It had broken a pledge, he said, to
the conscripts to allow them to select their regiments,
and if such was to be the policy of conscription he would
wash his hands of it.   This reprimand is illuminating.[59]
It laid down unmistakably the conditions upon which
Governor Vance would coöperate with the conscription
agencies.   The system must be flexible enough to meet
the local prejudices and the idiosyncrasies of his people.
He would not support a system of conscription that would
antagonize them and alienate them from him.   If their
rights were respected and they were handled with political tact by their friends they would be loyal, but they
would be rebellious if antagonized.   The West Pointers,
disciplined by the rule of thumb and ignorant of the

[56] In the late fall of 1862, Governor Vance made known his purpose
to organize independent troops for State defense.  *Jones' Diary,* I, 198.

[57] He said he "acquiesced in it as a great measure of necessity."  O. R.
ser. IV, vol. II, 465.

[58] He said that when he came into office conscription was at such a low
ebb he ordered his militia officers to help to ferret out the conscripts
and promised the conscripts if they would report for duty they would be
allowed to select their regiments.  The President and the Secretary of
War he claimed had authorized the promise, but when he got home he
found Major Mallett in possession of orders which ignored it.  He immediately wrote the Secretary that he could not be a party to such transac-
tions; if that was to be the policy of conscripion Major Mallett could
hunt down the conscripts as best he could.  O. R. ser. IV, vol. II, 114.

[59] O. R. ser. IV, vol. II, 114.  See President's reply, 154.

a b c's of human nature and of North Carolina politics, could never lead them. Because of his intuitive understanding of them and his popularity with them he should be accepted as the political weather vane of the State, and the Department should rely upon him to keep the people reconciled to conscription. "The opinions and advice of the old Union leaders," he wrote a few days later, "must be heeded with regard to the government of affairs in North Carolina." Without their "influence constantly and unremittingly given the present status cannot be maintained forty-eight hours." He was sure that the conscript law could not have been executed by one of different antecedents than his; and the enforcement of it in the future would tax heavily the power of his popularity, for "the waters of insubordination" were beginning "to surge more angrily." [60]

The fact that his suggestions, drawn from a superior knowledge of the political movements affecting conscription, should have received such scant attention compared to that given those of the West Point political novices chagrined him. But despite the nonchalant attitude of the Administration toward his advice, whenever his or his State's rights were involved he said he would feel it his duty to write fully and frankly about them. And so thus he became a consistent correspondent with the Richmond authorities and an occasional caller upon the President.

Governor Vance's plan spelled conflict. Generally speaking, there had to be uniformity in the policy of conscription, and the Department could not grant most of his requests for special modifications of the system to accomodate peculiar conditions in North Carolina. The

[60] O. R. ser. IV, vol. II, 146; ser. I, vol. LI, Pt. II, 765.

refusals irritated and disgusted him and he retaliated with obstructions.[61]

There were many conflicts between the Confederate and State authorities in North Carolina after 1862. Governor Vance pushed forward the protests which he had already begun, and other conflicts of a more serious nature were espoused. These transformed the Governor from a mild obstructionist to a bold defier, threatening at one time to make war on the Confederate Government for the maintenance of a sacred right of his State, and, at another, to withdraw the State troops from the field to protect the lives and property of his fellow-citizens.

Throughout the war Governor Vance wrangled with the Government over the subject of the employment of North Carolinians in the conscription service of the State. His eloquent advertisement of this naturally popular cause stimulated the anti-conscription peasant meetings in the western counties of the State to include the employment of "foreigners" in their list of objections to conscription.[62] The popular agitation that arose against "foreign domination" led the State's representatives in Congress to request the Secretary of War not to

[61] The critical attitude of the North Carolina authorities in the fall of 1862 caused the State's loyalty to be questioned. The legislature by a joint resolution, January 30, 1863, attempted to dispel this suspicion. It repudiated the charge that it desired "to conflict with the Confederate Government or to embarrass the President in the prosecution of the war" as "grossly untrue, illiberal, and slanderous"; and it pledged itself to "the most vigorous Constitutional war policy" (O. R. ser. IV, vol. II, 378). Whatever unction this resolution may have had for the Administration at the time, was soon neutralized by the conduct of Governor Vance, and finally, by the action of the legislature itself. Quite significantly, it promised to support only a "Constitutional war policy."

[62] N. C. *Standard,* July, 1863, to August, 1864 (*passim*). Cited in Schwab, 217.

employ citizens from other States as conscript officers in North Carolina.[63]

The appointment of Colonel August as commandant of conscripts in North Carolina in January, 1863, opened in a serious way this controversy. Governor Vance contested his appointment promptly. He thought it was an "obvious impropriety" and a bad policy to wound the sensibilities of his "people by the appointment of a citizen of another State to execute a law both harsh and odious"; and, moreover, it was a discourtesy to his people who had, according to the President's own admission, furnished far more conscripts than any other State.[64]

The Department consented to substitute Colonel Mallett for Colonel August, but was sorry that such susceptibility prevailed in North Carolina when it had not been displayed in other States where similar appointments had been made. It explained that the practice of appointing non-resident men to conscript duty in the various States was founded upon the belief that they would be less "affected by local association or feelings." [65]    The reason advanced did not satisfy Vance. He went to Richmond during the summer and protested against the presence in North Carolina of a number of Virginians and Marylanders in official capacity, each with "a brood of his own countrymen avoiding conscription and making themselves generally very obnoxious." The President promised, he said, to remove them and he returned "with

[63] For the facts of this controversy see O. R. ser. IV, vol. II, 375, 409, 411, 458, 787; *Ibid.,* ser. I, vol. LI, Pt. II, 818, 824, 830, 844; *Jones' Diary,* II, 39, 176.

[64] Governor Vance said that he had submitted in silence "to the many —very many—acts of the Administration" which had wounded the pride of the State; but the appointment of Colonel August was too "unjust and impolitic" not to be challenged. O. R. ser. IV, vol. II, 375.

[65] O. R. ser. IV, vol. II, 409.

high hopes and a comparatively easy heart and tried to satisfy the discontented by assuring them that there would henceforth be the most cordial understanding between the State and Confederate authorities." These officers were not removed promptly, whereupon he wrote Secretary Seddon that he was disgusted and "disheartened at being so often foiled" in his efforts to do something to reconcile his people to the Administration. "If I have not sufficient influence with the President," he implored, "to secure the removal of one man, even for reasons of policy, for God's sake let me know it." [66]

His persistent protests led the Government to use, whenever at all practicable, North Carolinians in the conscription service of the State. But all exceptions to the rule were vigorously protested by him. In the early part of 1864 he engaged the President in a censorious correspondence concerning the brutal conduct of some of the local conscript officers and the way the anti-Secessionists of North Carolina had been discriminated against by the Administration, both in the civil and military service.[67] President Davis refuted his imputations with dignity, but called a halt upon the correspondence when he felt that Governor Vance had exceeded the "proprieties of official intercourse." He requested that their future correspondence be restricted to matters that required official action.[68]

---

[66] O. R. ser. IV, vol. II, 787.

[67] Governor Vance charged that there had been "what seemed a studied exclusion of the anti-Secessionists from all the more important offices of the Government, even from those promotions in the army which many of them had won with their blood." The fact is the policy had been just the reverse. The Governor seems to have imbibed some of the supersensitiveness and naïve suspicion of his mountain environments.

[68] This correspondence may be found in the *Official Records,* ser. I, vol. LI, Pt. II, 818, 824, 830, 844.

The sharpest conflicts with the authorities of North Carolina over conscription were those pertaining to court decisions and the exemption of State officers.

The judicial obstructions to conscription in North Carolina have been encountered already.[69] In the spring of 1863 the adverse decisions of some of the local judges and of Chief Justice Pearson produced serious friction between the courts and the conscription authorities. The local courts were encouraged by Chief Justice Pearson's example, and they obstructed conscription right and left by the use of the writ of habeas corpus. They took conscripts and deserters from the custody of the enrolling officers and released them if there was a shadow of an excuse for such action. The enrolling officers became weary of this mischievous interference and ignored the orders of the courts.[70]

This sharp conflict between civil and military authority forced itself upon the attention of the State and Confederate executives. The Secretary of War complained to Governor Vance about the evil results of the conduct of the courts of North Carolina. He attributed the frequent desertions among North Carolina soldiers to the fact that the impression generally prevailed that if they should get within the jurisdiction of their courts they would be "permanently exonerated from the perils and hardships of military life." He hoped that the Governor would in some way restrain the courts. Vance deplored the fact that the Secretary of War had imbibed the idea, born of "political prejudice," that the North Carolina courts were mischievous and that conscription was poorly

[69] Pages 187-188 above.

[70] Examples of conflicts of this character are given in the *Sun*, June 6, 1863, and in the N. C. *Standard*, June 16, 1863.

functioning in the State. Since North Carolina had better executed the conscription law than any other State, he saw no cause for complaint against her, except that there was a "too ready" disposition on the part of her neighbors, and even of some of her own citizens, to believe evil of her. Instead of promising to use his influence to restrain the judiciary, he said it was his firm determination to uphold it. Since the Confederate Supreme Court had not been organized the decisions of the supreme court of North Carolina when formally rendered would be binding upon all parties.[71]

The Governor's threat to uphold the courts was not an empty one. He ordered the militia not to arrest any one as a conscript or deserter who had been discharged by a State judge, and to resist any such arrest by any person acting without authority from a court. Conflict was imminent and excitement ran high in and out of the State.[72] The Raleigh *State Journal* looked with "alarm upon the unsettled and conflicting claims." "The only honest course," it observed, "for a State of the Confederacy is to give her all to the contest now raging, or to quit the field at once. There can be no divided service compatible either with honor or safety." [73] The *Sun,* July 2, 1863, said there was considerable excitement, but some way out of the *débâcle* was hoped for. "Nothing but a spirit of compromise," it observed further, "between the State and Confederate governments will prevent anarchy and ruin, even whilst we are yet engaged

[71] O. R. ser. I, vol. LI, Pt. II, 714, 715.

[72] According to the N. C. *Standard,* July 7, 14, 1863, the legislature was offended at the Confederate Government for ignoring the supreme court. Cited in Schwab, 191.

[73] June 7, 1863. Cited in Moore's *Rebellion Record* (Rumors and Incidents), vol. 7, 72.

in a desperate struggle for national existence against a common foe."

There was another serious conflict a year later between the Government and Chief Justice Pearson; and, again, Governor Vance threatened to back the judge with the armed forces of the State. Judge Pearson declared the law abolishing substitution unconstitutional and proceeded, at chambers, to discharge the principals, the habeas corpus act to the contrary notwithstanding.[74] The War Department ordered the enrolling officers to ignore Judge Pearson's actions, and Governor Vance became indignant. He warned the Department that these orders meant "a direct and unavoidable collision of State and Confederate authorities." As much as he eschewed conflict with the Government or in any way to hinder its efficiency, he would call out the militia if necessary to protect persons discharged by Judge Pearson. This challenge drew fire from Richmond. The demand for men was so importunate that the issue could not be allowed to hang in the balance till the next regular session of the supreme court, as Vance proposed. Secretary Seddon informed him that, while he too deprecated greatly a conflict, the enrolling officers must go ahead as instructed, and if Judge Pearson usurped the authority to disregard the act of suspension "collision would only result from the wanton, unauthorized attempt by violence" to deter the officers. He said the President would be bound to protect the enrolling officers in the performance of their duties. The President also wrote Governor Vance that the conscription laws would be enforced in North Carolina as in the other States, and if Judge Pearson persisted in his "factious course" he would "not shrink from the issue." The

[74] See pages 46-47 and 187-188 above.

bold stand of the Administration reduced the Governor and the Judge,[75] and little more was heard of a conflict between the courts and conscript officers in North Carolina.

There was serious friction in North Carolina, as in most of the other Southern States, over the conscription of State officers. Governor Vance had not been in office long before he complained of the enrollment of local civil officers, and this produced a very strained relation between him and the Richmond authorities in the spring and summer of 1863. Commandant of conscripts, Colonel August (a fellow-North Carolinian), informed Governor Vance that he had counted on his aid rather than his opposition, and asked him to coöperate with the Bureau in a liberal-minded way to adjust any delicate questions that might arise. Vance replied that he would continue to support conscription and the Government so far as it might rightfully be done; beyond this he could not go. He had not belonged to "that class of politicians who made the 'night (and day) hideous' with cries for States' rights and was rather accused of consolidationism," yet he was not "quite willing to see the State of North Carolina in effect blotted from the map and her government abolished by the conscription of her officers." Under the exemption law the Bureau might claim all officers of the States;[76] he did not know that it would, but he could not trust it. "God forbid," he said, "that the rights, honor, and the existence itself of the States should rest only upon the grace and mercy of a bureau of conscription." He understood it to be his plain constitu-

---

[75] O. R. ser. IV, vol. III, 176, 197, 201.

[76] This was the case since all State officers were required to serve in the militia in cases of emergency.

tional duty to protect all State officers and agents whose services were necessary, and the State authorities alone could judge of the necessity. The State's claim upon its officers did not rest, he averred, upon the grace of Congress, or the discretion of those commissioned to execute its enactments, "but upon those higher and inalienable rights which by the genius of our Government are deemed inherent in and inseparable from the sovereign character of the State." He wanted to be informed at once whether the Confederate authorities were prepared to respect the rights of the States as to their officers.[77]

Thus, Governor Vance at the outset assumed a defiant attitude so far as the conscription of State officers was concerned. He challenged all the acts of Congress and of the Administration that were calculated to impair the police power of his State.[78]

To avoid conflict the enrolling officers were instructed to cease conscribing constables and justices of the peace until a conference with Governor Vance could be held and the laws of the State examined. President Davis wrote Vance that he had no power to exempt as a class the police of corporate towns, but in some instances they had been allowed temporary exemption upon the condition that they should join the local home guards and hold themselves in readiness for local military service.[79] He said it had been and was his policy in enforcing conscription "to comply as far as possible with the wishes

[77] O. R. ser. IV, vol. II, 465. He informed the President that the services of the justices of the peace, constables, and police officers were necessary to the well-being of the State, and added that their conscription would be "as insulting to the dignity as it is certainly violative of the rights and sovereignty of the State." *Ibid.,* 464.

[78] The North Carolina supreme court sustained him in the case of Johnson *vs.* Mallett.

[79] This was in harmony with the plan of local defense just adopted.

and views of the Governors of the several States in all cases where there [seemed] to be any fair doubt as to the intention of Congress." [80]

The year 1863, a critical year for the Confederacy as a whole, was particularly a critical one in North Carolina. In seditious public meetings the despotism of conscription was denounced, and there were many distressing conflicts between the authorities of the State and the Government over the enforcement of conscription. Governor Vance, though in virtual rebellion against Richmond several times, always protested that conscription was being more thoroughly enforced in North Carolina than elsewhere, and that he had, according to a decision of the supreme court of his State, exceeded his authority in promoting it. As an anti-climax to his battles with the Administration he issued a powerful proclamation to his people, whom he had helped to develop a bad feeling towards the Government, warning them against the transgression of Confederate law. He told them that the Confederate constitution and the laws passed in pursuance of it were the supreme law of the land and that as long as the laws remained on the statute book they would be enforced. [81]

The conflict over the enrollment of officers broke out afresh in the spring of 1864. Governor Vance was attuned for it by a captious correspondence with the President, the suspension of the writ of habeas corpus, and the collision over Chief Justice Pearson's decisions. He shared the general resentment of the States' rights men against the act suspending the writ, and had a particular grievance because he thought the act was aimed spe-

[80] O. R. ser. IV, vol. II, 633.
[81] Ibid., 794.

cifically at Judge Pearson and other obstructionists in North Carolina.[82]

The controversy was started over the case of one Daniel L. Russell (at a later time Governor of the State), who, while technically in the Confederate service, was elected to the position of "commissioner for distributing money and provisions for soldiers' families" and certified by Governor Vance. The Department refused to recognize the Governor's certificate in this case because Russell was in the service and was not elected to one of those offices specially recognized by the act of April 2, 1863.[83]  Governor Vance denied the right of the Government to Russell's service for three reasons. First, he was not in the service at the time of his election. Second, there was no difference between the meaning of "exemption" and "discharge" as used in the conscription acts.[84]  And third, in last analysis it made little difference whether Russell was in the service or not, or whether "exemption" and "discharge" were identical in meaning, for the State's right to its officers was in no sense dependent upon the action of Congress. After exchanging several notes with the Department to no advantage he defied it outright.  He wrote Secretary Seddon that he would not submit to Russell's enrollment "without resisting it by every means at [his] command."  The Sec-

[82] He pleaded earnestly with the President "to be chary of exercising the powers" conferred by it.  He felt compelled to add this word of expostulation because he knew that the President believed the suspension of the writ "to be the only way to secure North Carolina in the performance of her obligations to her confederates."  O. R. ser. I, vol. LI, Pt. II, 818.

[83] This act allowed persons in the service who were elected to certain State offices to be discharged.  Page 250 above.

[84] He cited Judge Pearson's strained interpretation in the Bradshaw case to support this proposition.

retary refused to be intimidated. He replied promptly: "The Department has conceded many things to the government of North Carolina with a view to secure a cordial coöperation of the government and people in the defense of the country . . . but it cannot make a concession of a principle so vital as the one contained in the question under discussion." The superior strength of the Government suggested the wisdom of yielding, and Governor Vance backed down a second time in a sharp tilt with Richmond.[85]

But the Governor did not lose the whole fight as to State officers. He took advantage of the trust reposed in him by the act of February 17, 1864, and certified every officer, however insignificant his duties, whose office was provided for by law. From this position he advanced finally to that of claiming "all persons in the actual employ of the State in any department where the law enjoins duties to be done which require the employment of such persons." That is, he claimed, like Governor Brown, all employees engaged in the manufacture of clothing and equipment for the State troops. Any other policy would lead to the State's being "shorn of its sovereignty and crippled in all its operations." [86] The legislature had already passed resolutions in direct conflict with some features of the Confederate exemption law, and Governor Vance undertook to enforce them to the letter.[87]

[85] O. R. ser. IV, vol. III, 375, 425, 530, 555.

[86] *Ibid.,* 754. He stretched his authority to claim factory laborers because he suspected the Government of conscribing the employees of the factories which had contracts with the State, with the deliberate purpose of forcing the State to abandon its practice of furnishing its troops. If the Government details to the factories should be curtailed he would have "to try tilts" with the Government. O. R. ser, IV, vol. III, 746.

[87] *Ibid.,* 754; the *Examiner,* June 9, 1864; *Jones' Diary,* II, 439.

The Secretary of War thought Vance was pressing the decision of the supreme court beyond its limits when he claimed the employees of factories, etc.[88]     Apparently the issue was never definitely settled.  As was the case in Georgia, it lost much of its prominence in the stirring events that terminated the war.

In a letter to Governor Bonham of South Carolina, September 23, 1864, Governor Vance divulged the secret of his certification of 16,000 or more persons.  He suggested that the great need for men in Lee's and Hood's armies might be supplied in part by giving up as many of the State officers as was compatible with efficient government and with the dignity and sovereignty of the States.  There were many "engaged in the various State departments who might be spared"; and there was "a large class of State officers in all the States withheld from service, not only on account of the necessity for them in administering the governments, but also because the principle of State sovereignty rendered it improper to allow the Confederate Government to conscript them." [89] He proposed a meeting of the governors east of the Mississippi, ostensibly for the purpose of adopting a uniform policy with respect to releasing some of the State officers.  The proposed meeting was held at Augusta, October 17, 1864, but it accomplished nothing so far as the subject of releasing State officers for service was concerned.  The sovereignty of the States still demanded

[88] O. R. ser. IV, vol. III, 755.  Judge J. A. Campbell also regarded the opinion erroneous "as militating against that supremacy which the Constitution ordains in respect to the legislation of the Confederate States in the subjects committed to them."

[89] Ibid., 685.  Similar letters were sent to the governors of Ala., Ga., Fla., Miss., S. C., Tenn., and Va.

that not a single officer should be surrendered to the Confederate Government.

Opposition to conscription by the three departments of government in North Carolina was very pronounced and its results were disastrous.[90]    Governor Vance's new faith in States' rights and his resentment because his vast store of information concerning his sensitive and peculiar people, upon whose good will his political success depended, was not utilized in the shaping of conscription in North Carolina, drove him into a stubborn opposition to its essential features.    Although it was "exceedingly unpleasant" for him "to refuse to do anything whatsoever which was requested by the Confederate authorities"; although he used his militia as no other governor did to enforce conscription, and protested often that he "assisted with zeal in its enforcement," and that it was working better in North Carolina than elsewhere, he must share with Governor Brown the notoriety of having been a stalwart obstructionist.    His support of conscription was of a very limited character, in fact inconsequential, compared to the grave obstructions he interposed.    At the crucial moments in his tilts with the Administration he played with the art of a past master upon the prejudices of the people and upon their distrust of Richmond.    They became uneasy and unruly.    Anything like a thorough-going conscription system was impossible under such circumstances.

The President had in Governors Brown and Vance

[90] The legislature nullified the act of Congress suspending the writ of habeas corpus (*Republican*, June 18, 1864).    According to the Florida *Union*, several members of the Senate early in 1865 launched a movement to have a conference of the governors for considering the crisis and a plan of reconstruction (February 18, 1865).

twin Nemeses with whom to contend. They made life uncomfortable for him. Controversial in character, anti-Davis in feeling, particularistic by nature and training, supinely self-confident by endowment and because of a spectacular rise in life, and unbending States' rightists in principle, they were admirably equipped to torment the souls of the military strategists at Richmond. Their patriotism was essentially local. They could not think consistently in terms of the whole Confederacy. They were simply allies to the other States, and often puny allies at that. They stood like divinely ordained sentinels upon the isolated peak of particularistic patriotism, flattering official prerogatives, and uncompromising personal prepossessions, and preached with equal skill two sermons for State protection: one against the devastating swords of the Federal troops, the other against the compressing tendrils of the "insatiable political octopus" at Richmond. Their conduct contributed much to the inefficacy of conscription in their respective States.

# CHAPTER XIII

## CONFEDERATE VERSUS STATE AUTHORITY IN THE UPPER SOUTH

THE upper South was the section of least political friction.[1a] There were no conflicts of any consequence after 1862 until the closing months of the War. In South Carolina, as Professor Stephenson has well said, "the prevailing view was that of experienced, disillusioned men who realized from the start that secession had burnt their bridges, and that now they must win the fight or change the whole current of their lives." [1b] There was a similar situation in Virginia.[2] The leadership was experienced and practical; the State had invested its best and most trusted talent in the civil and military councils of the Government; the Government was on the ground, it was not a mysterious something beyond the horizon that could be conjured by the imagination into the proportions of a monster, obsessed with a passion to consume the rights of the States and of the people; the enemy was always near and formidable; and, thanks to military strategy, at the climax of the war the Government ordered troops into Virginia from all sources and seemed to brood over the "Old Dominion." There were in Virginia, then, conditions and a leadership that tended

[1a] This chapter is a study of South Carolina and Virginia. Little evidence of conflict has been found in Tennessee.

[1b] *Op. cit.,* 75.

[2] The great journalists, Pollard and Rhett, played the roll of merciless critics in these States and did their part in creating an atmosphere of distrust and hostility toward the President.

always to keep the State authorities in line with the policies of the Government.

There was, however, some friction in Virginia in 1862 and 1864 over the Conscription of the V. M. I. cadets, and over the breaking up of the State regiments and the selection of officers for them. Governor Letcher was not in favor of conscription but he accepted it in good faith and offered no opposition to it, except as regards the State cadets.[3] His message to the legislature, January 7, 1863, stressing the necessity for coöperating with the Confederate Government, was a timely document.[4] Governor William Smith, his successor, exhibited a similar spirit and purpose. When some of the other governors set up extravagant claims for the exemption of State officers he certified with moderation, and urged that other governors should not shield unnecessary local functionaries.[5]

There was a serious conflict with the South Carolina authorities over exemption in the fall of 1862. The legislature passed a conscription law as a means of raising the State's quota of troops before the Confederate conscription act was passed. Thus after April 16th there were two conscription systems in the State: one emanating from Confederate authority, the other from

[3] He ordered the superintendent of the V. M. I. not to surrender a cadet until the constitutionality of the conscription act had been tested. The Secretary of War, "presuming that [the Governor desired] to avoid collisions between the authorities of the State and of the Confederacy," and that he would aid him "in adjusting the difference without a resort to force," proposed to make a test case for the State supreme court (O. R. ser. IV, vol. II, 123). The case was made, the act was upheld, and Governor Letcher allowed the cadets to be conscribed.

[4] The *Republican*, January 8, 1863.

[5] Governor Brown asserted that according to newspaper reports Governor Smith certified more men than he did (O. R. ser. IV, vol. III, 432). But the records of the Bureau do not support this assumption.

State authority. The systems overlapped and a question of precedency was raised. The Governor and Council (a rump body of secessionists) were not inclined to haul down the flag of State sovereignty in the contest.

Lieutenant John S. Preston reported, June 4th, that the State authorities would "persist in every form to require exemption under the State law" and that the enrollment of those within the Confederate conscription age, soon to be placed in his hands, would be expunged of all persons exempted by State law.[6] He ordered a new enrollment by the Confederate officers, and Governor Pickens and his Council prepared to issue a countervailing order.[7] President Davis accepted this challenge frankly and defended the exercise of central authority in a manner quite as able as extraordinary for a President of a coalition of sovereign States.[8] He expressed great surprise at the action of the Governor and Council and warned them of the dangers of their course. He said in part: "The issue thus presented to the Confederate Government is one which I am unable to avoid without violation of official duty. . . . If I do not misapprehend the meaning of these passages, the right is here broadly asserted that the State of South Carolina may at her pleasure relieve a portion of her citizens from obedience to laws of the Confederate Congress. . . . The right thus asserted is, to my mind, so devoid of foundation that I hestitate in attributing to you the intention of maintaining it, and still entertain the hope that I may have misapprehended your meaning. It is so very clear that the agreement of the States, as contained in the Constitution,

[6] O. R. ser. IV, vol. I, 1140, 1144, 1153.

[7] *Ibid.*, vol. II, 73.

[8] Secretary Seddon defended Confederate authority in a similar way in 1864. O. R. ser. I, vol. LII, Pt. II, 754.

to delegate to Congress the power to declare war and raise armies would be utterly defeated by the exercise of a power on the part of the States to exempt at their pleasure any or all of the citizens from service in the armies of the Confederacy, that I am at a loss how to illustrate so plain a proposition." The "assertion of such a right on the part of the State is tantamount to a denial of the right of the Confederate Government to enforce the exercise of the delegated power, and would render a confederacy an impracticable form of government. . . . The Confederate courts, as well as those of the State, possess ample powers for the redress of grievances, whether inflicted by legislation or executive usurpation, and the direct conflict of executive authorities presents a condition of affairs so grave and is suggestive of consequences so disastrous that I am sure you cannot contemplate them without deep-seated alarm." [9]

This strong argument and appeal caused the Governor and Council to desist from their course, but the issue was revived a year later. Governor Bonham requested the legislature to reconcile "as far as possible, the difference between the laws of the two governments"; it was his opinion that the State should, so far as consistent with its rights, conform to the Confederate laws. He proposed that the exemption issue should be submitted to a competent judicial tribunal.[10] Meanwhile, Superintendent Preston called upon him to dispel "all prepossessions against the operations of conscription," and to

[9] O. R. ser. IV, vol. II, 73. In the "Convention" a few days later it was proposed to nullify the conscription act, but the powerful address of Rhett in defense of conscription defeated the proposition. Stephenson, 72. The *Confederacy* referred to this convention as "irresponsible and remorseless."

[10] O. R. ser. IV, vol. II, 866; Moore, *Rebellion Record,* Doc. 172, 507.

secure a "concurrence of view and harmony of action between the Department and the authorities of [the] State." Preston's mission was fruitful, the issue was adjusted.[11]

There was no question about the soundness of the President's observations on the perilous consequences of discordant purposes and actions between the executives during the war, and he offered a fine antidote for secession. It would have been an excellent Jacksonian or Lincolnian state paper, but it was a strange document to emanate from the mind and pen of one who had shortly before endorsed a dissolution of the national system upon the principle of the competency of the respective States to judge and act for themselves.[12] It embodied the mature reflections of one who had been made responsible for upholding a national system. The principle of State potency had a utility when there was an old order to be demolished, but if invoked too often in the new political dispensation the national body politic would be wrecked by the tremors of revolution. Much to the chagrin of those whose duty it was to direct the fortunes of the nascent nation, it carried a dagger of self-destruction that men possessed of power and implacable logic threatened to draw when the central authority seemed too robust.

After the trouble over exemption in South Carolina was adjusted, no other serious friction developed until the end of 1864 when Sherman was preparing to invade the State. The threat of a terrible invasion led

[11] O. R. ser. IV, vol. II, 874. Governor Bonham did not try to shield insignificant State officers. Vol. III, 693; ser. I, vol. XXXV, Pt. II, 519.

[12] The fact that Davis originally opposed secession made this sort of argument easy for him.

the authorities to settle down to the grim business of preparing to save the State, when it was clear that requests for succor from Richmond were useless. The legislature passed a conscription act that conflicted with the Confederate law. The exemption feature of this act virtually nullified Confederate conscription, and Superintendent Preston said it was an explicit declaration that South Carolina would not furnish another soldier except upon her own terms. He was pained because "the first treason to the Confederate States in the form of law [had] been perpetrated in South Carolina." [13]

The advance of Sherman produced an irreparable breach between the government of South Carolina and the Confederate Government. Governor A. G. Magrath said in his inaugural address in December that it was the purpose of the dominant party in the State to prosecute the war and to check up on the exercise of power by the central Government. This erstwhile Confederate judge made the revolutionary proposition to Governor Vance that the Southeastern and Gulf States should pool their military resources and defend themselves independently of Richmond.[14] He claimed persons who were exempted by the new State law,[15] and General Lee was soon complaining that the South Carolina regiments were not being properly recruited. Thus, at the end of the war the State authorities of South Carolina, like those in many of the other States, were in virtual rebellion against the central Government.

[13] O. R. ser. IV, vol. III, 979.

[14] Stephenson, *The Day of the Confederacy*, 152-154.

[15] O. R. ser. IV, vol. III, 980, 1004. The *Whig* said that he ordered all able-bodied whites between 16 and 60, not already in the Confederate service, into the militia for the defense of the State. No exemptions were allowed, except under "special circumstances." January 5, 1865. Savannah *Republican*, January 4, 1865.

The conflict between State and Confederate authority over conscription was a most serious impediment to its effective enforcement. The factious intercessions of some of the governors presents a very striking contrast to the quiesence and cordial coöperation of our State governors in the World War. Their powerful arguments against the tyranny of the conscription system and their examples of seditious conduct; nonconforming legislative acts; and adverse court decisions, reinforced as they were by flaming newspaper editorials and the utterances and deeds of popular leaders, did much to produce that moral atrophy that led to wholesale skulking and deserting toward the close of the war. General J. B. Magruder said that there were large classes who were so anxious to stay at home "that they would unhesitatingly make use of that conflict to avoid military service altogether, and certainly that of the Confederate States." [16] Superintendent Preston noted that one of the great obstructions to conscription was the "active opposition to the law by State authorities." Upon another occasion he said: "The folly and wickedness of Governors Brown and Vance and the Legislature of South Carolina have . . . disintegrated the Confederacy. They have saved the Confederacy the shame of an idiotic suicide." [17]

The factious course of the governors during the last year of the war must have caused the President almost as much anxiety as the invading hordes. They quarrelled with him individually, and at times there was danger of joint action against him. For example, the

[16] O. R. ser. I, vol. XXXIV, Pt. III, 789.

[17] O. R. ser. IV, vol. III, 885, 979. It was Preston's opinion that military conscription would have disrupted the Confederacy if some of the State authorities had not.

Augusta meeting was intended rather more for the discussion of general war problems, and the problems of the governors in their dealings with the Richmond authorities, than for considering a common policy of giving up part of the State officers. The meeting was not inspired by a desire to uphold the hands of the President. The copious advice offered for the guidance of the authorities and the motes that were pulled out of the President's eyes indicate the spirit that prevailed. Consequently the revolutionary proposal of Governor Magrath in 1865 was the logical culmination, under very strenuous conditions, of months of strife and contemplated independent action.

President Davis fully appreciated from the outset the dangers of a conflict with the State authorities. This fact is evidenced by his message to Congress in August, 1862, and by many of his private letters and public utterances.[18] To Congress, he said: "If any legislation shall seem to you appropriate for adjusting differences of opinion, it will be my pleasure as well as duty to coöperate in any measure that may be devised for reconciling a just care for the public defense with a proper deference for the most scrupulous susceptibilities of the State authorities." [19] But conscription was contrary to the genius of the Confederate system and there would have been much bickering over it, even if the President had been less of a methodologist and had known more about the passions of men.

[18] In an address before the Mississippi legislature, December, 1862, he pleaded for coöperation. The Jackson *Mississippian*, quoted in the *Republican*, January 5, 1863.

[19] O. R. ser. IV, vol. II, 54.

# CHAPTER XIV

## THE CONCLUDING YEAR

WHEN Congress convened it addressed itself promptly to the consideration of the Administration's program for recruiting the armies. Substitution was forthwith abolished, and through January and the first half of February the other recommendations were earnestly deliberated upon.

Meanwhile newspaper editors and other public leaders took it upon themselves to guide Congress in the straight and narrow way. The Jacksonville *Republican* suggested three ways of filling the ranks without making levies upon immature youth and declining age. First, deserters and stragglers should be returned. The necessity of this was generally emphasized by the press and by civil and military leaders.[1] Second, the unnecessary garrisons should be withdrawn from the towns and cities, where they were of little use except to dun orderly citizens for passes. "Every provost marshal at a railway station

[1] The *Whig* said (quoted in the *Republican*, January 26th) there was a vast deal of complaint about absenteeism and desertion, and it was generally believed that the army had lost a third or more of its strength from these causes. The *Rebel* observed: "We hear a great deal of deserters and absentees" (*Republican*, January 23d). W. N. H. Smith, newly elected Congressman from North Carolina, is reported to have asserted that probably one-half of those on the muster roll were absent from duty. McPherson, *Political History of the Rebellion*, 121. The *Examiner* said the way to fill the armies was to collect stragglers (January 4, 1864).

must have a guard sufficient to do picket duty for a brigade." They "are an insufferable annoyance to the people where they are quartered. Their officious meddling with quiet citizens is a burlesque upon military rule, an outrage as intolerable as it is offensive and annoying." [2] The *Independent* of the same date pointed out still another way to add several thousands of the ages 18 to 45: there should be a consolidation of forces and the surplus officers resulting, as well as those holding sine-cures in the Government, should be reduced to ranks. It appeared absurd that brigadiers should be commanding regiments, colonels companies, and captains squads of ten or twelve men.

The governors urged the abolition of provost and post guards and passport agents upon railroads except where absolutely necessary.[3] Governor Brown with due apology ventured to suggest that it would be "infinitely better to make but little further drafts upon the producing class, and put the troops whose names are now on the muster-rolls . . . and especially the almost countless swarm of young, able-bodied officers, who are to be seen on all our railroad trains, and in all our hotels, into the Army." This, he claimed, would increase the armies 25 to 50 per cent.[4] There was much talk of the need for a strong government to suppress the evils of the time,[5] but the *Examiner* and its kind importuned the public never to trust its birthright to the unhampered discretion of Davis.[6] The Lynchburg *Virginian* flashed before the public an idea that was soon to be taken seriously, that

[2] January 23, 1864.
[3] O. R. ser. IV, vol. III, 735.
[4] *Ibid.*, 63.
[5] *Jones' Diary*, II, 123.
[6] January 12, 1864.

of putting the whole South under a military regime with General Lee in charge.[7]

Generals in the field voiced their anxiety for men. Johnston thought that 10,000 to 12,000 could be added to the army of Tennessee by substituting negroes for soldiers on detached duty.[8] The officers of Longstreet's army memorialized the authorities to put all men capable of bearing arms in the army.[9] Lee urged that every available recruit should be put in camp at once and trained for the spring campaigns. He thought much could be gained by restricting the privileges of volunteering. For example, a single company, the Rutledge Cavalry, in South Carolina was increased by volunteering so far beyond its complement that it was divided into four companies; and in North Carolina there was excessive volunteering in the heavy battery units at Wilmington and in the cavalry companies on the coast.[10] Bragg, since his discomfiture at Chattanooga, had taken up headquarters in Richmond and was using his influence on behalf of military conscription.

For the convenience of Congress the Bureau of Conscription undertook to ascertain the number of available men in the States east of the Mississippi, if the age limit should be raised to 55 years. Using such data as he could get, Colonel E. D. Blake, superintendent of the registration, estimated that there were 63,824 men between the ages of 45 and 55, and that about 70,000

[7] Diary, II, 123.

[8] O. R. ser. I, vol. XXXII, Pt. II, 511.

[9] Diary, vol. II, 126.

[10] O. R. ser. I, vol. XXXIII, 1087. He is reported to have said that if 20,000 men were added to his army and 40,000 to Johnston's they could cope successfully with the enemy. The Savannah Republican, February 1, 1864.

of those between 18 and 45 remained unaccounted for, but he doubted if more than 20,000 of the latter could be reached. His report was confessedly incomplete, especially as to Alabama and Mississippi, where it seems General Pillow's officers had not been good book-keepers.[11]

A new conscription act was passed February 17th.[12] It retained for the war those between 18 and 45 who were already in the service,[13] and lowered the age limit to 17 and raised it to 50. The new conscripts were to be organized as reserves for the defense of their respective States and for detail duty. By the creation of reserves for local defense it was proposed to release men already in the armies for action on the main battlefields, and to subject the whole man power of the Confederacy to a systematic distribution and to such use as the military strategy of the future might demand.[14] To encourage enlistment and to discourage desertion, a bounty of $100 in six per cent Government bonds was offered to all non-commissioned officers and privates who were in the service at the end of September and had not been absent without leave. The civil service, including re-cruiting for the army and navy, was reserved largely for

[11] O. R. ser. IV, vol. III, 103. One-fifth of the population was deducted as inaccessible to conscription because of the conquests of the enemy and disloyalty. No account was taken of those between the ages of 45 and 55 who might be exempted by the new act. It should be noticed, moreover, that Blake did not always quote the Census of 1860 accurately.

[12] *Ibid.*, 178. See *Jones' Diary* (vol. II, 127, 138, 129, 152) and the *Journals* for the different propositions considered.

[13] It should be noted in justice to these battle-scarred heroes that this feature of the act was scarcely necessary, for they had already inspired admiration throughout the country by their voluntary reënlistments.

[14] An experiment of this kind had been made the preceding fall by requisitioning the States for local defense troops, but it proved to be unsatisfactory. See page 239 above.

men fit for limited service only and for the senior reserves. The exemption system was radically changed,
and the President became in a large sense the custodian
and director of the agricultural and industrial interests
of the country. On the same day an act was passed
providing for the employment of not more than 20,000
free negroes and slaves for special work connected with
the army.[15]

The President's military program was fairly successful
before this Congress which was at least potentially hostile to him. It did not preëmpt the entire white labor
resources for the Government, nor did it gratify the
President by giving him complete control over exemptions and details. But it did create a local military
reserve from the youth and the aged; draft a considerable number of negroes for special service; take the able-
bodied out of the civil service; and enlarge greatly the
President's control over the productive enterprises of
the country. Enough was gained to placate his friends
and those who pinned their faith in a centralized executive control, and to frustrate his enemies and those generally who feared a military despotism.[16] However, the
concessions, as Jones keenly observed, were made to the
country instead of the President, and he and Congress
separated in a bad temper.[17]

It is obvious that in the revised system the purpose
of making the class between 18 and 45 bear the brunt
of the war still prevailed. General Grant's remark that
the Confederates were robbing the cradle and the grave

[15] O. R. ser. IV, vol. III, 208.
[16] The Mobile *Tribune* (quoted in Clarke County *Journal,* February
4th, by way of comment on the act in its preliminary stages) and the
*Examiner* illustrate the two viewpoints.
[17] *Diary,* vol. II, 133, 134, 161.

to fill their armies did not give due weight to this fact. The fundamental purpose of the act was to release the able-bodied between 18 and 45 for action on the main battlefields. It was proposed to accomplish this in three ways: (1) by the conscription of old men and boys to defend the States against raids and to do guard duty; (2) by the use of negroes to do the menial work in the armies; and (3) by limiting the number of exempted classes and authorizing the President to exempt and detail only so many, in addition, as were necessary to keep the shops and plows going.[18]

With the new means at hand the Administration braced itself for the great task before it. Measures were taken to push every vantage point of the new law. Jones predicted that there would be men enough to fill the armies if the Secretary of War and the conscription officers did not "strain the meshes of the seine too much," and he expected General Bragg to do his utmost to check any tendency of this kind.[19] From defeat at Chattanooga, General Bragg had been called to Richmond and made "supervising commander of all the armies," [20] with the duties of harmonizing military movements and of promoting military organization and efficiency. His position was that of chief military adviser to the President and supervisor ex-officio of the War Department and its bureaus. His part in conscription will appear in time; it is sufficient at this point to observe that his connection

[18] The act abolishing substitution carried this same purpose.

[19] *Diary*, vol. II, 139, 157.

[20] The *Examiner* sarcastically remarked that Johnston, Lee, and Beauregard would learn "with grateful emotions that the conqueror of Kentucky and Tennessee has been elevated to a position which his superiority deserves."

with the Bureau of Conscription seemed to bespeak action, rigidity, and efficiency.

The *Examiner* said that the new conscription act was generally accepted,[21] and there appeared to be foundation for the hope that the Confederate defenses would be stronger than ever in 1864. Did not the creation of State reserves, the revised exemption system, the system of Executive details, the use of negroes, and the provision for regular military aid to the enrolling officers point to this? But there were weaknesses and impediments that upset the general calculations.

First, it took a great deal of time to organize on the new basis. The Bureau could not secure a full corps of officers until the material was furnished by the new "invalid bill," and it was of "slow and gradual execution." Moreover, the officers supplied in this way knew nothing of conscription, and their high rank frequently made it difficult to adjust them to proper relations with the experienced officers retained by the law in the conscription business. Second, the morale of the people was at a low ebb. Most of those liable to conscription preferred claims for exemption or detail which justice and the law required to be carefully examined.[22] Third, a variety of obstacles were set in the way of the enrolling officers by the people, the courts, State authorities, and

[21] February 20th. The *Whig* and the Nashville *Dispatch* (February 29th) disagreed with the *Examiner*. According to these papers all classes were groaning under the burdens of the war and were casting about for means of averting starvation. The *Dispatch* said that the law caused a "great flutter" in some places and a stampeding to the North and to foreign parts.

[22] O. R. ser. IV, vol. III, 334. See pages 88-94 above for an account of how men kept out of service by advancing these claims. The *Whig* (quoted in the *Republican,* January 26th) said that the spirit of the people was so low that Lincoln could come and take them.

"demagoging politicians." And, fourth, the organization of the reserves was retarded by the opposition of the governors.[23]

Conflict with the State authorities over such matters as the suspension of the writ of habeas corpus, the appointment of army officers, and the exemption of State officers and employees was becoming general and almost constant. Even the Gulf States, in which there had been relatively little friction with State authority, began a real contest with the Confederate Government for their man power. These States had come to occupy a position of semi-isolation, and their governors felt constrained to organize the strongest possible local defense. They had the impulse to emulate the independent action of the Trans-Mississippi Department.[24] Conflict with State authority was a most serious obstacle to conscription.

The status of conscription in mid winter was not gratifying to the military leaders. Men were little inclined to take up quarters in the cold and disease-infested camps;[25] and those who had furnished substitutes dreaded the jeers and taunts of the veterans of the fields. General Lee said that only a few conscripts were

---

[23] See pages 239-249 above for an account of this.

[24] General E. K. Smith had the preceding fall called the leading jurists and statesmen of his department together to organize for self-defense. The President approved and General Smith took complete charge of affairs with only one obligation to the President; namely, that of following the system east of the river as closely as practicable. O. R. ser. I, vol. XXII, Pt. II, 949, 1005, 1010.

[25] The papers carried most tragical descriptions of deprivations and sufferings. Piteous appeals for food and clothing were made by the men in camp. The Nashville *Dispatch* asserted (February 29th, upon the authority of the *Whig*) that there were 3,000 barefooted men in Longstreet's corps alone and expressed a doubt shared by the *Whig,* January 1st, if the Government could feed and clothe more men than were then in camp.

coming to his army, and he offered to detail some of his officers temporarily to aid the enrolling officers.[26]   General Polk reported that a spirit of rebellion had developed in the pine-land counties of eastern Mississippi and in the River counties.   Conditions were as bad or worse in large areas in Alabama, especially in the northern part. It had become dangerous even for a pay master to enter this section without guard.   Any man in Confederate uniform was less welcome than a revenue officer,—the mountaineer's *bête noir* before the day of enrolling officers.[27]   Conditions had been bad for many months in Alabama and Mississippi, as was pointed out in the preceding chapter, but they probably were aggravated at this time by the irregularities involved in the transition from General Pillow's system back to the regular system.

General Polk, who was a zealous convert of military conscription, requested that he be given authority to put the rebellious conscripts of his department in the army. Secretary Seddon replied with kindness, pointing out the inherent weakness of military conscription, as it was revealed by the experiments of the preceding year, and assured him that the "efficient head of the Conscript Bureau" would soon establish order and efficiency in the conscription system.   Polk made good, however, with his demand for power to police his department.   Preston doubtless was willing that he should have the task.[28] Governor Watts requested authority to collect the conscripts in Alabama, but this, of course, was declined. Conscription by local civil or military authority, next to

[26] O. R. ser. I, vol. XXXIII, 1087.   The *Examiner,* January 20, 22, 1864.
[27] *Ibid.,* vol. XXXII, Pt. III, 725.   See same source, ser. IV, vol. III, 251, for Commandant Lockhart's statement of conditions in Alabama.
[28] See O. R. ser. I, vol. XXXII, Pt. III, 644, 723-726, for the Polk correspondence.

conscription by the generals commanding, Superintendent
Preston believed was the worst possible system. During
his six months in the Bureau he said there was not a single
man sent to the field by State authority. He saw no
reason for extraordinary devices of conscription if the
governors would support the Bureau and its agents
faithfully.[29]

In spite of all impediments the Bureau was making a
fair showing by the opening of spring. The rigorous
policy of the Government—exhibited by the suspension
of the writ of habeas corpus, the act for punishing those
who encouraged desertion or aided deserters, and the
refusal to suspend conscription in certain parts of North
Carolina, Louisiana, and Texas [30]—was producing good
results. This is attested by the fact that references in
the official papers to desertion were infrequent and the
rosters of the leading armies were enlarged. Superintendent Preston reported, on the basis of incomplete
returns, that the Bureau added 15,820 men to the army
between January 1st and April 1st, and more than as
many again had volunteered, largely in violation of law
and orders.[31] He admitted the results of conscription
since January 1st had not been equal to the expectations
of the public. Up to May 1st, however, he asserted that
no branch of the public service "was working with more
order and efficiency" than conscription, and that "all
obstacles and impediments . . . were yielding to the
intelligence, the indomitable zeal and devotion of the

[29] O. R. ser. IV, vol. III, 224.
[30] O. R. ser. I, vol. LIII, 324, 881, 985; ser. IV, vol. III, 189, 203.
[31] The report showed that 26,472 were exempted and 13,142 detailed,
making a total of 55,434 men disposed of. O. R. ser. IV, vol. III, 354,
363, 744. The *Republican* claimed (February 1st) that about 1,600 men
were added to the army of Tennessee during the last twenty days of
January, but most of them were returned absentees or deserters.

officers." "Large and rapid accessions to the Army" were being made. In the increased activity of the Bureau one sees the influence of General Bragg's presence in Richmond. He was known to be watching conscription with a critical eye.

Thus there was some foundation for the assuring tone of Secretary Seddon's report to the President on the eve of the campaigns against Richmond and Atlanta. It was his opinion that the Confederate forces approximated, relatively, more nearly than before the strength of their enemies.[32] They were outnumbered two to one, but by reason of holding the interior line they were numerically strong enough to defend themselves, if adequately equipped.

The experiences of the Bureau up to May 1st established certain cardinal facts about conscription. These Preston laid before the Secretary of War with frankness and solicitude. Under existing laws, orders, and conditions only a few more men could be furnished. So far as conscription from the general population was concerned, the Bureau might as well cease at the end of the year. The unnecessary details, able-bodied conscripts in the civil service of the States, and accretions by age were about the only sources of supply. Further drafts upon the small farmers and mechanics must be made with the utmost prudence, if at all. A sharp line must be drawn between the producers and the non-producers. This was a task of extracting the drones, or, as Preston said, "a system of delicate gleaning from the population of the country, involving the most laborious, patient, cautious, and intelligent re-investigation into the relations of every man to the public defense." It was a tedious and deli-

[32] O. R. ser. IV, vol. III, 327.

cate undertaking. Tact, zeal, and acute detection on the part of the officers, and the sympathetic support of the public were the requisites of success; but many of the officers with peculiar fitness and training had been taken from the conscription service, and "every authority, every prejudice, every interest, and every fear" opposed the efforts of those remaining.

These were the problems. Preston proposed to solve them as follows: (1) There should be a stern revocation of superfluous details;[33] (2) except for agriculture and manufacture, labor should be furnished from the exempted classes, reserves, light-duty conscripts, and the "invalid corps"; (3) the efficient officers taken from the Bureau should be restored to it; (4) an appeal should be made to the States to release the large number of able-bodied young men employed in their civil service; and (5) commanding officers should not be allowed again to conscript and recruit for special localities.

Congress met again in May but it did nothing to improve upon conscription. Ignoring Preston's recommendations, it would have enlarged one of the exemption classes but for the timely veto of the President.[34] It is one of the strange episodes of the War that Congress, instead of bending its efforts to give Lee every man possible, could have sat behind his beleaguered thin line and deliberated upon the expansion of the exemption system. Apparently it had too much confidence in the General and not enough in the President.

While the rival armies grappled in deadly combat in

[33] Preston said that not one detail in ten was necessary. No department of government, he charged, had complied with the law and he advised a rigid enforcement of it as soon as the reserves were organized.

[34] See pages 89-90 above.

the swamps of Virginia and on the hills of Northern
Georgia, such reports as came in indicated that conscription was not producing large results.  In East Louisiana
it was declared a failure, owing to the laxity and irregularities of the officers and the failure of the government
to support them.[35]  In Alabama and Mississippi, according to General Polk, the conscription officers were not
arresting many deserters, and in some of the counties the
Federal recruiting agents were organizing mounted regiments.[36]  From Western North Carolina came reports,
long since familiar, of violence and resistance.  However, Assistant Adjutant General Anderson made a swift
tour of inspection in the State and got the impression
that conscription was fairly successful there.[37]  And a
correspondent of the Charleston *Courier* wrote from
Lenoir, in the heart of the disaffected area: "Holdenism
is on the wane, and patriotic views are in the ascend-
ant." [38]  The reserves had not all been enrolled and
organized, and there was much quibbling with the governors about them.

According to the official reports there were only
148,418 men present for duty in the armies east of the
Mississippi June 30th.[39]  There were not, then, more
than 200,000 men present for duty in all of the armies,
which would make about 30,000 to 40,000 less than were
present for duty at the end of the preceding year.

[35] O. R. ser. IV, vol. III, 349.
[36] See report of Assistant Inspector General George B. Hodge, O. R.
ser. IV, vol. III, 445.  The Clarke County *Journal,* June 2d, reported that
General Polk's amnesty proclamation had caused thousands to return to
the armies within three weeks.  Some of these deserters had not been in
the service since the fall of Vicksburg.
[37] See O. R. ser. IV, vol. III, 353, 504, 541.
[38] Quoted in the Clarke County *Journal,* June 2d.
[39] O. R. ser. IV, vol. III, 520.

The terrible May and June days brought great glory and prestige to the Confederate arms. Grant's mighty army was given a stunning reversal at Cold Harbor, and Sherman was not able to reach Atlanta. Once again Southern hearts throbbed with hope. Conversely, in the North there was despair. More than 100,000 lives had been sacrificed and not a decisive victory for well-nigh a year. Hundreds of thousands began to entertain seriously the notion of peace, and the price of gold soared. The belief generally prevailed in the South that if neither Richmond nor Atlanta fell before the election President Lincoln would be defeated and peace would be restored. Thus it became a matter of enlightened policy to make a mighty effort to hold Grant and Sherman in check for a few more months.

The sober-minded among the civil and military leaders knew that the crisis was not over; rather it had just begun. Lee was rapidly wearing his forces down whipping Grant, and the Army of the West was clearly in straits. Here on the Western battle front a drama of great economic and political, as well as military, significance was being enacted, and North and South anxious eyes were bent upon it. There was impatience in the North at Sherman's tardiness, but Davis and his counsellors knew that he was surely, if slowly, succeeding. They began to comb the country for recruits with which to check him.

The new conscription law and the orders pursuant to it had not produced the results anticipated. It was expected that the abolition of substitution and the extraction of able-bodied conscripts from the civil service would result in the addition of large forces to the armies. But those who had furnished substitutes generally found ways to keep off the battlefield [40] and, according to the official papers, very few men fit for field duty had been turned over to the enrolling officers by the departments and bureaus. Even the departments and bureaus housed officially under the same roof as the President and the Secretary of War did not give up their men, though the Secretary at one time refused pay to the young and able-bodied clerks.[41] Generally speaking, those between 18 and 45 who became liable under the revised system made application for exemption or detail, expecting, if their applications were rejected, to get at least a few months' immunity while their cases made their slow and uncertain journey to Richmond and back.[42]

To expedite conscription the President ordered, July 1st, a rigid investigation of the departments and bureaus to see why they had not given over their able-bodied young men; the Secretary of war ordered that the practice of furloughing applicants for details until their cases were acted upon should be stopped; and measures were taken to get quicker action on all requests for exemption or detail.[43] General Bragg's report from Atlanta, July 26th, indicated that these measures produced immediate results in the army of the West.[44] But Lee's army was not being replenished.[45] Something else must be done.

[40] Page 48 above.

[41] *Jones' Diary*, vol. II, 144, 145. According to Jones the nephews, cousins, and pets of the authorities got increased pay, and were not generally mustered along with the rest when Richmond was threatened.

[42] See pages 91-92 above for an account of this.

[43] O. R. ser. IV, vol. III, 524, 531, 534, 578. It was the opinion of some of the inspectors that conscription could not be much improved until the Bureau and the local officers acted more promptly on the papers submitted to them (504-541).

[44] *Jones' Diary*, vol. II, 256.

[45] The *Diary*, II, 272. General Lee said that the Bureau of Conscription had ceased to send forward recruits. *Ibid.*, 274 (August 30th). A

September 3d Sherman occupied Atlanta and the South was stunned. If it needed more to frustrate and dishearten it, it was soon to have it in a series of disasters in the Valley of Virginia. Anything seemed possible; Sherman might move Richmondward through the Carolinas, or his long line of communications might be cut and the captor made captive. Certainly the Confederate cause was desperate. The menace of Sherman's victory and President Lincoln's call for 500,000 recruits made it imperative to use promptly every available means to increase the numbers and efficiency of the armies. Some, believing that the decisive stage had been reached, favored a rising in mass to expel or capture Sherman. A nation in arms for a few months might save a nation.[46]

The desperate resolve to put every available man in the field led to the resurrection of military conscription in modified form. General Bragg was the leading exponent in Richmond of military conscription. He had long since concluded that the Bureau of Conscription was utterly inadequate. He laid to its charge his failure in Tennessee, and was confident that its inefficiency would effect finally the downfall of the Confederacy. Though freighted with the pompous title of "general supervisor of the Confederate Armies,"—he had more befittingly been called "head of the military department of the interior" —he really had little to do except to supervise the agencies of supply to the armies. Lee and Johnston did not need the supervision of the deposed chieftain of the West.

few days earlier he had written: "Without some increase of strength, I cannot see how we are to escape the natural military consequences of the enemy's numerical superiority." September 2d found him making an urgent call for able-bodied men. White, *Robert E. Lee,* 412.

[46] O. R. ser. IV, vol. III, 757.

In the late spring General Bragg set on foot a series of inspections by which he expected to expose the evils of the conscript system and to force a radical reorganization of it, in spite of Preston's powerful pen and influence.[47]    Preston was quick to sense the project and prepared for defense.  Official Richmond was soon divided into two groups over the subject of conscription.  Essentially, though, it was Bragg's and Preston's fight; the former worked quietly through the President, the latter with a felicitous pen preached the funeral of Pillow's departed system to the President, the War Department, and to Congressmen and warned them against the resurrection of it.

The controversy began while Preston was away for a rest and the destinies of the Bureau were being directed by Colonels G. W. Lay and T. P. August.  Some of General Bragg's inspectors presumed to give orders to the commandants of conscripts, whereupon Colonel August protested vigorously.  He curtly told General Bragg that the Bureau was charged with the business of conscription and upon it rested the primary responsibility for the conduct of it; it would receive with attention and respect any suggestions he might have to make; it maintained its own system for obtaining information by inspection and reports and was accustomed to giving an attentive ear to complaints or suggestions from any source; if he were not satisfied and wanted to send out his inspectors-extraordinary it was very desirable that he should instruct them as to their proper relations to the

[47] Preston's influence made a distinct impression on Jones. He recorded in his *Diary* that this "millionaire" could stalk stiffly anywhere in Richmond (vol. II, 310).

conscript officers.[48]   The General had had friction with
officers before, but he had not been accustomed to receiving instructions from colonels.   He requested that young
August should be sent to the field and kept there long
enough to learn, at least, how to be respectful to his
superiors in rank.[49]

Superintendent Preston returned at this juncture and
with a few flourishes of his pen informed Secretary Seddon that the Colonel had seen enough service to get
wounded and to develop a disease that made it necessary
to take him from the field, if not enough to master the
fine points of military courtesy.[50]   He then directed his
attention to the reports of Bragg's inspectors.   These
reports were on the whole unfavorable to the Bureau.[51]
General Bragg said they revealed a "startling state of
affairs" in Georgia, Alabama, and Mississippi.   Immediately after the fall of Atlanta he advised a "complete
renovation of the Bureau and its ramifications." [52]   Preston defended his officers against the attacks of Bragg and
his "ignorant and prejudiced" "detectives."   He admitted that there were some structural weaknesses in the
system but contended earnestly for the soundness of the
principle upon which it was based; namely, that armies
should be recruited by organizations distinct from the
command of armies in the field.[53]   Charging that Bragg's

[48] O. R. ser. IV, vol. III, 568.

[49] *Jones' Diary*, vol. II, 278.

[50] O. R. ser. IV, vol. III, 630.

[51] *Ibid.*, 504, 539, 542, 578; *Jones' Diary*, vol. II, 223.

[52] Nothing but stern, rigid administration could correct the evils of
conscription. O. R. ser. IV, vol. III, 624.

[53] *Ibid.*, 630. He computed that if Pillow's system should be revived
and applied to the whole Confederacy it would take 6,000 officers and
36,000 men to maintain it, and expressed a doubt that Bragg himself, not
to mention the other generals, would favor maintaining the proportion of
men employed by Pillow.

"renovation" scheme was primarily a move to oust him, he very tactfully offered his resignation, requesting that the basic principle of the prevailing system should not be destroyed merely to effect a change of personnel. The President and Secretary Seddon were not quite ready to see him make a martyr of himself, so they induced him to withdraw his resignation. His splendid show of self-effacement added to the strength of his pen, and he used it with relentless zeal and eloquence to sustain the Bureau against the designs of Bragg.

But he had to yield ground. General Bragg a week later succeeded in getting the President to issue an order putting the generals of the reserve forces in control of conscription, "under the direction of the Secretary of War, through the Conscript Bureau." [54] The divided control set up by this order resulted in conflict between Superintendent Preston and the generals of reserves. Apparently it was made the duty of the general of reserves to enforce conscription in his State under the immediate direction of the Bureau, reporting regularly all particulars to it and referring all important questions, such as applications for exemption and detail, to it for decision. Preston said the President assured him that this was the purpose of the order.[55] The generals of reserves interpreted it to mean that they were in complete charge of conscription and that the Bureau of Conscrip-

[54] Jones claims that he suggested the idea to Bragg (*Diary*, vol. II, 290). Preston said this order showed that "the silent, but sure, legal working of the conscription authority overcoming popular prejudice, the opposition of State executives and judicial authorities, the weakness of its own agencies, the clamor of ignorant and interested officials, filling the ranks as far as the law allowed, was unappreciated." O. R. ser. IV, vol. III, 744. This plan provided for a system in each State similar to that of the Trans-Mississippi Department.

[55] O. R. ser. IV, vol. III, 737.

tion was merely a clerical channel through which to reach the War Department,—the fountain source of authority.[56] General Kemper, commanding the reserves in Virginia with headquarters in Richmond, felt that since he was daily in direct touch with the War Department he did not need the intermediary services of the Bureau. Preston vigorously protested that the Bureau was more than a medium of communication; that it was, as it had ever been, a special agency of the War Department for the supervision and direction of conscription.

General Kemper's independent action led to a spirited controversy with Superintendent Preston which lasted throughout the fall.[57] Time after time Preston called upon the President and the Department for an order clarifying the relations between the Bureau and General Kemper, but without success. Meanwhile he lectured the President and the War Department, and through them, "ignorant and presumptuous persons in high position" on the dangers of military conscription.

He reached the climax of his indictment of military conscription and of those who wanted to foist it upon the public in his communication to Secretary Seddon, November 5th. The movement, he said, resulted mainly from the "intrusion of a small and not very reputable system

[56] The really confusing feature was that with regard to the commandant of conscripts. He was put under the command of the general of reserves but was required to make reports and returns direct to the Bureau, which meant, as Preston contended, that he was not subordinate to the general of reserves, else there was the unusual situation of a subordinate officer reporting on the work of his superior. Preston and General Kemper hotly contested the question of control of the commandant of conscripts in Virginia.

[57] No evidence has been found of a serious conflict with the generals of reserves in the other States. See O. R. ser. IV, vol. III, 742, 744, 780, 785, 837, 854, 859, 894, and 946 for the leading facts of this significant controversy. See also *Jones' Diary*, vol. II, 310, 315, 347.

of police detection into the administration of a great national policy; espionage of Vidocq to upset the schemes of Carnot with his bureau for the public defense 'and his bureau for the public welfare.'" He feared that conscription was "destined to become nothing more than a ferocious and ignorant military outrage of public law and personal right, devastating the country and weakening the armies." There was danger that the story of Turkish military conscription in Egypt might be reenacted in the Confederacy. At the approach of the Pasha's conscription officers, men, women, and children fled from the villages to the deserts, and when the man-hunters returned from the pursuit the villages and fields were desolate and the deserts "white with the bleached bones of women and children." The imaginations of the President and General Bragg were not quite lively enough to establish an identity between the janizary and the man in gray. No new conscription orders were issued.

The Superintendent did not stop with analyzing the inherent weaknesses and dangers of conscription. He charged that it was a matter of record that military conscription had failed the preceding year, and as for General Kemper, he had only a "beggarly list" of conscripts to show for his toils. Kemper retorted that if he had been correctly informed he had conscripted more than half as many men in eighteen days as the Bureau of Conscription had in twelve months. He asked to be relieved of his command, and advised that the generals of reserves should be given control of conscription or they should be "relieved of their present irritating connection with that business." Adjutant and Inspector General Cooper recommended that a hard and fast line should be drawn between military functions in conscription and purely bureau duties, leaving the latter to the Bureau of Conscription.[58]    Certainly something needed to be done to terminate the friction between the agencies of conscription.

When Preston realized that he was fighting a losing battle he turned to his friend, Representative Miles of South Carolina, and requested him to use his influence to defeat military conscription.    He laid before Mr. Miles the gems of his now well-worn commentaries upon conscription.

One sees in the President's reply of silence to Preston's depositions and requests evidence of the division over conscription in official circles at Richmond.    There was a deadlock between the President, Bragg, and Cooper on the one side and Preston, Seddon, and Campbell on the other.    The President might have yielded to Bragg and cut the Gordian knot, but he could scarcely afford to convert more influential friends into enemies or to lose the service of his trained administrators at this critical time.    So Kemper was allowed virtually a free hand in Virginia, while the Bureau supervised conscription elsewhere.    Judge Campbell was Preston's mainstay in this controversy,[59] and according to Jones he and others at Richmond made it so uncomfortable for General Bragg that he was glad to go to the Western front.    By his efforts to energize the departments and bureaus and to drive their young and able-bodied employees to the battlefields, he became *persona non grata* to many Richmond

---

[58] O. R. ser. IV, vol. III, 855, 859, 946-948, 979.

[59] Jones said that Campbell was still running conscription, and "poor General Preston—indolent and ill—has been compelled to sign, sanction, and defend documents he knew nothing about." *Diary*, vol. II, 308.

functionaries.   But before he left he almost demolished the Bureau of Conscription.

The changes instituted in early September were an earnest of the dissatisfaction with the Bureau's work; and they represented a desperate effort to solve the riddle of adjusting the balance between the recognized needs of the army, the necessities of production and distribution, and the claims of the law and humanity.   At this time the Jacksonville *Republican* asserted that there were 200,000 men within conscript age at large, and the Richmond *Whig* said that none would deny that 50,000 men could be added to the army without serious detriment to the necessary industrial interests.[60]

The revocation of most of the details produced little results.   At the end of the year complaints were general that many fit young men were still employed in the non-fighting branches.[61]   Jones rejoiced early in October that fine looking farmers were "pouring in," who had not before reported because of immoderate details and "corruption in the business of conscription."   A few weeks later, however, he complained that Cabinet officers were getting their details back, and that in two months only about 3,000 men had been sent to the army as a result of the order of revocation.[62]   Those who had employed the details were reluctant to give them up, for trained help

[60] September 22d. It was claimed that there were 40,000 men in Virginia, alone, exempted and detailed who should be in the army. In Alabama the inspector's report showed that there were about 15,000 men fit for duty who were not in the field. The *Mercury,* November 9th.

[61] See pages 90-94 above.

[62] He noted early in December that the Bureau was "busily engaged in furloughing and detailing the rich slave owners." And General Lee complained that his army was being depleted by details, often for private and speculative purposes. *Diary,* vol. II, 307, 338, 344, 350.

was scarce and it was difficult to get light duty men.[63] Enough were taken, however, to produce alarm in some lines of work. November 15th the Senate committee on military affairs was instructed to inquire if the order revoking details required any modification by legislation to preserve the producing interests of the country.[64] A few weeks later the president of the Columbia and Augusta Railroad Company wrote the Secretary of War that he did not have enough contractors to build his road, which was imperatively necessary after Sherman occupied Savannah.[65]

The evidence does not bear out Preston's claim (December 18th) that "the present system has been efficacious," and before it was "rudely disturbed by the pestilent interference" of the military it had "commended itself . . . to the people, the States, the Congress, yourself [Secretary Seddon], and the President." [66] His earnest appeals for the perpetuation of the Bureau discredited his calculation at the beginning of the year that it would finish its work by the end of the year and could then be discontinued. The combined efforts of the Bureau and the generals of reserves were not sufficient to gather up the remnants of the fighting population.[67]

[63] The effort to create a reserve of light duty men to take the places of the young and able-bodied details was largely a failure. The light duty men, who former Senator Phelan of Mississippi said preferred to be no duty men, were allowed to stay at home. There being no person to whom application could be made for these men, the employers of details were strongly tempted to hold on to those they had. O. R. ser. IV, vol. III, 708. The retention of able-bodied young men became a matter of serious Congressional investigation. *Ibid.,* 943; the *Journal,* vol. IV, 261, 269, 300, 316, 330.

[64] The *Journal,* vol. IV, 268.

[65] O. R. ser. IV, vol. III, 968.

[66] *Ibid.,* 947.

[67] *Jones' Diary,* vol. II, 280, 281, 287, 288.

There were probably less than 20,000 men added to the armies during September and October.[68] Meantime General Lee inquired of the Secretary of War whether there was any prospect of obtaining an increase for his army. "If not," he warned, "it will be very difficult for us to maintain ourselves. . . . If we can get out our entire arms-bearing population in Virginia and North Carolina, and relieve all detailed men with negroes, we may be able, with the blessing of God, to keep the enemy in check to the beginning of winter." [69] Hood's army was less than half as large as Sherman's. So the latter could divide his command and send one-half to defeat Hood's frantic efforts to cut his line of communication, while with the other half he could set out with practically no opposition on his memorable march to Savannah.

When Hood's army was near the day of its annihilation and Sherman was well on his campaign of teaching Georgians and the world what war really was, new measures were adopted to increase the fighting force. An order was issued to rob the Georgia hospitals of all patients who were able to "travel"; and to take all exempted agriculturists and mechanics, except munition workers, and one-fifth of the ordnance and mining

[68] O. R. ser. IV, vol. III, 789, 859.
[69] O. R. ser. I, vol. XLII, Pt. III, 1134. See also *Jones' Diary*, vol. II, 281. The records show that there were 62,875 men present for duty in his command, October 31st, not including Kershaw's division of cavalry serving in the Valley district; while there were 74,747 present for duty November 30th. The aggregate present and absent at the latter date totaled 181,814. *Ibid.*, vol. XLII, Pt. III, 1186, 1236. Jones observed December 31st that Lee's army was diminishing rather than increasing, under the manipulations of the Bureau (*Diary*, vol. II, 371). This may have been true, but it should be borne in mind that Jones was prejudiced against the Bureau.

bureau.[70]  Another experiment with inspection as a means of driving men to the colors was made. Inspection had always been a considerable part of conscription activities, but the system set up by the order of December 1st was far more thoroughgoing and rigid than before. It in fact amounted to a detective's department within the Bureau with manifold duties, and instructions so copious that, as Preston said, no "treatise of moderate dimensions" could contain them.[71]  Besides their duties of instructing enrolling officers, of checking up on their every act and revising their decisions, of recommending changes for improving the service and the removal of incompetent officers, of promoting harmony between State authorities and the enrolling officers, and supervising the activities of exempts and details, the inspection officers were official advisers as to how every man of conscript age should be placed to render his best service. The watchwords of their duty were "visitation, scrutiny, revision and report." [72]

The new inspection system did not perfect the machinery of conscription. With the invasion of Georgia authority broke down in the lower South. Without the aid of a large military force it was no longer possible to recruit in this section for Johnston's and Lee's armies, and such force was not to be had. December 29th, In-

[70] Stephenson, *The Day of the Confederacy,* 150.  Many of the detailed men had already gone into the Confederate army and into the militia. They had no legal right to volunteer into the militia, but upon the recommendation of General Cobb they were not molested.

[71] O. R. ser. IV, vol. III, 887.  The machinery consisted of an inspector general, with headquarters in the Bureau, a State inspector, and Congressional district inspectors.

[72] In the Trans-Mississippi Department it was the duty of the enrolling officers and the commanders of their supporting forces to report each other for inefficiency, and regular inspectors were sent to each district to inspect all of them.  O. R. ser. I, vol. XLI, Pt. II, 1002.

spector H. W. Walter wrote Senator J. W. C. Watson
that he regarded the conscript department in Georgia,
Alabama, and Mississippi as "almost worthless."  He
said that there had been only 537 men between the ages
of 18 and 45 conscripted in Mississippi within the last
five months, and 302 of them deserted before leaving the
State.[73]  He believed that most of those of conscript age
had been conscribed and that the Bureau of Conscription
might as well be abolished.  The commandant of conscripts in Alabama said that it was "absolutely necessary" that the conscript officers "should be supplied with
an adequate and effective force." [74]  Howell Cobb, general of reserves in Georgia, wrote Seddon (December
25th) that it would take a whole army to enforce the
conscript law, if conditions in the other States were like
they were in Georgia, Alabama, and Tennessee.  Two
years of experience had demonstrated to him that the
effort to conscribe and send men to the old organizations
was a failure.  He recommended that the old organization should be consolidated and that men should be
allowed to volunteer into new organizations, holding
conscription in reserve as a threat to those who were not
inclined to volunteer.[75]

The failure of the Bureau of Conscription to return
deserters was as conspicuous as its failure to pick up the
scattering conscripts.  From all quarters came reports of

[73] The Bureau claimed to have put more than 1,000 in the army, but
Walter said many of these voluntarily surrendered themselves, and still
more were stragglers overstaying their furloughs. O. R. ser. IV, vol.
III, 976.                              [74] Ibid., 880.
[75] Ibid., 964.  This plan had become a sort of fetish with General Cobb.
Five days later Seddon wrote Cobb requesting his counsel as to any
other "possible" mode of recruitment than conscription, and as to the
practicability of employing slaves as soldiers.  Apparently he had not
received Cobb's communication. Ibid., 981.

numerous desertions and suggestions for returning the deserters. The practice was especially malignant in the lower South after the fall of Atlanta.[76] Terrible conditions in the army, unspeakable suffering in the homes of the poor, and a conviction that the cause was lost, led thousands who had endured with unsurpassed fortitude up to this time to take French leave of their commands. Some of the reservists deserted, even though they were called out solely for the defense of their States.[77] Not all of the deserters were "poor country clod-hoppers," but doubtless most of them were, and their desertion was due in part, as Jones asserted over and over again, to the deep-seated conviction that the wealthy were at home enjoying their usual comforts.[78] The feeble efforts of the Bureau, reënforced by the governors, the legislatures, and leading public men were not sufficient to restore many of them to their commands.

Toward the end of the year military leaders and many civil leaders were ready to abandon the Bureau of Conscription. But its failure was not due alone to its weaknesses. There was much truth in the contention of the Vice-President, the Secretary of War, Superintendent Preston, and others that the population was about exhausted.[79] The productive agencies, that were supposed

---

[76] O. R. ser. I, vol. XXXIX, Pt. III, 801; ser. IV, vol. III, 707, 880, 881, 976; Clarke County *Journal,* October 20th. It was reported from Texas that in some cases whole companies and battalions had deserted. O. R. ser. I, vol. XXXIV, Pt. III, 726.

[77] O. R. ser. IV, vol. III, 880.

[78] Jones remonstrated often in his *Diary* that because of "pernicious" partiality the higher class was not thrust into the trenches. He predicted that this situation would lead to the collapse of the Confederacy. Vol. II, 272, 277, 280, 305, 347.

[79] *Jones' Diary,* vol. II, 280; O. R. ser. III, vol. V, 696; ser. IV, vol. II, 694; vol. III, 976. Secretary Seddon said that the Bureau was operating creditably, considering its handicaps (*Ibid.,* 766).

by military leaders, soldiers, and anxious patriots to have
a surfeit of labor, were in fact seriously handicapped for
a lack of it; and they vied with the army for the scanty
remnant of the able-bodied. There were conscripts at
large but the number probably was not great.[80]

The failure of the Bureau of Conscription to collect
the scattered and unwilling fragments was due to several
causes. First, the controversy with the military conscriptionists distracted it. Superintendent Preston consumed
much time and thought in defense of the Bureau that
might have been applied profitably to improving upon its
services. Second, the officers of conscription were noto-
riously incompetent. Preston said that the agencies of
conscription were "extremely defective," and the commandant of conscripts of Georgia declared that there
were not twenty conscript officers in Georgia who had a
single qualification for their offices.[81] Third, the enrolling officers did not have adequate military backing.[82]
Even when the reserves were used in support of conscription, their equipment gave the appearance that they
had ransacked a museum. Their guns were nondescript,
rusty, and worn out, and their ammunition was scanty
and frequently did not fit.[83] Fourth, the machinery of

[80] The President shared the common belief that a considerable number
of conscripts in Georgia had not been reached (O. R. ser. IV, vol. III,
981). The estimate of Custis Jones (son of the famous war clerk) that
there were 550,000 available men was a mere speculation, although the
*Diary,* the faithful family record, carries the observation that there were
thus "enough for defense for several years yet, if the Bureau of Conscription were abolished and a better system adopted." Vol. II, 280, 399.

[81] O. R. ser. IV, vol. III, 863, 1049. See also pages 785, 853, 868, 869,
871, 894, 940.

[82] The supporting military force was probably relatively stronger in the
Trans-Mississippi Department than east of the River. O. R. ser. I, vol.
XLI, Pt. II, 1002.

[83] O. R. ser. I, vol. III, 881.

conscription was elaborate and complex, and therefore clumsy and slow of action. It needed to be simplified, centralized, and energized. Superintendent Preston was conscious of its weaknesses and recommended the reforms necessary to make it "active and energetic . . . simple and orderly in structure, uniform and rapid in operation." Fifth, the independent action of State authorities, which became alarmingly prevalent toward the end of the year, was a great hindrance to the Bureau of Conscription.

The recommendations of the military conscriptionists that the Bureau of Conscription should be abolished and a military department of the interior, under the direction of "a general-in-chief of the reserves and conscription," set up in its stead did not find place in the President's recommendations to Congress.[84] The President and the Secretary of War recommended that class exemption should be abolished and that a general militia law should be passed for purposes of local defense. They concurred in the opinion that there were as many of military age as could be advantageously employed in the active service. Each favored a more extensive use of slaves for labor purposes, and they submitted for public reflection that it might become necessary to use slaves as soldiers.[85]

The military program which inspired so much hope at the beginning of the year was in disrepute before

[84] Preston said that as far as he had been able to ascertain the features of their scheme, it was "a cumbrous, confused mass of indigested regulations, the offspring of utter ignorance of the nature of the duties to be performed, of the condition of the country, and the wants of the public service . . . a mere military experiment on the vitals of the country." O. R. ser. IV, vol. III, 947.

[85] Ibid., 756, 796.

the end of it. It had proved to be insufficient as to recruitment, and 100,000 deserters were said to be at large.[86] The fighting of the year had laid waste Lee's chief bases of supply and reduced the Confederacy to the Carolinas and a part of Virginia. The people were in despair and without faith in their President. The peace men and the President's enemies were encouraged to action. Former Senator James Phelan observed: "The infernal hydra of reconstruction is again stirring its envenomed heads."[87] The President's enemies were conspiring to depose him and to set General Lee up in his place with Cromwellian powers. Worst of all, perhaps, the State authorities in Georgia and the Carolinas were in virtual revolt against Richmond.

The cause of the President and the country was desperate. Faithless and torn to pieces by every species of friction, ranging from the question as to whether General Bragg should address Commissary-General Northrop according to military etiquette to the bitter contests between the President and Congress and the President and the governors, the Confederacy was tottering on its last legs while Sherman was enjoying his Christmas repast in Savannah. No system of recruitment could prosper under the conditions that prevailed. The Confederate sun was low in the West, but the end was not yet.

[86] Judge Campbell thought that Superintendent Preston and others had probably overstated the number of deserters. "But the evil," he admitted, "is one of enormous magnitude, and the means of the Department to apply a corrective have diminished in proportion to its increase."

[87] He said that there was only a "Spartan band" of genuine patriots in Mississippi, "whilst the timid, the traitor, and the time-server are 'legion.'" O. R. ser. IV, vol. III, 707.

# CHAPTER XV

## THE LAST DAYS

WHEN Grant resumed his drive on Richmond and Sherman started north to meet him it was understood that a decision would soon be made in favor of independence or re-union. The tide of time and the fortunes of war were about to bring the contending forces to the decisive hour. There could be no question about results if Lee's and Johnston's armies were not enlarged and adequately equipped and provisioned. Secretary Seddon expressed the Administration's view when he wrote to General Cobb: "Soldiers are our greatest necessity"; and no duties were "of such immediate and vital importance as those which minister to the recruitment of our armies." [1]

The people sensed the gravity of the hour, and there was gloom and deep despondency throughout the land. Friendly patriots, who had notions as to how the Confederacy could save itself, put to a severe test the President's claim that he read all letters addressed to him; while his enemies spared no effort to ridicule and revile him. There was a tremendous hue and cry against him in the press. The editors of the *Examiner* and *Mercury,* overcome with wrath and disgust, boldly propagated the idea of overthrowing him; [2] while many other papers,

[1] O. R. ser. IV, vol. III, 981, 1030.
[2] The *Mercury* said that "a more inefficient organization never dis-

placed by the fortunes of war in the hands of Northern Union men, chanted the funeral dirge of the Confederacy and vied with the *Mercury* and the *Examiner* in literary composition upon the weakness and wickedness of the President.

Numerous expedients were proposed. The *Examiner* said three courses of action were needed: (1) the enforcement of the conscription law and the inflexible punishment of all deserters by death; (2) the energizing of the commissary department so it would supply the army without looking for help from abroad; and (3) the selection of the best officers of the army for defense.[3] Some advocated the arming of slaves, while others thought a general plan of abolition might induce England and France to espouse the Confederate cause. The plan that attracted most attention in the first weeks of the year was that of making General Lee military dictator. The *Examiner* probably expressed a popular sentiment when it advised: "In the name of God let Lee save us, if he will: no one else can." There was a general feeling that this great chieftain could, if allowed, go down into the pit like a second Heracles and bring back the fair Alcestis of victory. The movement gathered such momentum that some of the States considered calling conventions for the purpose of deposing Davis, and probably nothing but the unqualified disapproval of the General himself defeated it.[4]

graced the science of War." Never was a great power and opportunity "so frittered away, so broken down, so misapplied, so utterly disorganized, by an ineradicable vice of unscrupulous administration." January 10, 1865.

[3] February 20, 1865.

[4] The *Examiner*, January 9th, 12th, 17th, 21st; *Atlantic Monthly*, 107: 192. The making of Lee "General in Chief" of the army was a by-product of this movement.

The Bureau of Conscription and the auxiliary State reserve forces were confessedly inadequate for the work before them. Considerable numbers of conscripts had never been reached,[5] and a vast number of deserters, according to the Richmond authorities,[6] were at large and were so bold that they did not go to the trouble to hide themselves.[7] The return of these men was regarded the great necessity of the hour.[8] From all of the States reports came in that the enrolling officers were incompetent or unprincipled, and the generals of reserves claimed that their forces could not give effective aid until they were relieved of general military duty. Superintendent Preston said the service never would "be performed satisfactorily until intelligent and suitable officers [were] selected and permanently assigned to duty."[9] There was truth in the extravagant observation of the *Examiner* that: "Enrolling officers apparently make a clean sweep of the country on paper, and after a documentary manner," but they did not produce the men. The Bureau "is too cumbrous and slow in action, admits of too many references and red tape, so that those who are desirous of avoiding service can do so by mere delay and circumlocution; months and even years pass, the enrolled conscript grows old or he has removed to another part of

[5] O. R. ser. IV, 981, 1009, 1049.

[6] It was asserted in Richmond that 72,000 men deserted between October 1, 1864, and February 4, 1865. *The Annual Cyclopædia,* 1865, 188.

[7] Preston said the deserters were the more numerous class in some communities. The vicious element among them instituted a reign of terror. It is significant that not all of the deserters belonged to the regular forces: some of them were details, and others belonged to the local defense units. O. R. ser. IV, vol. III, 1007, 1065, 1101, 1119, 1121, 1122, 1145, 1146; the *Mercury,* January 10, 1865; the Clarke County *Journal,* January 26, 1865; the *Examiner,* February 20, 1865.

[8] O. R. ser. IV, vol. III, 1119, 1168.

[9] *Ibid.,* 1048.

the country, and his papers require a reference to the military authorities of the State or district; and so enrolling officers are always pouring our fighting material into a tub of the Danaides, pierced with an hundred auger holes." [10]

Congress revised some minor features of the conscript laws; abolished the Bureau of Conscription; and after months of desultory deliberation passed an act for the arming of slaves and prepared to adjourn. It rejected flatly the President's propositions for the abolition of class exemptions [11] and for a general militia law. Judge Campbell's report on military, financial, and political conditions, accompanied by reports from the departments of supply, alarmed the President.[12] He transmitted the reports secretly to Congress without comment; and wrote a special message urging it not to adjourn and scolding it for its tardiness and for its failure to enact the military legislation recommended by him. He urged with renewed vigor the abolition of class exemptions and the passage of a general militia law, so that the State militia might be put on a firmer footing and be subjected in a systematic way to the call of the Confederate Government.[13] To these demands he added the necessity for suspending the writ of habeas corpus.[14]

This message exhibited not only impatience and anxiety, but also President Davis' conception of the relative functions of the President, as Commander-in-Chief of

[10] February 20, 1865.

[11] Pages 101-105 above.

[12] Campbell claimed later that he was convinced of the futility of trying to continue hostilities and advised President Davis to open negotiations for peace. Letter to Curtis, *Century Magazine,* October, 1865, 951.

[13] He regarded a general military law as the measure most needed to afford an effective increase of the military strength.

[14] O. R. ser. IV, vol. III, 1133.

the military forces, and of Congress in time of war. Congress had, of course, power to make laws to raise and preserve armies, but he believed that the President's recommendations should be accepted by Congress as a guide in its military legislation. With impatience and apparent astonishment he remonstrated: "The recommendation to abolish all class exemptions has not met your favor, although still deemed by me a valuable and important measure." This statement was accepted by zealous Congressmen, and by the President's enemies in and out of Congress, as the height of Executive dogmatism and intolerance; and with similar utterances it gave the anti-Administration forces and the hostile press a fine theme for exposition.

The conflict found its way into the papers. The Montgomery *Advertiser,* for example, observed: "It seems that the President is not yet satisfied with his power. He wants the system of exemption by classes abandoned. . . . The exemption by classes for special pursuits and professions, he says is not defensible in theory. Of course not—it conflicts very materially with that omnipotent military authority which he and Mr. Secretary Seddon would exercise over the civil, as well as military affairs of this country. They know so much better than Congress, or the whole Confederacy, what the necessities of the people are. They, fortunate beings, live in Richmond, the center of all intelligence, and these poor witless Congressmen reside in the dark corners of this benighted land. The many know nothing, the few everything. If this theory is carried out . . . all will be merged at once into a narrow, self-willed military despotism, from which we may never recover." [15]

[15] Quoted in the Clarke County *Journal,* November 17, 1864.

The efforts of the President to force through his military measures on the basis of his constitutional powers and of expert military opinion produced a storm of indignation in Congress. His enemies, supported by those who were jealous for the maintenance of the power and prestige of Congress, determined to measure strength with him. He, they thought, had hurled down the gauge of battle and they could do nothing less than accept it. "Congress would be derelict in its duty to permit its legitimate and constitutional influence to be destroyed by Executive admonitions, such as those contained in the message under consideration, without some public exposition of its conduct." [16] The President's insistent demand that he should be given full power over exemptions "presents the question whether the representatives of the people or the Executive shall decide what persons shall remain at home in pursuits indispensable to the vital interests of the country." [17] Thus the battle was on; criminations and recriminations sizzled back and forth, while the Federal cannons roared audibly and ominously in the nearby forests.

The President complained because the power to make details was taken from him, and he was told that it was revoked because he and the Secretary of War had abused it. He was chagrined because Congress would not see the wisdom of leaving exemption to the exercise of Executive discretion, but was informed that a matter of such vital consequences could not be intrusted to him; and since it involved the very fundamental question of the relative powers of the Executive and Congress in the raising of armies, Congress would lay it to rest by retain-

[16] O. R. ser. IV, vol. III, 1152.
[17] *Ibid.*, 1145,

ing its control over exemption. Finally, he was compelled by a profound conviction to advise Congress that the military measures passed by it were in his judgment insufficient, only to be told curtly that Congress might reasonably be excused for not having expanded Executive control more "until some satisfactory assurances are given of the ability to control and employ the means long since placed at the disposal of the Executive Department of the Government." [18] The Senate expressed a regret "that the views of the legislative department of the Government have not met the favor of the Executive, and that he should deem it both necessary and proper to express dissatisfaction with the matured opinion of Congress." [19]

The special message so antagonized Congress that it could not approach the President's recommendations with open-mindedness. It modified some features of the new exemption act but held out against the abolition of class exemptions. Likewise it stood by its former decision not to enact a general militia law, and refused to suspend the writ of habeas corpus. As to the former, it was opposed to it because if the conscript laws were enforced a militia law could operate only on those who were necessary for police purposes in the States and for arresting deserters; concerning the latter, it was unwilling to antagonize the people who were definitely arrayed against the suspension of the writ.[20]

The most significant military legislation done by Con-

[18] O. R. ser. IV, vol. III, 1146.

[19] *Ibid.,* 1150.

[20] North Carolina, Georgia, and Mississippi had already expressed through their legislatures great repugnance to the legislation of Congress suspending the writ. See O. R. ser. IV, vol. III, 1144, 1152.

gress in this its final session was the act providing for the
enrollment of slaves. The President was authorized to
ask the masters for any number of slaves thought by him
to be necessary.[21] If he did not receive a sufficient
number by the volunteer method, he was authorized to
requisition the States for their quota of 300,000 men to
be raised "irrespective of color," providing that not more
than twenty-five per cent of the male slaves between the
ages of 18 and 45 in any State could be called out. The
slaves were to be subject to the same regulations as white
soldiers, but military service would not affect the status
of the slaves without the consent of their masters and of
the State in which they resided. The War Department
took advantage of the indefiniteness of this feature of
the act and interpreted it with a view to military necessity. In the order published for the promulgation of the
act it assumed that a master might confer "the rights of
freedman" upon the slave when he volunteered.[22]

This was a desperate act and Congress passed it only
under the compulsion of public necessity and public
opinion. It was the outgrowth of several years of think-
ing which crystallized rapidly under the distressing
conditions that obtained in the winter of 1864-1865. As
early as 1861 some persons conceived the idea of arming negroes. Louisiana used a regiment of free negroes
in the defense of New Orleans,[23] and the legislature of
Tennessee passed an act, September 3, 1861, to receive

[21] The recruiting officers were ordered not to accept any slaves without
their own and their master's consent. The Adjutant and Inspector General's office assumed control of the recruiting service.

[22] O. R. ser. IV, vol. III, 1161.

[23] Four other negro regiments were later organized in the department.
O. R. ser. I, vol. XV, 556, 559; ser. IV, vol. I, 625, 1020.

into the military service all free negroes between 15 and 50.[24] The matter did not receive serious attention before 1864. However, in the fall of 1863 the Alabama legislature urged upon the President's attention the propriety of considering the use of slaves "in some effective way"; [25] and General P. R. Cleburne of the Army of Tennessee formulated a plan for the employment of slaves as soldiers.[26] President Davis thought it was "injurious" to discuss the subject at that time, but in his annual message to Congress he recommended the use of negroes on Government works.[27] Congress passed an act, February 14, 1864, authorizing the use of free negroes and slaves as proposed by the President.[28] The States had used slaves, more or less, from the beginning upon defense works, but this was the first definite step taken by the Confederate Government to use negroes in a military way.

Throughout 1864 there was much talk among the people and the soldiers about arming the slaves.[29] The discussion was particularly earnest toward the end of the year, owing to the desperate military situation. At the Augusta meeting of the governors General Cleburne's plan of enrolling slaves was endorsed; [30] and the President and the Secretary of War recommended a more ex-

---

[24] O. R. ser. IV, vol. I, 409. The Virginia legislature considered seriously a similar bill in the following February. *Miss. Val. Hist. Rev.*, 6: 34.
[25] *Ibid.*, vol. II, 767.
[26] O. R. ser. I, vol. LII, Pt. II, 586, 593, 596, 598, 606, 608.
[27] O. R. ser. IV, vol. II, 998.
[28] *Ibid.*, vol. III, 208. Not more than 20,000 slaves could be so used.
[29] Nathaniel W. Stephenson, "The Question of Arming the Slaves," *American Historical Review*, 18: 295; Pollard, *Life of Jefferson Davis*, 44.
[30] Governor Watts of Alabama was not present when the resolution adopting it was passed, and a few weeks later he denounced it to the legislature. *Annual Cyclopædia*, 1864, 11, 196, 202.

tensive use of slaves for labor purposes, while putting out
a "feeler" on the more serious matter of using them as
soldiers.[31]  This "feeler" stimulated discussion and the
sources—*Official Records,* the *Journals* of Congress,
newspapers, and personal memoirs and recollections—
show that it became the most absorbing question during
the momentous winter months.[32]

Leadership was sharply divided.  Men like General
Howell Cobb, Senators R. M. T. Hunter and Louis T.
Wigfall, Congressmen H. S. Foote and H. C. Chambers,
and Governor Brown pointed out forcibly the objections
to arming the slaves, and the *Mercury* and its kind
searched their expansive vocabularies for fitting words
of condemnation.  General Lee, Judah P. Benjamin,
Governor Smith of Virginia, and Senator Brown ably met
the arguments against it, on the basis of military necessity.  The cardinal points of the opposition were: (1)
the arming of slaves would be a repudiation of the
theories and traditions of the South; (2) it would mean
the abolition of slavery, for if "the negro was fit to be
a soldier, he was not fit to be a slave"; [33] (3) it would be
an abandonment of the ground upon which the States
seceded if they allowed Congress to interfere with the
institution of slavery; and (4) it would be an offense to
the white soldiers and many of them would lay down
their arms.[34]  Congressman Chambers was "ashamed to

[31] O. R. ser. IV, vol. III, 790, 959.

[32] Professor Stephenson has pointed out that many public leaders and
journalists understood that the President was in favor of arming the
slaves. *Amer. Hist. Rev.,* 18:297.

[33] Pollard, *Life of Jefferson Davis,* 453.

[34] The *Mercury* warned that "if the slaves were armed, South Carolina
could no longer have an interest in prosecuting the war." Pollard, *Life
of Jefferson Davis,* 452. O. R. ser. I, XLVI, Pt. II, 1229; *Amer. Hist.
Rev.,* 18: 295.

debate the question." General Cobb thought the proposition was the "most pernicious idea that had been suggested since the war began." It was a source of deep "mortification and regret" that the great and good Lee had endorsed it.[35] General Lee, who was the mainstay of the advocates of arming slaves, put the matter squarely on the basis of military necessity. He observed pointedly: "We must decide whether slavery shall be extinguished by our enemies and the slaves be used against us, or use them ourselves at the risk of the effects which may be produced upon our social institutions." [36]

While Congress tried to demolish the project with condemnatory resolutions, and the President waited for public opinion concerning it to ripen, the friends of it called upon General Lee for his opinion and through him tested the sentiment of his soldiers.[37] The strong convictions of General Lee, who was generally looked to at this dark hour for guidance, in favor of it and the endorsement of it by his army; [38] the failure of the Hampton Roads Conference; and the enactment of a law for arming the slaves by the Virginia legislature induced Congress to yield.

It had been a mooted question among the friends of

[35] O. R. ser. IV, vol. III, 1009.

[36] Letter to Senator Andrew Hunter of the Virginia legislature. O. R. ser. IV, vol. III, 1012.

[37] It was in reply to the inquiries of Senator Andrew Hunter, Congressman Barksdale of Mississippi, and Secretary of State Judah P. Benjamin that General Lee expressed his views. O. R. ser. IV, vol. III, 1012; ser. I, vol. XLVI, Pt. II, 1236, 1229; McCabe, *Life and Campaigns of General Robert E. Lee,* 574. McCabe claims that Lee was in favor of enrolling negroes the preceding fall and training them during the winter months, 576.

[38] General J. B. Gordon, commanding the second corps of Lee's army, reported that but few soldiers in his corps were opposed to it. O. R. ser. I, vol. LI, Pt. II, 1063.

the project as to whether the slaves should be promised
freedom as a reward for their service, and, if so, whether
it should be granted when they entered the service or at
the end of the war. General Lee thought any act for enrolling them should be accompanied by a "well-digested
plan of gradual and general emancipation." He believed
that it "would be neither just nor wise, . . . to require
them to serve as slaves." [39]

Congress was not willing to take so desperate a step,
nor did General Lee recommend that it should.[40] It
adhered to the political traditions of the South by refusing to interfere with slavery,—leaving the question
of freeing the slaves to the States and providing for
the raising of negro troops through the States.[41] The
order for putting the act into operation emphasized
manumission by the masters at the time the slaves
should enlist.[42]

A definite invitation to the States, like that proposed
by General Lee, would not have impaired the power of
the States over slavery. Congress might have taken
a more courageous position on the question without over-
stepping its constitutional authority or Southern traditions, but the fact that the Virginia legislature had just
repudiated the idea of emancipation doubtless had a de-

[39] O. R. ser. IV, vol. III, 1012; McCabe, *Life and Campaigns of General Robert E. Lee,* 574.

[40] He recommended emancipation to the Virginia legislature (O. R.
ser. IV, vol. III, 1012). He thought that Congress should only authorize
the President to call upon the States for such as they were willing to
contribute, "with the condition of emancipation to all enrolled." Mc-
Cabe, *op. cit.,* 575.

[41] The act of the Virginia legislature (March 6th) providing for the
arming of slaves probably helped to preëmpt the matter for the States.
O. R. ser. I, vol. XLVI, Pt. III, 1315; LI, Pt. II, 1068.

[42] O. R. ser. IV, vol. III, 1161. 'See also ser. I, vol. XLVI, Pt. III, 1354,
1366, 1367, 1370; *Jones' Diary,* vol. II, 450, 451, 456, 457, 461.

terrent influence upon Congress.[43]   General Lee had suggested a call upon the States for slaves, upon the condition of emancipation by the States, as an experiment, but Congress probably felt that if Virginia, the real battleground of the Confederacy, would not free the slaves who helped to defend her there was no use to call upon the States for slaves upon such condition.  Watchful waiting with regard to the Virginia legislature, European reaction, the peace movement, and the designs of the President and his despised Secretary of State produced a dilatoriness that was painful and hazardous.  But if Congress delayed action, it did no worse than the Virginia legislature, which had the question of arming the slaves before it for about three months.

President Davis played a negative role in the movement for arming the slaves.  Probably this was the wisest policy because of the strong opposition to him in Congress and throughout the country.  By the latter part of February he seems to have been fully converted to the views of Secretary Benjamin and General Lee, if, indeed, he had not been in sympathy with their views all the while.  Benjamin's letter to Frederick A. Porcher of Charleston (December 21, 1864) indicated that President Davis was then only waiting for public opinion to ripen on the subject.  Professor Stephenson is doubtless correct in his opinion that Secretary Benjamin spoke for the Administration in his famous address, the night of February 17th.  On February 21st President Davis wrote Honorable John Forsyth, editor of the *Register*

[43] The provision that nothing in the act should be construed to affect the relation of master and slave, "except by consent of the owners and of the States in which they may reside," may have been intended for a suggestion to the States rather than a caution as to the interpretation of the act.

*and Advertiser,* Mobile, Alabama: "It is now becoming daily more evident to all reflecting persons that we are reduced to choosing whether the negroes shall fight for or against us, and that all arguments as to the positive advantages or disadvantages of employing them are beside the question." [44]  In his special message to Congress March 13th, he complained about its delay in passing the bill for employing slaves as soldiers. Even though it came late, "much benefit" was anticipated from it.[45]

It was generally conceded by those who championed arming the slaves that the white men must still bear the brunt of the war. The all important question was how to put the maximum number of them on the firing line, that is, how to gather up the fragments of the conscript population and to drive the hosts of deserters back to their commands.[46]  General Howell Cobb, a loyal patriot and trusted friend of the Administration, thought "the freest, broadest and most unrestricted system of volunteering" was the true policy and could not "be too soon resorted to." The only way, in fact, to save the army was to allow the people to volunteer and form new

[44] O. R. ser. IV, vol. III, 1110.

[45] O. R. ser. IV, vol. III, 1133. In this discussion of the question of arming the slaves I have relied mainly upon the *Official Records,* ser. IV, vol. III, 756 *et seq.,* and the *Journals.* I have also availed myself of the benefits of Professor Nathaniel W. Stephenson's brief but illuminating article in the *American Historical Review,* 18:295 f, and of Professor T. R. Hay's full discussion in the *Mississippi Valley Historical Review,* 6:34 f.

[46] President Davis decided to try once more a proclamation of amnesty. He promised for the last time pardon to all absentees and deserters if they would return to the ranks within twenty days. (*Annual Cyclopædia,* 1865, 193.) Rendezvous camps were established for the purpose of collecting and promptly returning deserters. Clarke County *Journal,* March 30, 1865.

organizations. The President and Secretary Seddon did not think the plan feasible, owing among other reasons, to sentiment in the army and the opposition of generals in the field to the raising of new organizations.[47]

General Lee and Superintendent Preston formulated plans for reaching the deserters. General Lee believed that if the States would pass laws debarring them from political rights, and such civil rights as acquiring title to property they would feel compelled to go to camp. As a supplement he would have Government agents and employees, and the State constabulary and reserves put on an efficient basis for returning deserters. Preston believed they could be reached only (1) by the States setting up special courts with simple and quick procedure for the crime of desertion and backing them with all civil power and machinery; and (2) by using the reserves solely as an auxiliary to conscription, or by creating a new reserve out of boys between 16 and 17 and of men between 50 and 60 for this special duty.[48]

While Congress deliberated at length upon plans of military reform and civil and military leaders interchanged opinions, the conscription service broke down almost completely. General Preston's opinion that little could be done under existing conditions is borne out by the records. The decline of general morale, the independent action of the States, the incompetency of conscript officers, and the inefficiency of the reserves as a supporting arm consigned conscription to irretrievable failure. It was of little importance that the reserves

[47] O. R. ser. IV, vol. III, 1009, 1030.
[48] O. R. ser. IV, vol. III, 1119, 1121. Each one of these plans was open to the objection that it required State action and there was no way to get it, certainly not in time to be of any service in the spring campaigns.

were taken out of the general service in February [49] and
assigned solely to conscription duty.   They were composed mainly of old men who had large estates, families, and dependents and who were more inclined to look
after them than deserters.   Indeed, Preston said there
were as many deserters among them as among the regulars.[50]   They were a spiritless, incoherent, and miserably
equipped force; and the character of their six months'
service as an auxiliary to conscription was not such as
to hold out hope in the future, unless they could be transformed along the lines suggested by General Lee.[51]

When the Bureau of Conscription was abolished conscription was turned over to the generals of reserves.[52]
A special assistant adjutant general was set up in the
place of the Superintendent of the Bureau, with the duty
of supervising the routine of conscription and of acting
as intermediary between the generals of reserves and the
War Department concerning very important matters.
The abolition of the Bureau simplified the machinery of
conscription somewhat and put conscription essentially on
a military basis.   The commandant of conscripts now
was the commander of the reserves, and it was his duty to
coördinate and direct the two agencies.[53]

There is nothing to show that the new system pro-

[49] O. R. ser. IV, vol. III, 1113.

[50] Ibid., 1119.

[51] Ibid., 1119, 1121.

[52] The Bureau was abolished March 9, 1865.  O. R. ser. IV, vol.
III, 1176.

[53] The act prevented the use of able-bodied conscripts as conscript
officers.  Jones claimed that President Davis ignored the act abolishing
the Bureau because he disapproved of some of the details of it; and
Colonel Lay was again acting superintendent.  He attributed this in
part to Preston's wealth.  Diary, vol. II, 456, 463.  I have found no
orders emanating from the Bureau after the act abolishing it was passed.

duced tangible results before the collapse at App mattox. The efforts at reform; the slight revisions of the exemption and detail systems; the assignment of the reserve forces to the sole duty of aiding conscription; the consolidation of depleted units and the assignment of superfluous officers to the ranks;[54] the resort to military conscription; and the provision for converting slaves into soldiers were of little consequence. Letters "poured into the Department" asking for authority to raise and command negro troops;[55] newspapers carried advertisements calling for negro enlistments, and orders were issued by the War Department[56] for their enrollment, but only a few were organized.[57] Whatever merits the changes instituted may have had, the end came before they were well under way. Johnston with a handful of men dodged about in the Carolinas in front of Sherman, and Lee arose on the last day with a small band of underfed, scantily clothed, and half-equipped patriots.

By 1865 the Confederacy had spent its strength and the masses would have welcomed peace. The transportation system had broken down and there was terrible suffering in the armies and among much of the civilian population for lack of food and clothing. The administration stood thoroughly discredited with the people,

[54] It was estimated that this measure of consolidation would add at least 10,000 soldiers. *Annual Cyclopædia*, 1865, 190.

[55] *Jones' Diary*, vol. II, 450, 461.

[56] O. R. ser. I, vol. XLVI, Pt. III, 1354, 1366, 1367, 1370; ser. IV, vol. III, 1144, 1161, 1193.

[57] Pollard sarcastically remarked that the act resulted in the organization of two companies "from some negro vagabonds in Richmond, which were allowed to give balls at Libby Prison and were exhibited in fine, fresh uniforms on Capitol Square, as decoys to obtain sable recruits. But the mass of the colored brethren looked on the parade with unenvious eyes and little boys exhibited the early prejudices of race by pelting the fine uniforms with mud." Pollard, *Life of Jefferson Davis*, 456.

and the States took measures to corral for self-protection all able-bodied men who had not been actually enrolled in the armies. There was division and wrangling of the most malignant sort among the leaders. Francis P. Blair, Sr., while on his special mission found the leaders so distrustful of each other that none dared "to assume the responsibility of making advances, or agreeing to terms which would lead to peace. Davis is environed with enemies, who watch his every motion, and are ready" at the first move toward a settlement "to spring upon and overwhelm him."[58] A feeling of hostility and a jealousy for Congressional prerogatives led Congress into aggressive opposition to the President. It adjourned apparently with more pride in its victory over him than in the military laws enacted by it. The Confederacy was a house divided against itself, and successful recruitment was impossible. The abundance of able and ambitious leaders, civil and military, proved to be a liability rather than an asset to the Confederate cause.

[58] Quoted in the Jacksonville (Fla.) *Union*, February 11, 1865.

# CHAPTER XVI

## DID CONSCRIPTION FAIL?

THE enforcement of the conscript laws was attended by difficulties that inhered in a system of compulsory service among a proud and free people. Conscription was not only contrary to the spirit of the people but to the genius of the Confederate political system. It seemed unnatural that the new government, just set up as the agent of the sovereign States, should exercise such compelling and far-reaching authority over the people, independently of the States. Public leaders generally recognized the necessity of conscription,[1] and their influence and the hard facts of war gradually reconciled the public to it; but there was always strong opposition to it. Leaders who never became reconciled to it, and conflicts with State authorities in the enforcement of it seriously impaired its efficiency.

The system had many imperfections. Substitution was a serious mistake, and class exemptions provided altogether too easy a means for evading service. A judicious selective system, supported by a policy of executive detail, would have effected much greater economy in the disposition of men. The machinery of conscription was not fully set up in all of the States until the latter part

[1] President Davis told the Mississippi legislature that there was no more reason to expect voluntary service in the army than voluntary labor upon the public roads or the voluntary payment of taxes. Savannah *Republican*, January 14, 1863.

of 1863, and then it was too cumbrous and its processes too elaborate. The official personnel of the service was often inefficient. The generals who superintended the work before Preston seem to have had only a secondary interest in the work, at least they did not push it aggressively; and complaints persisted throughout the war that the enrolling officers were ignorant, incompetent, and corrupt.[2] Finally, conscription would have been less odious if it had been made the exclusive policy of raising armies at the outset. It might then have been regarded as a scientific way of allocating the man power of the country and of distributing fairly the burdens of war. But the volunteer system was tried the first year, and after conscription was adopted volunteering was still allowed. This made conscription appear to be a device for coercing derelicts, hence the taint that attached to the conscript.

In the absence of complete records it is impossible to place a satisfactory estimate upon the value of conscription. A system of recruitment that enabled the Confederacy to maintain itself against tremendous odds for so long a time deserves a more sympathetic consideration than it has customarily had.[3] It rendered a distinct service by systematizing and centralizing the military system. Of more importance, it saved the Confederacy

[2] No one was bolder in the assertion that enrolling officers were incompetent than Superintendent Preston; but, as the *Courier* (March 4, 1863) pointed out, complaints were sometimes registered against good officers by the derelicts, and candidates for office found it helpful to denounce them before prejudiced audiences. See O. R. ser. I, vol. XVII, Pt. II, 788; ser. IV, vol. II, 307, 411, 849; vol. III, 785, 855-857, 863, 868, 866-914, 894, 940, 946, 1030, 1048.

[3] For adverse opinions of conscription see Fleming, *The Civil War and Reconstruction in Alabama*, 98; Brooks, "Conscription in the Confederate States of America," *Military Historian and Economist*, vol. I, No. 4, 441.

in the summer of 1862 by keeping the seasoned twelve-month's troops in the army and by stimulating extensive volunteering.[4] Many of the volunteers might have gone into the service of their own volition later, but the conscription act gave them to the service just at the moment when they were absolutely necessary to check the onrush of the enemy. The powerful armies built up in the summer and fall of 1862 were the backbone of the Confederate military system that distinguished itself on the bloody battlefields of 1863 and 1864.

It is impossible to say how many men passed through the channels of conscription. Superintendent Preston's final report, February 1865, showed that 177,121 men, east of the Mississippi, had been disposed of by the conscription service.[5] The report was confessedly incomplete. It did not include the men put into the service by General Pillow in 1863 from Alabama, Mississippi, and West Tennessee, nor the State reserves that probably totaled 50,000 or more;[6] and the number of exempts and details was probably understated 40,000 to 50,000.[7] It does not seem extravagant to conclude that the conscription service was probably directly responsible for

[4] The Richmond authorities and leaders generally, including the enemies of conscription, accredited it with performing these services. See, for example, O. R. ser. IV, vol. II, 34, 42, 128, 279, 580; the *Examiner*, January 12, 1864. The *Examiner* said it not only overcame the deficiencies of the voluntary system, but changed the character of the army "from the desultory character of prompt enthusiasm to that of permanent and organized discipline."

[5] Of this number 81,993 had been put into the army (O. R. ser. IV, vol. III, 1101). But Preston estimated, November, 1863, that 75,000 men had been disposed of by the conscription service in Virginia, the Carolinas, and Georgia. Of these 37,500 had actually been added to the army. O. R. ser. IV, vol. II, 939.

[6] The enrollment of the reserves was not under the jurisdiction of the Bureau of Conscription.

[7] Pages 107-108 above.

the assignment of 300,000 men in the Cis-Mississippi area. According to the Richmond authorities, leading newspapers, and some of the old veterans, themselves, conscription was chiefly responsible for most of the volunteering. Men of conscript age were urged by recruiting officers to volunteer so as to avoid the odium of conscription, and to get the bounty and the privilege of selecting the arm of service and the unit with which to serve.[8] Secretary Seddon estimated that 100,000 men were added to the armies in 1863, and that three-fourths of them volunteered but the Bureau of Conscription did not receive credit for them. Superintendent Preston claimed that most of the volunteers joined the service to avoid the odium of conscription, and therefore the conscription service should be accredited with them.[9]

If conscription is to be accredited with having directly or indirectly put most of the men in the service after the first year of the war, it would be possible to place a fair estimate upon it, if the total enrollment in the Confederate armies were known. But the question of total enrollment has been one of controversial discussion since the Civil War, and we seem to be no nearer a common agreement than at the outset. The question will continue to be a matter of speculation until more complete records are unearthed. The number actually enrolled probably lies between the usual Southern estimate of 600,000 and the Northern estimate of 1,100,000. When the final count is made the enrollment, including the State reserves and other local defense troops, will probably total

[8] For example see O. R. ser. I, vol. XXXIV, Pt. II, 1092; vol. LIII, 372; ser. III, vol. V, 696; ser. IV, vol. II, 171, 694, 723; vol. III, 1059, 1101; the *Enquirer,* June 20, 1862; the *Daily Courier,* April 2, 1863; the *Examiner,* January 12 and 14, 1864.

[9] Report of February, 1865; O. R. ser. IV, vol. III, 1099.

850,000 to 900,000.[10] If to this number the exempts and details are added it will be seen that most of the military population was reached and allocated, if temporarily and improperly in many instances. While the figures upon which this deduction is made are conjectural, they do not seem extravagant, in view of such testimony as we have, and they will serve to emphasize a fact generally accepted, that, as things go in war, the South gave very liberally of its military population.

The opinion has prevailed that the net results of conscription did not compensate for the opposition it aroused and for the trouble it produced among leaders. This, of course, and the failure properly to distribute men between the various war necessities stand to its discredit. The evidence is convincing that it utterly failed

[10] A. B. Casselman and Cornelius B. Hite have recently reviewed the testimony as to numbers (*Current History,* January, 1923, page 653; May, page 251); the former concluding that the total enrollment was probably above 1,000,000, the latter that it was close around the 600,000 mark. The estimates by the Southern State historical societies total 1,052,000. Confederate leaders generally have estimated the number at 600,000 (*op. cit.,* May No., page 251), but the late Dr. Randolph H. McKim, the most brilliant commentator upon this subject in recent years, understood that the estimate of 600,000 was that of the men "actually serving with the colors" (*op. cit.* January No., page 655). The editor of *DeBow's Review* estimated the fighting population, allowing one out of four for exemption, at a little more than 1,000,000 (quoted in the *Courier,* August 12, 1863). One J. W. Ellis of Raleigh estimated, January 29, 1865, that probably 1,000,000 men had been enrolled (O. R. ser. IV, vol. III, 1041); and the Mobile *Register and Advertiser* estimated the total fighting population at about 1,000,000 (quoted in the Columbus *Sun,* August 14, 1863). Secretary of War Geo. W. Randolph estimated, October 20, 1862, that if three-sevenths were allowed for exempts there would remain a net fighting population of 551,428 between the ages of 18 and 45 (O. R. ser. IV, vol. II, 132). The Richmond *Dispatch* and the Knoxville *Register* calculated that conscription should yield 700,000 men between the ages of 18 and 40 (quoted in Clarke County *Journal,* January 15, 1863, and the *Republican,* January 16, 1863); and the House Committee on Military Affairs estimated the army at 500,000, April 16, 1865 (O. R. ser. IV, vol. III, 1146).

during the last six or eight months of the war. Its
failure was due to the loss of a large portion of the
South, the belief that the war was hopelessly lost, and
to the fact that the Government's power of compulsion
had completely broken down. There is no ground for
assuming that any other system could have at this time
produced material results. The chief task was to return
deserters, but the conscription service failed to do it,
according to Superintendent Preston's own avowal, in
the grand total of 100,000 or more. It has been assumed
that conscripts did not make good soldiers, and that
most deserters were conscripts. This assumption ignores
the significant fact, pointed out by the Mobile *Register
and Advertiser*,[11] that many men who waited to be conscribed were not moral slackers, but they waited because
of their private obligations and the necessities of their
dependents. When they were conscribed they took up
their arms in good faith. Vice-President Stephens and
some other prominent leaders expressed doubts that conscripts would make good soldiers, and some of the generals were prejudiced against them. But long before the
war was over the generals pleaded for conscripts; and
the glory of Confederate arms in 1863 and 1864 was
established in large part by the valor of men who had
directly or indirectly gone into the service under the pressure of conscription. Doubtless many of the deserters
were conscripts, but there was much said in the winter
of 1864-1865 about men deserting who had cheerfully
and bravely fought from the beginning.[12] Truth of the
matter is, the hardships of camp life, privations of the
homefolks, and the loss of confidence in the chances for

[11] Quoted in the *Whig*, August 23, 1862.
[12] See, for example, O. R., ser. IV, vol. III, 1043.

victory induced many men to desert, regardless of how they got into the army. If volunteers lacked zeal because conscription drove them to volunteer, and deserted, it is reasonable to suppose that in most cases they would not have volunteered but for conscription.

The alternatives to Confederate conscription were conscription by the States and volunteering. There were many persons who endorsed the principle of conscription but believed that it would be more effective and more compatible with the Confederate political system if done by the States. State conscription probably would have been more agreeable to the average man, and might have secured more recruits, if the State authorities had kept on good terms with the Richmond Government. Even if the States had conscribed their quotas promptly, State conscription would still have been open to the objection that it would have made difficult the problem of coördinating the forces and establishing a central control over them. As to volunteering, it was made the exclusive method of recruitment the first year of the war, but did not secure enough men to meet the demands of 1862. Besides, it was open to men throughout the war who were zealous to get into the ranks. It ought to be said in fairness, however, that conscription took some of the glory out of volunteering, and it probably blunted the edge of public opinion which otherwise might have driven many men to volunteer. It is a significant commentary on volunteering that three States resorted to conscription to furnish their quotas before Confederate conscription was adopted; and the States generally fell back on conscription to raise their local defense troops in 1863 and 1864. As regards the relative value of systems of recruitment, much weight should be given to the opinions of the Richmond authorities. Their faith in conscription remained unshaken to the end.[13]

Over against the friction, confusion, and dereliction depicted in this narrative stands out in bold relief the fact of general sacrifices unsurpassed in the annals of military history. Nor is conscription a contradiction of the cheerfulness with which the sacrifices were made. There is much truth in Lord Charnwood's observation that the general patriotism of the people is not to be judged so much by the failure of the purely voluntary system as by the success of the system which succeeded it.[14] The dereliction of many sets in a brighter light the heroic devotion of the masses. The unsurpassed sacrifices and heroism of the Southern armies and civilian population—the proudest and most sacred tradition of the South—stand unassailed.

[13] Even General Cobb, who favored getting back on the volunteer basis after the summer of 1862, thought the conscript law should be left on the statute book as a threat to those who would not be inclined to volunteer.

[14] Lord Charnwood said this of the North; it might as truly be said of the South. *Abraham Lincoln*, 365.

# INDEX

Alabama, conditions in, 125, 148, 151-3, 202, 211, 221, 317, 322, 331; exemption, 93, 95, 106; conflict with Confederate authority, 242-4, 251-3.

Aliens, 31, 60, 61.

August, Thomas P., 284, 289, 321.

Beauregard, General P. G. T., 147, 199.

Benjamin, Judah P., favors arming of slaves, 345, 348.

Blake, E. D., 307.

Bonham, Governor Milledge L., 111, 294, 301.

Bounties, 7, 14, 308.

Bragg, General Braxton, on exemption and substitution, 39-40; sets up bureau of conscription under General Pillow, 192; approves Pillow's system, 195, 215; supervisor of military affairs, 310; attack on Bureau of Conscription, 307, 315, 320, 321-6.

Brown, Governor Joseph E., protests against conscription, 23-4, 123, 155, 230-2, 233, 255-6; officers certified, 95; defies President, 257, 260, 270 276; criticizes Georgia supreme court, 170; obstructs conscription, 256; tilt with Richmond, 255-279; press opinion of, 261; correspondence with General Cobb, 267-69; opposes arming slaves, 345; in virtual rebellion against Richmond, 278.

Bureau of Conscription, 78, 80, 83, 112, 161, 208-9, 217; estimate of available men east of the Mississippi in 1864, 307; Bragg's influence on, 307, 310, 326; reasons for failure, 332-4; movement to abolish, 332, 338; abolished, 339.

Campbell, Judge John A., on activities of courts, 184; dominates Bureau of Conscription, 208, 209; opinion of Pillow's system, 212; conditions in N. C., S. C., Ga., and Ala., 221; on desertions, 209, 335; Supt. Preston's mainstay, 326.

Camps of Instruction, 114-116.

Chambers, H. C., 345.

Clark, Governor Henry T., 232, 234.

Clark, Governor Charles, in conflict with Richmond, 244-6, 251.

Clay, Senator Clement C., Jr., 165, 192.

Cleburne, General P. R., favors arming slaves, 344.

Clopton, David, on failure of volunteer system, 13.

Cobb, General Howell, favors volunteering, 331, 349, 361; on conscription, 153; supporter of the President, 258; tilt with Governor Brown, 267-9; on conditions in Ga. (1864); against arming slaves, 345, 346.

Conflict, between Confederate and State government, 106, 123, 132, 228-236; causes of in lower South, 237-9; results, 253, 295-6, 303-4, 312. See index under various States.

Congress, quarrel with the President over military policy, 102-5.

Conscription Act of April 16, 1862, 13-14; reasons for it, 12-14; popular attitude toward, 13, 17-26, 123, 134-5, 148; efforts to enforce, 96, 218, 225; machinery and processes, 114-6; evasion of, 131, 221, 225, 240; enforcement of, 96, 218, 225; results of 124,

127-8, 130-3; second act, 138, 140; conditions, 156, 209, 211, 215, 219-24; results, 156-58, 199-201, 222-6; press on remedies, 305-6} Act of Feb. 16, 1864, 308; problem of enforcement, 142, 153-4, 219-20; results, 314-15, 317-18, 328-9, 335; character of officers, 93, 112, 311, 316, 333, 338, 355; drastic measures, 319-20, 327, 343, 351; proposed remedies, 158, 306, 337, 350; breaks down, 350, 353, 358; inherent difficulties, 118, 227, 304, 311, 330, 354; imperfections, 316, 353-4; services, 355-6; estimates of numbers furnished, 356, 358.

Cooper, Samuel, 88, 213, 222; recommends administrative changes as to conscription, 325.

Courts, character of decisions, 162-3, 171, 176; Confederate court system incomplete, 164-6, 181, 189; uphold constitutionality of conscription, 168-9, 181; importance of State courts, 167-8, 171-6; on substitution, 177; concurrent powers, 171-2; variety of cases in, 176-81; leading decisions of, 168-71, 174, 177-81; policy of administration as to decisions, 181-2; minor courts cause trouble, 181-7, 189, 286; effects of court decisions, 188-90.

Davis, President Jefferson, favors conscription, 13, 14; recommends change in exemption system, 81; vetoes act extending exemption, 90; resolves to put men in the field, 99; conflict with Governor and Council of S. C., 123, 299-301; commends conscription, 132; swing around circle, 72, 143, 158; recommends abolition of class exemption, 101-2, 339; on speculation, 150; recommends suspension of writ of *habeas corpus*, 188, 339; in trouble, 204-5, 227; urged to become dictator, 205; calls out men between 35 and 40, 142; between 40 and 45, 207; proclamation of amnesty to deserters, 221; tries to tone up people, 224; plans to reform conscription, 132; opposition to him, 226, 305, 353; calls upon States to organize local defense troops, 239; military program for 1864, 225-6; tries to put able-bodied clerks, etc., in the field, 99, 319; favors general militia law, 338-9; movement to depose him, 335-7; on arming slaves, 334, 349; conflict with Congress over exemptions, etc., 102-5, 339-42; policy as to governors, 13, 220, 223, 225, 229, 237, 276, 285, 303-4, 323, 326, 333; For conflict with governors *see* index under names of governors.

Desertions, 129, 158, 202, 304; reasons for, 148-51, 332, 359; deserters and conscripts defiant, 211, 214, 219-21; Lee's and Preston's plan as to, 350; number of, 335, 338, 359.

Details, 76, 77, 90, 96, 103, 111; limited service details, 86, 328; abuses, 77, 91, 225, 311, 319, 327; system unsatisfactory, 90-2, 99.

Dunwoody, John, 28, 120, 260.

Examinations, medical, 69, 93, 97, 112, 125-7.

Exemption, the problem, 15, 51; reasons for it, 53, 110, 232; act of April 21, 1862, 53; act of October 11, 1862, 67; amendatory acts, 67, 68, 72-3, 89, 316; act of February 17, 1864, 83-4; opposition to exemption of manufacturers, 63-4; extended by Secretary of War, 62; press on it, 65-6; efforts to enforce it, 69, 80, 85; exemption of overseers unpopular, 70-2, 75, 143, 144-5; "twenty-nigger" law amended, 73; frauds, 54-63, 82, 88, 111-2, 143, 201, 225, 311; statutory-executive exemption, 82-3, 309; Act of 1864 not satisfactory, 88-92, 94, 97-100; Administration favors abolition of class exemption, 81, 131, 339; conflict over exemption of State officers, 94-5, 249-250, 265-8,

286-7, 289-292; probable number of exempts 106-9; results, 71, 75, 78-80, 112-13, 143-4, 201.

Florida, 95, 157.
Foote, Henry S., 23, 123, 345.
Fort Sumpter, effects of fall of, 4.

Georgia, conditions in, 152, 155, 202, 221, 317, 321, 331; exempts in, 79, 93, 95, 100, 107; conflict in, 255-278.
Greer, General Elkanah, on courts in the Trans-Mississippi Department, 185.

Habeas Corpus, suspended, 47, 86, 188; conflict over suspension of, 238-9, 270, 280, 342.
Herbert, Caleb C., 137.
Hill, Senator Benjamin H., 159, 164, 258.
Hill, General Daniel H., on planter exempts, 71; conscription in N. C., 199.
Hindman, General Thomas C., 33, 128-9.
Holden, William W., 220, 271.
Holmes, General Theophilus, 148.
Hunter, Senator Robert M. T., 345.

Inspection, 218, 321-2, 330-1.

Jackson, General Thomas J., 33.
Johnson, Senator Herschel V., 26, 123, 156, 258-9.
Johnston, General Joseph E., 193, 198; in control of conscription in Department No. 2, 207-8; approves Pillow's work, 213, 215; calls for men, 307.

Kemper, James L., on exempts and details, 90, 97, 108; commander of reserves in Va., 324; tilt with Superintendent Preston, 324-5.
Kenan, A. H., 10, 25.

Lay, George W., 201, 220, 321.
Lee, General Robert E., 97, 108, 198, 318, 327; on courts, 186; on conscription, 209, 312; movement to make him dictator, 306,

334, 337; favors limiting privilege of volunteering, 307; needs men, 329, favors arming slaves, 302, 345-7.
Letcher, Governor John, on conscription, 123, 232.
Louisiana, number of exempts, 107; conditions in, 147, 317; conflict in, 248-9.
Lubbock, Governor Francis R., on conscription, 232, 247, 254.

Magrath, Governor Andrew G., 108; as Confederate judge upholds conscription, 124, 168; in conflict with Richmond, 302, 304.
Magruder, General John B., brings Governor Murrah to terms, 347-8, 303.
Melton, C. D., 220.
Military Conscription, 192-4, 207-13, 217; revived, 320-26, 328, 334.
Milton, Governor John, on conscription, 63, 232; on exemption, 65, 68, 75; sets fine example, 235, 253.
Mississippi, exemption in, 93, 95, 107; conditions in, 128, 148, 151-2, 202, 211, 313, 317, 321, 331; conflict in, 243-6.
Moore, Governor Thomas O., 64; tilt with Richmond, 249.
Murrah, Governor Pendleton, conflict with conscription authorities, 247.

North Carolina, exemption in, 79, 95, 107; conditions in, 97, 148, 202-3, 320-1, 282, 317; conflict in, 47, 187, 279-296.

Oldham, Senator Williamson S., 23, 137.
Orr, Senator James L., opposed to conscription, 23.

Partisan Rangers, 121-2.
Pearson, Chief Justice Richmond M., causes trouble, 23, 46, 47, 178, 181, 187, 188, 286, 288.
Pettus, Governor John J., attitude toward conscription, 232; tilt

with Richmond, 65, 128, 158, 243-4.

Phelan, Senator James, on exemption, 71; on condition of conscription, 152, 154, 328, 335.

Pickens, Governor Francis W., in conflict with President over conscription, 123, 298-9; for enforcement of the law, 154; cooperates, 234.

Pillow, General Gideon J., in charge of conscription in Dept. No. 2, 192-4, 207-13, 223; removed, 195, 213; in conflict with Bureau of Conscription, 192-3, 212, 217; results of work, 108, 195-7, 212-14, 308, 313, 322.

Polk, General Leonidas, on conditions in Ala. and Miss., 313, 317; favors military conscription, 313.

Preston, John L., on details, 87, 99; on substitution, 38, 48; on exemption 79, 80, 87, 88, 92, 111, 215; favors abolition of class exemption, 101; superintendent of conscription, 215; condemns Pillow's system, 197, 217; plans improvement of conscription, 215-6, 218, 315-6; criticizes government of N. C., S. C., and Ga. for opposition, 303; defends conscription, 314, 326, 328, 332; offers to resign, 323; conflict with Bragg, 321-3; on desertion, 338; reasons for breakdown of conscription, 328, 335, 355; on numbers, 222, 240, 299, 300, 302, 303, 313, 334, 350, 356, 359.

Rains, Gabriel J., 193.

Randolph, George W., Secretary of War, 33, 40, 76, 116, 142, 158, 358.

Rector, Governor Henry M., 147; defies Richmond, 128, 246.

Reserves, Junior and Senior, 240; generals of given conscription duties, 323, 351; given complete control of conscription, 351.

Rhett, Robert Barnwell, favors conscription, 25, 205, 230

Seddon, James A., Secretary of War, on conscription, 154; on

courts, 182; reprimands Pillow, 194; opinion of Pillow's system, 212; conflict with governors of Ala., Ga., Miss., and N. C., 241, 263-4, 269-70, 277, 286, 288, 292-3, 336; on conditions of Army, 198, 315; favors arming slaves, 222, 223, 224, 234, 319; 332, 333, 334, 343, 357.

Simms, General William E., 137.

Shorter, Governor John G., attitude toward conscription, 160, 234; on conscription in Ala., 152, 158, 209; on courts, 185.

Slaves, movement to arm, 337, 339, 343-49.

Smith, General E. K., 148, 186, 249, 312.

Smith, Governor William, supports Administration, 298; on minor courts in Va., 185; favors arming slaves, 345.

South Carolina, exemptions in, 79, 95, 107; conditions in, 219-21, 297; conflict in, 123, 298-9, 302.

Speculation, 149, 151.

Stephens, Alexander H., against conscription, 23; opinion of Davis, 270-1; against Davis, 271-3; believes population about exhausted, 332; thought conscripts would not fight, 28, 231, 288, 359.

Stephens, Linton, denounces conscription 24, 170, 257; author of denunciatory resolutions, 274.

Substitution, reasons for, 27; popular attitude toward, 27, 33, 36, 39, 42, 44; process of, 27; price of substitutes, 29-30; frauds, 29, 31-3, 37, 41, 319; constitutional questions involved in, 34-6, 43, 45-6; produced class friction, 49-50; condemned by General Bragg and staff, 39-40; number of substitutes, 40; principals evade service, 48; abolished, 44; results, 50.

Tennessee, exemptions in, 107; conditions in, 148, 151, 202, 211, 247, 331.

Texas, conditions in, 153, 155, 157, 202; conflict in, 246-8.

Thomas, Judge T. W., 126, 183.

Toombs, Robert, against conscription, 23-4; warns against despotism, 206; in anti-Davis faction in Ga., 274.

Trans-Mississippi Department, exemptions in, 106; conditions in, 128, 147, 185, 221, 226, 312, 330, 333.

Twelve-months' men, 14, 16, 116, 133.

Vance, Governor Zebulon B., officers certified, 95; on conscription, 156; appeal to slackers, 203; conflict with Richmond, 47, 279-96.

Volunteering, 1-10; allowed after conscription was adopted, 14, 15, 119, 191, 215, 223, 355, 360; effects on conscription, 109, 215, 223, 314, 357.

Virginia, exemption in, 79, 82, 95, 97, 106-8, 327; conditions in, 97, 219, 297; conflict in, 298; arming slaves, 346-8.

Walthall, W. T., on conditions in Ala., 153, 193, 216, 331.

Walter, H. W., on conditions in Ala., Ga., and Miss., 93, 331.

Watts, Governor Thomas H., Attorney-General, 116-7, 168; governor, in conflict with Richmond, 242-4, 251-3; asks for authority to collect conscripts, 313.

Wigfall, Senator Louis T., favors conscription, 25, 137, 165; opposed arming slaves, 345.

Yancy, Senator William L., endorses conscription, 25; ready to abandon it, 133; opposes conscription of minor state officers, 137-8; defends conscription before Alabama legislature, 60, 159; estimate of size of army at end of 1863, 157.